WITHDRAWN

Later Medieval Philosophy

189
M334L

Later Medieval Philosophy (1150-1350)
An Introduction

John Marenbon

ROUTLEDGE & KEGAN PAUL
London and New York

TO SHEILA

First published in 1987 by
Routledge & Kegan Paul Ltd
11 New Fetter Lane, London EC4P 4EE

Published in the USA by
Routledge & Kegan Paul Inc.
in association with Methuen Inc.
29 West 35th Street, New York, NY 10001

Set in 10/11pt Bembo
by Falcon Graphic Art Ltd, Wallington, Surrey
and printed in Great Britain
by TJ Press (Padstow) Ltd,
Padstow, Cornwall

© John Marenbon 1987

No part of this book may be reproduced in any form without permission from the
publisher except for the quotation of brief passages in criticism

Library of Congress Cataloging in Publication Data

Marenbon, John.
Later medieval philosophy (1150-1350).
Sequel to: Early medieval philosophy (480-1150).
Bibliography: p.
Includes index.
1. Philosophy, Medieval. I. Title.
B721.M344   1987   189   87-4958

British Library CIP Data also available

ISBN 0–7102–0286–5

Contents

ALLEGHENY COLLEGE LIBRARY

88-454

Acknowledgments

I should like to thank Dr S. Lawlor for comments on early versions
of this book; the anonymous reader engaged by my publisher and
Dr O. Letwin for their very thorough and valuable criticisms of a
later draft.

John Marenbon, Trinity College, Cambridge, 2 June 1986.

References to primary sources

References to primary works are made in brackets within the text. The abbreviations used for the names of individual works are explained when they are first used, and they are listed on page 192. In accord with normal scholarly practice, texts in *quaestio*-form (for a full discussion of this form, see below, pp. 27–34) are cited according to their own divisions and sub-divisions. But the abbreviations often used within references ('q' for question; 'd' for distinction; 'a' for article) have been suppressed. In this *Introduction*, a roman numeral refers to the Book or Part; the first arabic numeral to the question or distinction; the second arabic numeral – where appropriate – to the article within a question, or the question within a distinction. For example, 'I, 4, 3' would designate Part I, question 4, article 3, if the reference were to, say, Aquinas's *Summa Theologiae*, or Book I, distinction 4, question 3, if the reference were to a *Sentence* commentary. (This system has also been used for the Books, chapters and sections of Aquinas's *Summa Contra Gentiles*, and the Books, *lectiones* and sections of his commentaries on Aristotle.) References made in this way apply to any edition or translation. Other texts are cited by page (and line) number of the editions given in the Bibliography, Section I.

Introduction

This book is not a history of later medieval philosophy, but an introduction to it. A history would offer the reader an account, however abbreviated, of thought in the later Middle Ages; this introduction is intended rather to help him begin his own study of the subject. It aims to provide some of the important information without which medieval philosophical texts will tend to baffle or mislead, and to give some detailed examples of how later medieval thinkers argued. Part One examines the organization of studies in medieval universities, the forms of writing and techniques of thought, the presuppositions and aims of thirteenth- and fourteenth-century scholars. Part Two examines in detail the way in which some important later medieval thinkers discussed a difficult and central question: the nature of intellectual knowledge.

Readers with predominantly philosophical concerns may feel that Part One is irrelevant to them, whilst those with strongly historical interests may find Part Two unnecessarily detailed, technical and limited in scope. But the main purpose of this book will be frustrated if its two parts are treated as alternative rather than complementary. The study of medieval thought calls for the skills of both the historian and the philosopher: the historian's, in order to understand the presuppositions and aims which made the concerns of thinkers in the Middle Ages so different from those of modern philosophy; the philosopher's, because the achievements of medieval thinkers can only be appreciated by the close philosophical analysis of their reasoning.

In the later Middle Ages, sophisticated abstract thought took place in universities. The first chapter of Part One, therefore, examines the nature of medieval universities, the complex structure of their courses, the methods used for learning and teaching and the different literary forms in which the writings of university men survive. Chapter 2 looks at the techniques of logic which a thirteenth- or fourteenth-century scholar would assimilate during his education – the tools of medieval thought. Chapter 3 discusses the translation and dissemination of Aristotelian and Arabic philosophical texts; and Chapter 4 considers some reactions to the threats and challenges which this material presented. The Conclusion to Part One describes some of the ways in which historians and philosophers nowadays approach medieval philosophy and explains how the method of 'historical analysis' adopted in Part Two differs from them.

Intellectual knowledge was by no means the only philosophical topic discussed in the later Middle Ages. It is chosen for detailed study in Part Two because it provides a particularly clear illustration of the manner, aims and achievements of thirteenth- and fourteenth-century abstract thought. Most of the outstanding later medieval thinkers discussed the topic in detail and arrived at very different conclusions. Their various treatments depend, in most cases, both on their understanding of ancient Greek thought (especially Aristotle's) and on their function as Christian theologians. Although intellectual knowledge does not exactly correspond to any single concept used in modern philosophy, many of the questions which medieval thinkers raised about it are closely related to those which interest philosophers today. And medieval discussions of the subject can be made comprehensible – unlike many topics in ethics or the philosophy of mind and action – without too much explanation of purely theological doctrines.

The individual writers whose discussions of intellectual knowledge are examined are taken from different parts of the period from 1230 to about 1340. The selection of Aquinas (Chapter 7), Duns Scotus (Chapter 10) and William of Ockham (Chapter 11) for extended attention requires little justification: their pre-eminence is widely and justly accepted. The choice of other thinkers for detailed study cannot but seem a little arbitrary, in a book which makes no claims to be comprehensive. The size and richness of the philosophical material from the mid-thirteenth century onwards suggested that the interesting, but lesser thinkers of the period 1150–1230 should receive only a general treatment in Part One. William of Auvergne (Chapter 6) is chosen as the most complex thinker of the first generation to explore and react to the implications of Artistotle and Avicenna; Martin and Boethius of Dacia, and Radulphus Brito (Chapter 8), because from their work can be gauged the achievements and the limitations of the later thirteenth-century arts faculties. Henry of Ghent (Chapter 9) was the most adventurous of the theologians between Aquinas and Duns Scotus; a close study of his arguments indicates that he was a far more powerful thinker than is allowed by most histories of philosophy, where he is labelled rather inappropriately as a Platonist or an Augustinian. Among the outstanding writers who are *not* treated in detail in Part Two are Robert Grosseteste, Roger Bacon, Albert the Great, Siger of Brabant, Bonaventure, Godfrey of Fontaines, Hervaeus Natalis, Meister Eckhart, Thomas Bradwardine and John Buridan. And a glance at any text book will reveal how easily many more names could be added to this list. Part Two is intended only to provide a sample of some later medieval treatments of one group of problems. Like Part One, it should not be regarded as any more than an introduction to the subject.

It is never possible to delimit the history of thought into neat and precise periods. But the middle of the twelfth century is, for many reasons, an appropriate date from which to begin an introduction to later medieval thought. In 1150 a remarkable period in the history of thought was drawing to a close. Abelard and Hugh of St Victor had died in the previous decade. Within a few years Gilbert of Poitiers and Bernard of Clairvaux would be dead, Thierry of Chartres would have retired from intellectual life, and William of Conches disappeared from the record. Abelard and Gilbert each had considerable influence on some logicians and theologians of the succeeding decades; but their followers had to accommodate themselves to the new techniques which were transforming intellectual life. From 1150 onwards, the forms of later scholastic debate were elaborated, its logical tools developed; many of the antique and Arab texts which would be so influential were translated; and the loosely organized schools of Paris began to become a university.

Part One

1 Teaching and learning in the universities

In the later Middle Ages, sophisticated abstract thinkers were trained in universities and usually taught there. For the period up to 1350 two universities are of outstanding importance for the historian of philosophy: Paris and Oxford. There were indeed other large, respected and earlier established universities, like Bologna, Salerno and Montpellier: but Bologna specialized in law, Salerno and Montpellier in medicine. Only later in the fourteenth century did other universities – such as Cambridge, Prague, Vienna and Heidelberg – begin to become important centres for the study of logic and theology.

The institutional development of Paris and Oxford as universities

The reputation of Paris as the place to study logic and theology was already well established early in the twelfth century. A number of other towns in France had cathedral schools which gained eminence in a particular field: Laon, for instance, was a centre for theology, Chartres for Platonic and scientific studies. But no town rivalled Paris in the variety of its teachers. Masters were allowed to set up schools there on payment of a small fee to the bishop and so teaching was not limited to the cathedral school of Notre Dame: there was, for example, a school on Mte St Geveviève, founded by Abelard, and the logician Adam of Balsham and his followers taught near the Petit Pont. During the later twelfth century this conglomeration of Parisian schools began to develop the institutional organization which would characterize the later medieval university: faculties became distinct, an order of studies was fixed and a pattern of degrees established to mark a student's academic progress. The intellectual celebrity of the town increased further and pupils came there to study not only from France, but also from England, Germany, Spain, Portugal, the Low Countries, Denmark and Italy.

The University of Oxford grew later and less gradually. An undistinguished school in the early twelfth century, it had become by about 1250 the second most important centre of the study of logic, philosophy and theology. Throughout the thirteenth century, however, Paris maintained its supremacy; and masters who made a name for themselves in Oxford regularly completed their academic careers by going to Paris. Only in the 1320s did the intellectual standing of Oxford start to equal, if not eclipse, the older university.

The growth of Paris and Oxford preceded the regular use of a terminology to differentiate between universities and other educational establishments. By the late fourteenth century, the term *studium generale* had become the usual designation of a university; a plain *studium* was a school of lesser scope and pretentions. A concept which became associated in university documents with the idea of a *studium generale* was the *ius ubique docendi* – the right of those who gained qualifications at the *studium* to teach at any other university. In practice this right was often disregarded – especially by the masters of Paris and Oxford.

The universities were subject to two kinds of institutional rule. Externally, the relations between their members and the civic authorities were defined and controlled; internally, the order, method and duration of academic studies were regulated. It was valuable for a ruler to have a university in his domain: its presence both brought economic stimulation and provided educated men who could work as administrators. By threatening to go elsewhere – and sometimes actually doing so – the masters at Paris, Oxford and elsewhere were able to obtain privileges for themselves and their students from the secular government. A charter of 1200 (*Chartularium no.* 1) granted members of Paris university the right to be tried by ecclesiastical courts even if they were not clerics and imposed severe penalties on townsmen guilty of violence against the students; whilst in Oxford, the university authorities gradually came to control most aspects of civic life. So far from their work being subject to secular political constraints, medieval scholars won for themselves a legally privileged status in society and enjoyed special liberties. Their intellectual freedoms, however, were to some extent limited by the local church leaders and by the papacy. The condemnation of various books and doctrines, and the uncertain response to these proscriptions, provide a measure of the control which the ecclesiastical authorities were able to exercise, and of its limitations (see below, pp. 17, 69, 72-4).

The internal regulation of the universities derives from three main sources: the pattern of studies followed in the schools since the early Middle Ages; the system which grew up in early twelfth-century Paris, whereby individual masters were licensed to teach by the Chancellor of Notre Dame, the original cathedral school; and the status, recognized in Paris by the early thirteenth century, of the masters and scholars as a guild (*universitas*). Before someone could be admitted to the guild as a master, a number of years had to be spent as an apprentice, various accomplishments had to be demonstrated and certain ceremonies performed. Against the background of these different influences, the form and methods of studies in the medieval university slowly developed. It is best to examine them in two stages: their development in the decades after 1150, before the schools of Paris had fully become a university; and the form which they had reached by the mid-thirteenth century and which, with minor variations, they retained until the end of the Middle Ages.

Methods and organization of studies before the thirteenth century

(1) Texts, commentaries and the origin of the faculties

From its very beginnings, medieval education was based around authoritative texts. Teaching consisted in expounding them; learning was a process of familiarization with their contents. By understanding a text, the student came to know a subject. Each area had its own authorities: in grammar there were Donatus and Priscian, in logic Aristotle. The Bible had a special position as the supremely authoritative work, and the subject which came by the mid-thirteenth century to be described as theology grew out of the study of it.

Such a system of education might seem inimical to independent thought and to make philosophical speculation impossible. But the dividing line between understanding another's thoughts and working out one's own is often uncertain, and never more so than in the Middle Ages. Attempts to explain Aristotle or Boethius or Priscian led scholars to investigate problems and propose solutions which the ancient authors had never envisaged, and commentary was often the vehicle for original thought. By the twelfth century, medieval scholars had become ingenious at explaining why their own clear and sophisticated ideas were merely the correct interpretation of an apparently crude and muddled authoritative text: a particularly clear example is Gilbert of Poitiers's commentary (c.1140) on Boethius's *Opuscula Sacra*.

Although there survives a considerable number of theological or broadly philosophical works by schoolmasters from the ninth to twelfth centuries which do not directly reflect the teaching of the schools and which have a polished literary form – John Scottus's *Periphyseon*; the prosimetra of Bernard Silvestris and Alan of Lille; Abelard's *Colloquium* – the main written products of the schools in this period took the form of glosses and commentaries. Sometimes scholars went on to produce quasi-independent handbooks to a discipline; but they were not *completely* independent, because they would generally follow the subject-matter and order of the authoritative texts (for example, Abelard's *Dialectica* or Peter Helias's *Summa super Priscianum*).

The position of the Bible as the supreme authority made it the goal of study. The seven liberal arts tended to be regarded as a propaedeutic to learning about Christian doctrine through commentary on the Bible. The liberal arts were themselves divided into the trivium — grammar, logic and rhetoric – and the quadrivium of subjects considered to be mathematical – arithmetic, geometry, astronomy and music; but the quadrivium was frequently neglected, and rhetoric did not receive the attention given to grammar and logic. A knowledge of grammar was self-evidently a prerequisite for any further learning, and at least an elementary grasp of logic was thought almost as necessary. A pattern of education was therefore already established in the earlier Middle Ages in which a training in grammar and logic led on to theology. In the twelfth century the careers of a number of masters followed a pattern which reinforces the notion of theology as a superior discipline. William of Champeaux and his brilliant pupil, Abelard, had each become celebrated as a teacher of logic before he decided to study theology. During the following decades it became a regular feature of scholastic life for a teacher of arts to go on to become a student, and then finally a teacher, of theology.

(2) The beginnings of the *quaestio*-technique

It was among the theologians in the later twelfth century that a development took place in the method of teaching which would have the profoundest effects on medieval intellectual life. Its product, the *quaestio*-technique, was fundamental to the method of teaching and thinking of the universities.

Early twelfth-century theologians often described their works as sentences, *quaestiones* or *summae*. Sentences were enunciations or explorations of doctrine which may once have been, but no longer formed part of the commentary on a biblical text. *Quaestiones* juxtaposed authoritative statements which seemed to contradict each other. A *summa* collected together points or problems of dogma in an orderly, comprehensive manner. But such definitions obscure the extent to which the three procedures were interrelated: sentences led scholars to consider the instances where authorities disagreed and so to formulate *quaestiones*, and *summae* organized these individual discussions. In his *Sentences* (probably written 1255–7), Peter the Lombard, who taught at the cathedral school in Paris, succeeded in bringing these procedures into even closer conjunction. On some occasions Peter is content merely to quote the Bible or the Fathers, or to summarize their texts, just as Anselm of Laon had done in some of his more dogmatic sentences. More often Peter uses the form of a *quaestio*, setting out authorities which seem to support opposed solutions before resolving their differences and giving an answer. He organizes all this material into a *summa*, an orderly consideration of all the main theological problems debated by his contemporaries.

The Lombard's *Sentences* are related to his teaching at the cathedral school, but probably not directly based on it. Accounts of theological teaching in the mid-twelfth century suggest that it consisted of commentary on the Bible. No doubt doctrinal problems were raised in the course of exegesis, but they were probably discussed as they occurred. There is a set of glosses on *Romans* by Peter which seems to be the direct product of this sort of teaching. But the compilation of the *Sentences* was a literary activity in which Peter brought together in a thematic order discussions which had occurred in the course of his biblical exegesis (such as those preserved in the glosses to *Romans*), and added to them other material from the Bible, the Fathers and the theologians of the recent past, such as Hugh of St Victor, so as to provide a comprehensive doctrinal handbook. In doing so, Peter was following the normal practice of his times for compiling a *summa*: for example, his contemporary Robert of Melun used his own *Questiones de Divina Pagina* and *Questiones de Epistolis Pauli* as sources for his *Sentences*.

Peter the Lombard was a sober scholar, reverential towards his authorities and zealous for orthodoxy. If he indulged in argument, it was to solve genuine problems about doctrine. Those who taught theology in Paris in the later decades of the century were more attracted to reasoning for its own sake. For example, in the *Sentences* of Peter of Poitiers (probably written between 1167 and 1170), questions on which there is general agreement are omitted, whilst those where the authorities seem contradictory are developed at great length, and the author deploys sophisticated logical and linguistic techniques to reach his solutions. A technical vocabulary of argument is more widespread and developed than in earlier writing: 'some say in reply to this argument' (*ad hoc quidam dicunt*); 'it should be said in reply to this' (*ad hoc dicendum*); 'but against this it is objected' (*sed contra hoc obicitur*); 'an objection might be put thus' (*ita instantia dari possit/ita possit instari*). And the author will sometimes give a series of arguments and then raise objections to each in turn. Some chapters are devoted to a particular, controversial question – for example, 'Can God do whatever he has been able to do?' (i, 8), or 'Is God's prescience the cause of the things which happen or vice versa?' i, 13). A similar emphasis on controversy is evident in the slightly later *Summa* by Simon of Tournai. In these works of the later twelfth century the main features of the fully developed thirteenth-century *quaestio*-technique are already present: a problem is divided into a series of discrete questions, which can be answered 'yes' or 'no'. The writer assembles citations and arguments for each of the two replies, and not only does he explain why his response is correct, but also why the material he has adduced for the opposite solution does not in fact vindicate it.

How much does the development of the *quaestio*-technique by authors like Peter depend on the *logica nova* – the books of Aristotelian logic newly available in the mid-twelfth century (see below, pp. 35–6)? One of them, the *Topics*, is a textbook for a type of argument-contest, in which a questioner tries to force an answerer into self-contradiction. In his *Metalogicon* (1159) John of Salisbury enthuses about the value of the *Topics* and describes (iii, 10) the method of disputation which the book teaches. It is therefore tempting to believe that the development of the *quaestio*-technique was encouraged by disputations conducted according to the principles of the *Topics*. The *Disputationes* of Simon of Tournai, a teacher of theology in Paris, seem to bear out this view. Written before the end of the century, the work appears to record a set of independent disputes about doctrinal problems which took place with Simon as master, charged with providing a solution once opposing arguments had been presented to him. The dispute, then, can be presented as an activity separate from the exegesis of scripture, which developed in the later twelfth century under the aegis of Aristotelian logic and which shaped the way in which theological method was elaborated.

There are, however, many reasons for rejecting this view. Despite John of Salisbury's advocacy, Aristotle's *Topics* was not a very popular book; and, in any case, the procedure it describes bears little resemblance to that of the *quaestio*. A *quaestio* is designed to reconcile texts which appear contradictory; the elenchic debate described in the *Topics* has nothing to do with texts nor does it aim at the resolution of any problem. In his passages about disputation, John of Salisbury seems rather to have been talking about an ideal which he read in Aristotle than the practices of his contemporaries.

The *quaestio*-technique used by Peter of Poitiers and his contemporaries is better explained as an elaboration of what he learned from Peter the Lombard than through the influence of logic or disputations. The Lombard's *Sentences* were enormously popular as soon as they were written. By 1165, less than a decade after their composition, three sets of glosses to them had already been written. Peter of Poitiers, so different in interests and temperament from his namesake, none the less used the Lombard's *Sentences* closely, ordering his own work according to their general scheme, following them in doctrine and often in detail and using them throughout as a dossier of patristic quotations. Simon of Tournai was the author of a literal abbreviation of the *Sentences*, and when he came to write his own *Summa* he followed the Lombard in his general arrangement of material. His *Disputationes* can be seen as records of the development of a literary procedure into oral teaching. The *quaestiones* it contains are considerably simpler in form than those of contemporary and earlier works based on the *Sentences*; and it seems much more probable that they represent an attempt to use in the classroom techniques which had been learned and developed in following on from the Lombard's work, than an independent tradition.

Historians who use the *logica nova* and the practice of disputation to explain the development of the *quaestio*-technique tend to separate the method of theological speculation from its contents. They see the method as characterized by an intellectual energy and openness to rational speculation which is accounted for by influences external to theology: in particular, by Aristotle's logic. The account of later twelfth-century theology which has been put forward above in opposition to this view has very different implications. It maintains that the method and content of later medieval theology were inextricably connected. The *quaestio*-technique developed because of the special characteristics of the textbook of theology, the Bible. Everything in the Bible was accepted by the theologians as true, but often scriptural statements seemed contradictory. The more systematically theologians wished to organize their doctrinal discussions, the less possible it became to ignore these contradictions; and other contradictions, too, between different patristic authors or between Christian writers and pagan philosophers became evident and were drawn into the discussion. Gradually, the *quaestio*-technique became, not just a method for organizing theological *summae*, but a way of thought which could be used in any subject and which shaped the practice of teaching in the medieval universities.

University organization from the thirteenth century

(1) The faculty of arts

In 1215 Robert of Courçon, as papal legate, issued a set of instructions about the content and organization of studies in Paris (*Chartularium* no. 20): many of their provisions no doubt rehearse what had already become common practice. Robert's statutes suggest that one of the main features of medieval university education was now definitely established at Paris. A student would begin by studying arts and, at a fairly young age (Robert gives twenty-one as a minimum), become a teacher of arts. Only then might he become a student of theology and, after another lengthy period of study, teach the subject. There were two other 'higher' disciplines (not covered by Robert's provisions) besides that of theology: medicine and law. In the 1170s or 1180s – to judge from Alexander of Nequam's career – a student could combine work in all three higher subjects; but even by 1215 theology was already too demanding a discipline to leave room for other academic interests.

One of the main reasons why Paris had become an outstanding centre for study at the turn of the twelfth century was the freedom which masters had there in setting up schools. They needed only to buy a licence from the chancellor of the cathedral in order to be allowed to teach. But by the early thirteenth century, academic careers in Paris had become highly regulated. Recognition as a master of arts required a long course of study and various examinations (see below, pp.20–4) and in the faculty of theology the number of magisterial teaching-posts (or 'chairs') was strictly limited. Similar restrictions were in force at other medieval universities.

In size the arts faculty was by far the largest in medieval universities. Many students did not continue their studies beyond arts; many, indeed, followed only part of the arts course. In Paris, for instance, only about a third of the university belonged to the three higher faculties; and there were, in most medieval universities, many more students of law than theology. The arts masters in Paris were divided into four Nations (the French – which included masters from Spain and Italy – the Norman, the Picard and the English-German), each of which had its own schools and was responsible for much of the organization of a student's academic life. The four Nations of the Paris arts faculty elected a rector, who was in practice the head of the university. The arts faculty was therefore in the somewhat odd position of being institutionally predominant within the university and yet intellectually subordinate to the higher faculties: when a scholar had become a fully qualified teacher of arts, he was merely ready to begin his studies in theology, law or medicine.

(2) The mendicants in the university

Most of the great thirteenth- and fourteenth-century theologians were members of the mendicant orders. For instance, Albert the Great and St Thomas Aquinas were Dominicans. The mendicants, especially the Dominicans and Franciscans, had quite quickly established their own schools, in which the full range of arts and theology (although not medicine or law) came to be taught. Just as universities like Paris drew students from all over Europe, so the mendicants' schools included not only *scolae provinciales* for students from a particular area, but *studia generalia* to which students from elsewhere could be assigned. There was a tendency to choose convents in university towns as the place for these schools, especially the *studia generalia*, perhaps in order to attract to the order intellectually able recruits from the university; but at first mendicant scholars showed no wish to play a direct part in university teaching. However, during a long strike by the secular masters in 1229–30, the friars kept on teaching and opened their schools to secular students of theology. The Dominican, Roland of Cremona, thus became the first mendicant theology master in Paris university. The number of mendicant masters increased rapidly, because secular masters became members of an order but continued with their teaching. For instance, Alexander of Hales became the first of

ALLEGHENY COLLEGE LIBRARY

the Franciscan masters in the university when he converted to the order in about 1231. When a member of an order finished his period of magisterial teaching, he passed the chair on to another of his confraternity. As a result, by 1254 the secular masters in Paris had no more than three out of fifteen chairs in the theology faculty.

The resentment of the secular masters, whose careers had been made so much more difficult by the mendicants, and whose unity and power as a guild was threatened by a set of colleagues not bound by its rules, resulted in a series of quarrels between 1253 and 1256: the seculars passed various measures directed against the mendicants, who appealed to the papacy for support. When the seculars set out their position (*Chartularium* 230), Pope Innocent IV was inclined to support them. But his successor, Alexander IV took the mendicants' part, and the outcome was that the secular masters, despite their threats to dissolve the university, had to accept the role of the mendicants in teaching theology. In Oxford the mendicants were accepted with far less acrimony, although there were some quarrels with the seculars, especially in the early fourteenth century.

Unlike secular students, mendicants did not take an arts degree at university before they began their course in theology. But they received an equally thorough training in the arts at one of their order's *studia*, usually away from the great universities. And, in the fourteenth century especially, the *studia* in non-university towns like London were sometimes the setting for advanced work in theology too. A Franciscan statute of 1336, for instance, requires members of the order who wish to comment on the *Sentences* at Paris, Oxford or Cambridge to have lectured on them previously in a *studium* elsewhere (such as London, York or Norwich).

(3) Methods of teaching in the thirteenth and fourteenth centuries

Various elementary scholastic exercises were used in the arts faculty; and it was part of a master of theology's task to preach university sermons. But the two main methods of teaching used in the medieval universities were the 'reading' of set-texts and disputations.

(i) Reading
The earliest list of set-books for the arts faculty is contained in Robert of Courçon's statutes (see above, p.14). He prescribes Aristotle's logic and *Ethics*, Priscian and, less specifically, some other grammatical works, and some rhetorical and mathematical

texts. Robert's statutes are famous for forbidding the use as set-books of Aristotle's *Metaphysics* and books of 'natural philosophy' (see below, pp. 54–5). But by 1255 (cf. *Chartularium no.* 246) most of Aristotle's works – including the *Metaphysics, Physics* and *De anima* – were prescribed for students of arts in Paris. From about this time onwards, the arts course in every medieval university involved the study of a wide range of Aristotelian texts. The new books did not, however, replace the grammatical and logical texts or diminish their importance. Aristotle's non-logical works came to occupy the position which the quadrivium had traditionally held in relation to the trivium. Grammar and logic remained the beginning and foundation of all learning, the primary sources of intellectual method.

Although for the theologians the main text to be studied had been, and always to an extent remained, the Bible, in the 1220s another set-book was added to their curriculum. From the time they were composed, the *Sentences* of Peter the Lombard had been influential (see above, pp. 11–13). Their form had been imitated and a number of literal commentaries on them, had been written. There had been opposition to the Lombard's trinitarian views; but at the Lateran Council of 1215 the teaching of the *Sentences* on the Trinity was adopted as the Church's. After such official commendation, the decision of Alexander of Hales early in the 1220s to use the *Sentences* as a text to be 'read' in his Parisian theology lectures is hardly surprising. From Alexander's time to Luther's, the *Sentences* joined the Bible as the textbook of the theology faculty.

When medieval university documents prescribe set books to be 'read' (the Latin term is *legere*, and it will be rendered as *read* – in italics – henceforth), they are referring to a very different process from the modern reader's private and somewhat passive assimilation. Texts *read* were texts expounded. Early medieval masters had sometimes limited themselves to brief, literal explanations of their texts, and sometimes produced lengthy commentaries in which they developed their own views in detail. In the universities these two approaches became regularized as a feature of the curriculum. Texts could be *read* 'cursorily' (*cursorie*) or 'ordinarily' (*ordinarie*). Cursory *reading* was limited to presenting the sense of a text, without discussing the problems it raised, and so the records of these *readings* are not of the greatest interest to the historian. The ordinary *readings* of texts, by contrast, was as much an opportunity for the development of new ideas as for the exposition of old ones.

The method used by theology masters for ordinary *reading* of the Bible was a formalization of exegetical techniques developed in earlier centuries for studying secular texts. First, the master would divide the text to be studied into sections and sub-sections; then he would proceed to expound it, beginning with a literal explanation but moving into wider ranging discussion and allegorical exegesis as he found necessary. The method for ordinary *reading* of the theologian's other textbook, the *Sentences*, was rather different. Early and mid-thirteenth-century *Sentence* commentaries – such as those by Alexander of Hales and Aquinas – do indeed divide up each section of the Lombard's text and expound it literally; but then follow a series of *quaestiones* on the problems raised by that section of the *Sentences*. But after this time it became usual to omit the introductory division and exposition of the text. *Reading* the *Sentences* amounted to composing *quaestiones* on the problems discussed in each part of the text. In the fourteenth century, even the links between the *quaestiones* and the Lombard's topics and ordering became loose: a theologian *reading* a given book of the *Sentences* would feel bound to make his *quaestiones* relate to the general area of theology dealt with in the whole book, but otherwise he would be free to discuss in them the particular theological problems which were currently at issue.

From the 1250s onwards, arts masters too were fond of using *quaestiones* in the ordinary *reading* of their set-texts. Detailed exposition of the text, section by section, would be followed by a series of *quaestiones* on the problems which had been raised. Normally these *quaestiones* are simple in form. Only a few arguments against the chosen solution are advanced, and the counter-argument to them is often a simple appeal to the text being discussed.

The methods of *reading* in medieval universities were, then, well adapted to the different types of work studied. The Bible, the sacred repository of truth, was *read* in a way which closely linked any wider discussion with the text itself. Aristotle and the other authorities of the arts faculty were valued because they were thought, in general, to put forward the best rational explanations of the problems they examined. Accordingly, they were *read* in a way which allowed these problems to be raised in general terms, but which looked back to the authoritative texts for their solutions. Peter the Lombard's *Sentences* was useful as an index of the main areas of theological debate and, in most cases, as a guide to the Church's view on them. But it was neither a sacred text nor one of great intellectual force. It was therefore *read* in a way which allowed scholars to concentrate on the theological problems themselves, leaving the text itself very much in the background.

(ii) Disputation

The *quaestio*, in all probability, was developed as a literary form (see above, pp. 12–14). The arguments for and against a position, the solution and the counter-arguments were all the work or choice of a single author. This remained the case when *quaestiones* were used in *reading* the *Sentences* or arts texts. The *quaestio*-commentaries which derive from these sessions should be thought to give a picture of debate between teacher and pupils: they are the words of the teacher, copied down by his students or from his own notes. In disputations, however, the *quaestio* provided the vehicle for genuine argument and counter-argument between those present.

Disputations in the theology faculty were of two main sorts – *quaestiones ordinariae/disputatae* ('ordinary disputations') and *quaestiones de quolibet* ('quodlibetal disputations, quodlibets'). Both types took place under the aegis of a master. Ordinary disputations were, in the main, intended as exercise and instruction for the master's own pupils. The master decided on a thesis or set of theses – short statements of position answerable by 'yes' or 'no' – to be debated. Very often he would select these carefully, so that their discussion, in a single disputation or over a number of them, would provide a systematic treatment of a particular topic. Each disputation had two sessions. In the first session, the pupils conducted most of the argument, although the master intervened whenever he thought it useful. The pupils could each contribute in one of two ways: as an 'objector' (*opponens, quaerens*), putting forward arguments against the thesis) or as a 'responder' (*respondens*), countering the objector's arguments. A responder's task was usually more difficult than that of an objector, since he was expected to set out his own general views on the problem at issue before answering the objection itself. In the second section, the master summarized the various arguments given by his pupils for and against the thesis and 'determined' the question at issue by giving his own answer and the reasonings which led him to it.

Ordinary disputations in the theology faculty were frequent and regular (often taking place once a week); and it was part of a master's duty to conduct them. Quodlibetal disputations were rarer – for instance, in later thirteenth-century Paris they took place just twice a year. No master was obliged to organize quodlibets, although participation in them was considered a necessary part of a theology student's training. Whereas the participants in an ordinary disputation were a master's own pupils, quodlibets were attended by students from all over the university. It was for one of the audience, not the master, to raise the problem to be discussed, and he had complete freedom of choice in doing so: quodlibets were disputes about anything (*de quolibet*) raised by anyone (*a quolibet*). Usually, in raising a problem, a student put forward a position and supported it with reasoning. A responder – another student, but not necessarily a pupil of the presiding master – countered his arguments. During a single session, a number of different theses, raised by different participants, were debated in this way. At a second session – as in an ordinary disputation – the master determined, summarizing the arguments given on each side of the questions and proposing his own solutions.

In the arts faculty there were three sorts of disputation: *de sophismatibus, de quaestione* and *de quolibet*. Disputations *de sophismatibus* or (*sophismata*) were about logic (though sometimes, late in the Middle Ages, *sophisma* was used as a word for any disputation in the arts faculty); disputations *de quaestione* were about the *scientiae reales* – branches of knowledge such as physics which concern things, rather than methods of reasoning about them. Disputations *de quolibet* were, as the name implies, open. Much less information about disputations in the arts faculty survives than for the theologians. It appears that they followed much the same form; but magisterial determination may not have constituted a separate session, and often the disputations amounted to little more than scholastic exercises.

(4) A university student's career

The institutional aspects of university life, the curricula of the faculties and the various methods of teaching combine to give the later medieval university student's career its characteristic form. Its details are best summarized in a table (see below, Table 1). But it is important to emphasize that, although the general pattern of university studies remained remarkably constant from the mid-thirteenth century until the end of the Middle Ages, in detail they varied much more, from decade to decade and from student to student, than statutes and other official documents – which provide most of the historian's evidence – might suggest. If we were to describe a modern student's academic career solely on the basis of his university's statutes and ordinances, how far from the truth our account would be!

Table 1   **A student's career at university**

Duration in years	Description	Main academic activities
Arts faculty		
2	Undergraduate	Attends ordinary and cursory *readings* of grammatical, logical and some other Aristotelian works, and disputations
2	Undergraduate	As above; also responds in disputations
after which	admitted to determine	
3 (at Oxford; variable at Paris)	Bachelor	Determination (determining at disputes); attends ordinary *readings* and disputes as before and also of further material (such as Aristotle's natural philosophy and metaphysics and texts concerning the *quadrivium*); responding at disputations; giving cursory *readings*
after which	licence; inception as master	Participates in special disputations etc.
2 (but can be continued beyond the two years necessary)	Master: necessary regency	Gives ordinary *readings*, determines at disputations

Theology faculty

7 (later reduced to 6)		Attends ordinary and cursory *readings* of Bible, attends *readings* of *Sentences*, and disputations
2	*Cursus/ baccalaureus biblicus*	Attends ordinary *readings* and disputations as before; gives cursory *readings* of Bible; responds in disputations
2; but 1 by fourteenth century	*Baccalaureus sententiarius*	Gives (ordinary) *reading* of *Sentences*
4	*Baccalaureus formatus*	Takes part in disputations and attends university functions
after which	inception as master	Participates in special disputations etc.
usually limited	Regent master	Gives ordinary *readings* of Bible and determines at disputations

[The figures given for the theology faculty relate to Paris; at Oxford the course became shorter; and there the stage of *baccalaureus biblicus* usually came after that of *sententiarius*.]

The student came to university at about fourteen or fifteen and entered the faculty of arts. His career there was divided into three stages. For at least four years he was an undergraduate: he had to attend ordinary and cursory *readings* mainly of logical and grammatical works, but also of some other Aristotelian texts. He also had to attend disputations; and, after his first two years, he had to act as responder in them. When the student and his teacher had satisfied a board of masters that he had fulfilled these requirements and was a person of moral probity, he was admitted to 'determine'. A series of disputations took place during Lent which were like ordinary disputations except that it was not the presiding master, but the student so admitted who determined, giving his solution to the problems which had been raised. It is most probable that the student was regarded as a bachelor (*baccalaureus*) once he had been admitted to determine; certainly he was one after determining.

As a bachelor, the student continued to attend ordinary readings, both of texts he had previously studied and of some new ones. He acted as responder in disputes and was allowed to give cursory *readings* himself. He completed this stage of his career (which lasted for three years at Oxford) by receiving his 'licence' – a relic of the time when masters had to be licensed by the chancellor of a cathedral school – and incepting as a master of arts. Inception marked the student's full entry into the guild of masters: it involved taking the part of objector in a disputation (the *vesperies*), giving a short *reading* and taking part in a further disputation (the investiture). One of the oaths taken by intending masters was that, for at least two years, he would teach in the university. These two years are therefore known as a master's 'necessary regency'. Masters gave ordinary *readings*, and determined at disputations.

After he fulfilled his necessary regency, an arts master could go on teaching for as long as he wished. But there were few who remained arts masters for very long (Roger Bacon, Siger of Brabant, Boethius of Dacia, Radulphus Brito and John Buridan are among these exceptions): most began study in the theology faculty or else sought a position outside academic life.

Before he could enter the faculty of theology, a student had to be a master of arts or to have received an equally thorough training in a mendicant *studium*. During the first part of his course – which lasted originally for six or seven years – the student had to attend ordinary and cursory *readings* of the Bible, ordinary *readings* of the *Sentences* (and perhaps also cursory *readings* of them), disputations and other functions of the faculty. He then became a bachelor and, in Paris, for the first two years, was a *cursor biblicus* – he was required to give cursory *readings* of the Bible and act as responder in disputations, in addition to attending ordinary *readings* and disputes as previously. For the next two years, he became a *baccalaureus sententiarius*: during this time he was devoted to *reading* the *Sentences* – a function which demanded a thorough and sophisticated knowledge of theology and which provided more junior members of the faculty, who were obliged to attend, with one of their most important forms of instruction. The student then spent a period – at least four years at Paris– as a *baccalaureus formatus*, during which he was obliged to take part in disputations and other university functions.

The student was now ready to become a master of theology, but he could do so only if there were a Chair free for him: William of Ockham ('the Venerable Inceptor') was not the only distinguished theologian who completed all the requirements for mastership, but was unable to incept because none of his order's university Chairs became available. Just as a master of arts incepted by taking part in special disputations, so in the theology faculty inception involved a set of disputations divided into three sessions. The new master took various roles, including that of determiner; and a number of other masters and bachelors participated. As regent master (a master holding a Chair and engaged in teaching) he gave ordinary *readings* of the Bible, choosing their frequency and texts as he wished; presided and determined at disputations. Masters of theology were also required to preach sermons (as were students of theology at all levels).

Masters of theology did not usually stay in their chairs for long. If they were members of an order, they would probably be encouraged to vacate their position for a colleague who was ready to incept. Some masters of theology were promoted to high positions in the Church or within their order – for instance, Bonaventure was made Minister General of the Franciscans three years after he incepted. Mendicant masters were often sent to teach at one of their order's *studia* or to found a new *studium*. For instance, Albert the Great was made responsible for organizing a new Dominican *studium* in Cologne; and Duns Scotus spent the last years of his short life teaching at the Franciscan *studium* in the same town. Aquinas was given the job of starting a Dominican *studium* in Rome; and Ockham taught at the Franciscan house in London.

The forms of logical, philosophical and theological writing

The pattern of university studies is of great importance to the historian of medieval philosophy because most of the texts he uses are either the records of university teaching and exercises (*Sentence* commentaries, *quaestio*-commentaries on Aristotle, disputations) or are related to the work of the university (textbooks, monographs, polemics).

(1) Types of text which record university teaching

The spoken university teaching of a *sententiarius* or master could become a written text in one of two ways. It might be copied down by one of his pupils – a *reportatio*; or it might be prepared for publication by the master himself, either from his own notes or from those of a pupil – an *ordinatio*. *Reportationes* often record what a particular listener found interesting (or was able to understand); an *ordinatio* gave a scholar the chance to make his thought clearer or, if he thought necessary, to alter it. Ordinary *readings* of Aristotle or the *Sentences* often are recorded as *reportationes* and sometimes have been put into an *ordinatio* by their authors. The first session of a disputation – more an exercise for pupils than an opportunity for a master to develop doctrine – was not usually recorded; but a few *reportationes* survive, from which a picture of these has emerged. The second session of a disputation, however, where the master summarized and determined, was very often recorded, revised and published by the master as the expression of his views.

Many works from the medieval universities consist of a set of *quaestiones*. From which type of teaching and from what stage in its author's professional career does such a text derive? Sometimes, as well as *quaestiones*, a work has passages of section-by-section commentary. If the text commented belongs to the curriculum of the arts faculty, then the commentary and *quaestiones* record the ordinary *readings* of a master of arts; if the *Sentences* are its object, then the work is that of a *baccalaureus sententiarius* – unless it dates from before about 1250, when it ceased to be the custom for masters to *read* the *Sentences* (but see below).

Very often, however, sets of *quaestiones* survive which include no passages of commentary. Only some of them are records of (the second sessions of) disputations; and these are usually identified by the large number of arguments given for and against each thesis (for example, Aquinas's *Quaestiones de Veritate* and his *Quaestiones de Anima*). Others are almost certainly records of arts masters' ordinary *readings* from which the sections of literal exposition have been omitted (for instance, many texts of Siger of Brabant's commentaries), or records of a bachelor's *reading* of the *Sentences*, which may never have included any literal exposition (see above, p. 18). It is not, however, inevitably the case that *quaestiones* on the *Sentences* are the work of a bachelor, since the *quaestiones disputatae* of a few later thirteenth-, fourteenth- and fifteenth-century masters are based on the plan of the *Sentences*.

Not every text which records university teaching consists of *quaestiones*. Besides the records of ordinary *readings* of the Bible, some manuscripts preserve what were probably cursory *readings* of Aristotle. And some commentaries are products of a time when the forms of university teaching were less regular than they became from the mid-thirteenth century. For example, there is a gloss by

Stephen Langton on the *Sentences* which does not seem to record merely a 'cursory reading' and yet is certainly not a full *quaestio-*commentary of the sort Alexander of Hales was to introduce. Or there is the *De Anima* of John Blund, which probably records his arts teaching in Oxford or Paris at the turn of the thirteenth century. This treatise sometimes uses the vocabulary of the *quaestio* but it is neither divided into questions, nor does it comment a text paragraph by paragraph, but is arranged as a discursive account of doctrine on the soul.

(2) Types of university text which do not record university teaching

Masters of arts and theology were authors of many sorts of textbooks, which did not record any particular type of university teaching, although they were usually, though not always, written to be read by students there. The grandest sort of textbook is exemplified by Aquinas's two *summae*. The *Summa Theologiae* [ST] was intended to provide a more systematic treatment of Christian doctrine to replace the Lombard's *Sentences* as a textbook for theologians (an aim achieved only in the sixteenth century). His earlier *Summa Contra Gentiles* [SG] had been written to provide a handbook to Christian doctrine especially for those engaged in missionary work with the Muslim. In the *Summa Theologiae*, but not the *Summa Contra Gentiles*, Aquinas adopted the *quaestio*-form. Such elaborate textbooks are very rare in the thirteenth and fourteenth centuries. Most are manuals dedicated to a particular subject, normally a technical one such as logic or grammar. For example, there are the manuals of the early thirteenth-century 'terminist' logicians (see below, pp. 41–7); specialized treatises on parts of logic like syncategoremata or obligations; and more philosophically ambitious introductions such as Ockham's *Summa totius Logicae*.

Monographs, written simply from a wish to explore a particular intellectual problem in depth, were very rare indeed. Aquinas (so often an exception to the rule so far as the form of his work is concerned) produced a few examples, including an early work (more of definition than discussion) about being, *De Esse et Essentia* and a later piece on angels, *De Substantiis Separatis*. But monographs were more frequently written as a direct result of controversies, in order to combat a particular view or thinker. For example, Aquinas and Boethius of Dacia wrote treatises in connection with a dispute about Aristotle's contention that the world is eternal (see below, pp. 71–2); Aquinas wrote about the intellect in response to an erroneous view which he had heard propounded (see below, pp. 68–71); and Giles of Rome wrote a monograph attacking more generally the *Errors of the Philosophers.*

There are also at least two sets of commentaries on Aristotle which do not record the public *reading* of texts. Albert the Great, distressed at what he felt to be a widespread ignorance of Aristotle, wrote a set of commentaries on his works, using the type of discursive exposition favoured by the Arab philosopher, Avicenna (see below, pp.59–60), where the commentary forms an independent work which can substitute for the text it sets out to explain. Albert's pupil, Aquinas, produced towards the end of his life a series of commentaries on Aristotle which both expound the philosopher's texts in a clear and literal way and, on many occasions, include passages of wider discussion and explanation which make them among the fullest and most sophisticated expositions of Aquinas's own doctrine in many areas (see below, pp.79, 125–7).

Even these textbooks, monographs and commentaries, which were written as literary works rather than delivered as lectures, use the technical style typical of university *readings* and disputations, without rhetorical flourishes, any ornamentation, or any attempt to persuade a reader other than by the logic of reasoning. The attention to phrasing and form characteristic of earlier twelfth-century authors is almost entirely missing. Bonaventure's *Itinerarium Viae Mentis Humanae ad Deum* – the very title of which stands out among the list of later medieval theological works – is almost alone among the books of university men in having the stylistic and affective qualities which had once been cultivated by medieval thinkers.

The form and later development of the *quaestio*

Much of the writing by later medieval thinkers, it will now be clear, consists of *quaestiones*. What was the exact form of a *quaestio*? How did it develop in the thirteenth and fourteenth centuries? And what can be gathered from this about the goals and presuppositions of the writers who used this technique?

(1) The form of the *quaestio* in the middle and late thirteenth century

The table below (Table 2) shows the relatively simple form of the *quaestio* common in the middle and late thirteenth century.

Table 2   **The form of a *quaestio***

[In this example, the author wishes to argue that *p* (for instance, that God exists): *p* will be called the 'preferred' position and not–*p* the 'contrary' position]

I	STATEMENT OF THE PROBLEM; 'It is asked (*quaeritur*) whether it is the case that *p*': e.g. 'It is asked whether God exists' [*sometimes a group of related questions will be posed and then answered in turn*]
II	STATEMENT OF THE CONTRARY POSITION (not–*p*), usually introduced by the phrase *uidetur quod* ('it seems that'): e.g. 'it seems that God does not exist'; followed by individual ARGUMENTS – from authority and/or reason – IN SUPPORT OF THIS POSITION.
III	ARGUMENT(S) – from authority or reason – FOR THE PREFERRED POSITION (*p*), usually introduced by the phrase *sed contra* ('but against [this]'): e.g. 'But against this is what is said in *Exodus* . . .'
IV	The author's own SOLUTION OF THE PROBLEM and EXPLANATION of why it is the case that *p*, introduced by the words *respondeo dicendum* ('I reply that it ought to be said that . . .'): e.g. 'I reply that it ought to be said that God can be proved to exist . . .'
V	REFUTATION, one by one, OF THE ARGUMENTS FOR THE CONTRARY POSITION

Aquinas discusses whether God exists following this format in his *Summa Theologiae* (1,2,3). His solution to the problem (section IV) consists of his famous exposition of the 'five ways'. Another article from the *Summa* (1,85,1) will furnish a rather more typical example of the balance between reasoning and quotation of authority in a *quaestio*. The question posed is 'whether our intellect knows corporeal and material things by abstraction from *phantasmata*' (see below, pp. 123–9 for an extended discussion of the problem itself). Aquinas believes that this is indeed the method of human intellectual knowledge. He therefore begins his *quaestio* by proposing the position contrary to this. It *seems*, he says, that our intellects do *not* understand in this way; and he goes on to give five separate arguments which bear out this position. Two of these are pure pieces of reasoning, three of them are based on authority, citing a text of Aristotle's and drawing out its implications. After these arguments comes the phrase *sed contra* and another argument, also based on the authority of Aristotle, which supports Aquinas's own favoured position. Aquinas then gives his own, detailed argument for thinking that our intellects do understand by abstraction from *phantasmata* – the 'body' of the *quaestio* – and concludes by explaining in turn why each of the arguments for the opposite position is not conclusive. In this particular *quaestio*, these refutations involve lengthy discussion; but in the *Summa* – as in many other works – there are often occasions where the author's own detailed argument in the body of the *quaestio* makes such discussion unnecessary: 'the reply to the objections is obvious' (*patet responsio ad obiecta*). The number of arguments given here for the opposite position is average or more than average for the *Summa* (and also for a mid-thirteenth-century *Sentences* commentary). But a *quaestio* which derives from (the second session of) a theological disputation would usually have many more such opposing arguments – perhaps fifteen or twenty. Since each opposing argument usually demanded a reply, these *quaestiones* are considerably longer than those in the *Summa* (four or five thousand words as against eight hundred to a thousand), and their material is differently balanced, with much more space devoted to the objections and replies than to the author's own solution.

In Aquinas's *quaestio* on the intellect and abstraction the only authority adduced for the opposing arguments and the *sed contra* is Aristotle; this is not unusual for a *quaestio* about the soul and its ways of knowledge, a subject for which Aristotle's *De Anima* was of paramount importance. But writers chose from a wide range of authorities, depending on the topic of the *quaestio*. Aristotle was very often cited, as were other ancient, Arab and Jewish authors; but so are the Bible, Augustine, pseudo-Dionysius, Boethius and the other Fathers of the Church. The works of contemporaries or near-contemporaries do not provide material for these arguments, but thinkers of the eleventh and twelfth centuries, like Anselm and Hugh of St Victor, are sometimes quoted. A single *quaestio* might include individual opposing arguments taken from a combination of these types of sacred and secular authority.

The use of authorities, and the manner of that use, is the feature which most separates the thirteenth-century *quaestio* from the philosophical methods more familiar to a modern reader. Modern philosophers will not find it strange that it was thought essential to anticipate the possible arguments which might be advanced against a view and to show why they are not convincing; nor that these arguments were sometimes explicitly taken from other authors. Many a modern philosophical article begins by presenting the views of other philosophers on its subject and explaining why they are inadequate. But the quotation of authorities in a *quaestio* was not merely a way of presenting arguments which happened to have been formulated by others. The quotations, like the texts from which they were taken, are authoritative. They often do not derive their power from the coherence of the argument they put forward, but from the identity of their authors. Indeed, the authoritative quotations rarely propose a train of reasoning: they merely state a position, the implications of which the medieval writer would sometimes find it necessary to make explicit. This was especially true of the Bible – the most authoritative, but usually the least argumentative, text which could be adduced. When, at the end of the *quaestio*, the writer came to dismissing the arguments for the opposing solution, he might refute those which had claimed to be based on reason, but he would not usually reject in any straightforward way those which were quoted from authorities. Rather, he would 'solve' (*solvere*) the objections, by explaining why in context the author did not mean what he appeared to be saying or why his view was not really incompatible with the favoured position.

Modern commentators will often ignore every part of a thirteenth-century *quaestio* except for the 'body', the writer's own reply to the initial question. They are not without some justification. The body of the *quaestio* gave the medieval thinker a chance to develop his own arguments in the direction he thought fit and to arrive at an individual position far subtler than a simple positive or negative reply to the question. None the less, the body of a *quaestio* stands in a complex and important relation to the other three parts. The first two parts of a *quaestio* show the reason why the discussion in the third part, the body, is necessary. There is a contradiction: a contradiction between a position which the author wishes to hold and which has authoritative or rational backing (adduced in the second, *sed contra*, section) and a series of statements – seemingly-plausible arguments and/or quotations from authorities. The discussion in the body of the *quaestio* is designed to remove the contradiction by investigating the problem more deeply. Sometimes it does this so effectively that the fourth part of the *quaestio* can be omitted; at other times it is necessary to work out explicitly the solution to each of the opposing arguments. To a modern reader the grouping of replies to the opposing arguments at the end of a *quaestio* seems strange and formalistic: surely the place for them is immediately after the arguments which they concern and before the writer's own reasonings. To a thirteenth-century scholar immediate reply to these arguments would have seemed precipitate: it was only in the light of the deeper discussion which they occasioned that they could be solved.

Thirteenth-century *quaestiones* were not uniformly as integrated as this description would suggest. In some the reply to an opposing argument might occasion detailed consideration of a new aspect of the problem, or another problem altogether, not treated in the body of the *quaestio*. In others the body might form a brief, almost independent treatise, for which the opposing arguments and their solutions seem to offer an excuse rather than a reason.

(2) The form of the *quaestio* in the fourteenth century

By the beginning of the fourteenth century the *quaestio* used by many theologians to comment on the *Sentences* had taken on a form very different from that which would have been familiar to their predecessors fifty years before. Each *quaestio* was much, much longer: Duns Scotus stretches some to more than twenty thousand words. The practice of beginning with arguments for the opposing view and ending with their solution was retained, but often it was little more than a formality – the opposing arguments are few and the solutions perfunctory. The body of the *quaestio* occupies almost all the space. But it no longer just presents the writer's own views. Sections are devoted to presenting the positions of other thinkers, often contemporaries or from the previous generation. Arguments will follow against each of these views (often against each individual aspect of each view). Eventually the writer will put forward his own position, but he may well then propose a series of *dubia* or *instantia*, arguments against his own position. In countering these he will often modify and refine his own arguments. Such a structure was not fixed or regular, but could be adapted to suit the problem and the nature of the writer's disagreements with his colleagues. The scheme of two *quaestiones* from the *Sentence* commentaries of two leading fourteenth-century theologians – Duns Scotus and William of Ockham – illustrates the possibilities of the form.

Table 3 **The form of fourteenth-century *quaestiones***

(a)   *Scheme of a* quaestio *by Duns Scotus* (0 *1,*3 *pars* 3,1) (for a discussion of the content of this *quaestio*, see below, pp. 155–6)

I	Brief arguments for opposing position
II	Brief argument for favoured position
III	Opinions of others – (1) Henry of Ghent
	(2) Godfrey of Fontaines
IV	Arguments against III – (1) Against III 1, for three different types of reason – a, b, c
	(2) Against III 2, for one type of reason
V	Writer's own position on the problem
VI	Why Aristotle and Augustine can be said to support this view
VII	Arguments against I
VIII	Arguments against arguments which were given in defence of III –
	(1) against those in defence of III 1
	(2) against those in defence of III 2

(b)	*Scheme of a* quaestio *by William of Ockham (O 1,3,6)* (for a discussion of the content of this *quaestio*, see below, pp. 177–8).
I	Single authoritative argument for opposing position
II	Very brief argument for favoured position by reference to earlier discussion in Ockham's own work
III	Opinions of others – (1) Aquinas
	(2) Henry of Ghent
IV	Arguments from authority and reason in favour of III 1 and III 2
V	Arguments against III 1 and III 2, including counter-arguments against anticipated replies
VI	Writer's own position on the problem
VII	Arguments against IV. (This section is very long and complicated: there are counter-arguments to many of the arguments, which are then refuted in turn)
VIII	One brief sentence in reply to I

There are three important aspects to the shift in method illustrated by these two examples. First, if each *quaestio* was so long, writers could deal only with a limited number of *quaestiones*: in the fourteenth century *Sentence* commentaries became less and less a treatment of all the problems raised by the Lombard's text, and ever more a series of discussion about the issues which fascinated thinkers of the time (see above, p.18). Second, the views of contemporary and near-contemporary thinkers play a very large role in discussion. Thanks to an efficient system of copying manuscripts in the universities, a writer would often have at his disposal texts of his immediate predecessors' *Sentence* commentaries: he could quote their arguments verbatim and analyse them in detail. Third, authorities are indeed adduced with respect, but only in connection with the views which the writer wishes to present himself or with the views of contemporaries which he wishes to refute. No longer would it be reasonable to say that the *quaestio* was based on a clash of authoritative views and was intended primarily to solve the contradiction. The freely formed fourteenth-century *quaestio* has become a vehicle for self-sustaining debate between professional thinkers: thinkers who, unlike their modern counterparts, still feel that they cannot contradict their authorities, but whose problems and interests are not themselves determined by the authorities. Originally, the ordinary *reading* of the *Sentence*s had been based on authoritative texts in two ways: each *quaestio* was based around authoritative texts, and the Lombard's work itself was expounded through these *quaestiones*. By the early fourteenth century both the Lombard's texts and those of the authorities had lost their motivating power and scholars, though still deeply respectful of authorities, no longer were interpreters of books but setters of problems and investigators of their solutions.

(3) Addendum: a note on nomenclature – *distinctions, articles* and *quaestiones*

The individual *quaestiones* which make up most medieval university texts do not usually follow each other in an unbroken series: they are arranged in groups and sub-groups, which articulate the main divisions of a topic. In many sets of *quaestiones ordinariae*, or in a textbook like Aquinas's *Summa Theologiae*, individual *quaestiones* on the same topic are called 'articles' (*articuli*) and each set of articles on different aspects of the same subject constitutes what is called (rather confusingly) a question (*quaestio*). For instance, the fourth question of Part 1 of Aquinas's *Summa* is about the perfection of

God: it consists of three articles (that is, individual *quaestiones*) – whether God is perfect; whether the perfections of all things are in God; and whether any created thing can be similar to God. In *Sentence* commentaries there is a slightly different system of grouping. Peter the Lombard divided his work into books and chapters; but when Alexander of Hales commented on it, he introduced his own division of each book into 'distinctions' (*distinctiones*), each dealing with a single main topic. Alexander's arrangement was adopted by his successors, and commentaries on the *Sentences* were divided into books, sub-divided into distinctions and further sub-divided into questions. For example, the *quaestio* by Ockham schematized above (Table 3) relates to the Book 1 of the *Sentences* (which is about God); and, in particular, to Distinction 3 (which is about the Trinity); and it is the sixth *quaestio* about topics relating to that distinction.

2 The techniques of logic

From the curriculum alone of medieval Paris and Oxford it is clear that students who stayed the course received a very thorough logical training in the arts faculty. The texts studied by historians of later medieval philosophy are almost all the work of either masters in the arts faculty or of bachelors or masters of theology. All, therefore, were written by men who had been fully trained in logic – whether at university or at a mendicant *studium*. When they went on to do more original work in arts or theology, both their identification of problems and the ways they tackled them were profoundly influenced by the intellectual procedures they had learned in their earlier education. Later medieval thought would seem very puzzling to a modern reader without some knowledge of these logical techniques.

Logic played three main parts in medieval intellectual life: as a tool, used for almost every sort of abstract speculation (logic as a technique); as a speculative subject in which far-ranging abstract problems were raised and discussed (philosophical logic); and as a discipline developed for its own sake according to its own rules (formal logic). The achievements of thirteenth- and fourteenth-century scholars in formal logic, already the object of several modern appreciations, are beyond the scope of this survey. Some aspects of their philosophical logic will be discussed in later chapters (see below, pp.139–43, 181–2). But here logic will be considered so far as possible simply in its role as technique.

The *logica vetus*, *logica nova* and *logica modernorum*

By the twelfth century, medieval logicians were familiar (in translation) with two of Aristotle's logical works, the *Categories* and the *De Interpretatione*; with Porphyry's *Isagoge*, a standard

introduction to Aristotelian logic. They also knew a number of
pieces by Boethius, which transmitted much of the late antique
logical tradition: his commentaries on the *Isagoge*, *Categories* and *De
Interpretatione*, his treatise on topical reasoning – *De topicis differentiis*
and his two monographs on the syllogism. This long-familiar
material came to be known in the later Middle Ages as the *logica
vetus* ('old logic').

Around the middle of the twelfth century, three other parts of
Aristotle's logic came into use: the *Prior Analytics*, the *De Sophisticis
Elenchis* and the *Topics*. The *Posterior Analytics* was also available in
Latin by this time, but it was not thoroughly studied until the 1230s
(see below, pp. 56–7). These four recently recovered logical books
of Aristotle's were known as the *logica nova* ('new logic').

Later medieval logicians also developed certain branches of their
subject which Aristotle had neglected: the two most important
were the theory of the properties of terms (*proprietates terminorum*)
and the theory of consequences (*consequentiae*). The newly-devised
branches of logic were known as *logica modernorum* ('contemporary
logic'). Despite their titles, it would be very wrong to think that the
'new logic' replaced the old, or that 'contemporary logic' out-
moded them both (although it is true that some of Boethius's
commentaries and handbooks fell out of use). Twentieth-century
historians of formal logic, understandably impressed by the complexity and originality of the *logica modernorum*, have given it the
bulk of their attention; but up to 1350 and beyond a student's
training would be based solidly on the old and the new logic as well
as the logical discoveries of his contemporaries.

Logic and a conceptual vocabulary: the *Isagoge* and the *Categories*

Porphyry's *Isagoge* and Aristotle's *Categories* were usually the first
two logical texts the medieval student would read. They provided
him with some of the most important terms in his conceptual
vocabulary. Porphyry offers a brief introduction to five basic
concepts (the five 'predicables') which the reader must know in
order to understand the *Categories*: genus, difference (*differentia*),
species, property (*proprium*) and accident (*accidens*). These terms
were basic in the medieval thinker's vocabulary. A species (for
example, 'man') is predicated of many things which differ in
number but are linked by some set of defining characteristics (for
instance, individual men); a genus (for example, 'animal') is
predicated of many things which differ in species but are linked by

some more general set of defining characteristics (men, horses, cows and so on). The same class can be both genus and species, since it can be regarded both as a subset of a more general class, or a general class with more specific subsets: 'rational animal', for instance, is a species of 'animal' but the genus of 'man'. That by which a species is distinguished from its genus is a specific difference: the specific difference 'rational' makes the genus 'animal' into its species 'rational animal', whilst the further specific difference 'mortal' turns 'rational animal' into its species 'man'. Properties are the characteristics of species. They are of different sorts: (1) those which occur in one species only, (a) but not in every member of it *or* (b) in every member of it but not always *or* (c) in every member of it always; and (2) those which occur in every member of a species but also in other species. Among the properties of man, for instance, are measuring (1a), turning grey with age (1b), being able to laugh (1c) and having two feet (2). An accident is that which 'comes into being and passes away apart from the destruction of the subject': it can be separable – as sleeping is to a man – or inseparable – as being black is to a crow. But being black is still regarded as an accident of the crow, since it is possible to conceive of a white crow.

The most influential parts of the *Categories* in the later Middle Ages were probably the various sets of distinctions which Aristotle makes near to the beginning of the work. Aristotle begins his treatise (1a1–15) by distinguishing three ways in which words can be used: equivocally, where the same word applies to things different in substance ('bank' – of a river, or where money is deposited); univocally, where the same word applies to things which are common in definition (as 'animal' is used of men and cows, which are indeed both animals); and denominatively, when something takes its name from something related to it with only a superficial change (for instance, 'grammarian' from 'grammar'). In the next section (1a16–19) he makes another distinction among things said: some are complex (*secundum complexionem*), some are simple (*sine complexione*). Expressions which include more than one term, like 'the man runs', are complex; simple expressions consist of a single term, like 'man' or 'runs'. Aristotle goes on (1a20–b9) to make yet another distinction. Some things can be said 'of a subject' (*de subiecto*) but never be 'in a subject' (*in subiecto*): 'man', for instance, can be said *of* an individual as its subject, but can never be in him as its subject. Some things, on the contrary, can be in a subject but not said of it: the particular white is in a particular white thing as its subject. Some things can be in a subject and said of a subject: knowledge, for instance, can be in the soul as its subject but also said of grammar as its subject. Finally, there are those things which are neither said of a subject nor in a subject, such as the individual man or horse. These distinctions of Aristotle's linked with the concepts discussed by Porphyry and gave the student a means of describing the logical relations between these concepts and the items of which they are predicated. The genus or species is said of its individual member as its subject; an accident is in its subject; the individual substance is neither said of nor in a subject.

The terms and way of thought learnt from the *Isagoge* and *Categories* were so widespread and fundamental in the later Middle Ages that it would be artificial to pick a set of particular passages to illustrate their use. For example, the theories about intellectual knowledge, which are examined in detail in Part Two, would be impossible without the terms and principles assimilated from these logical texts.

Logic and argument: *De Interpretatione* and the *Prior Analytics*

(1) Syllogistic reasoning

If the first two books of the logical corpus provided students with a set of invaluable terms and concepts, from the *De Interpretatione*, *Prior Analytics* and the works on the topics they learned how to link terms together into an argument. Syllogistic argument is explained in part of the *De Interpretatione* and receives fuller treatment in the *Prior Analytics*. Syllogisms formalize a very common type of argument where, from knowing how two different things are each related to a third thing, the relations between the first two are deduced. An informal, everyday example of such an argument might be: 'That burglar only stole from the bedroom; but I kept some of my cash elsewhere and so I can be sure that the burglar did not steal all my cash'. In formalizing such arguments, Aristotle did not interest himself in terms which denote a single, specified individual, like 'Socrates' or 'that burglar' (singular terms), but only in those which designate either all the members of a class ('all men', 'all burglars') or else some of them ('some men', 'some burglars'). Since any statement can be affirmative or negative, the theory of the syllogism is therefore concerned with four types of statement: universal affirmative ('Every man is a burglar'); universal negative ('no man is a burglar'); particular affirmative ('Some man is a burglar') and particular negative ('Some man is not a burglar').

Every syllogism contains two premisses ('major' and 'minor') – each asserting a relation between a common term (the 'middle term') and one of two different terms (the 'extremes' of the syllogism); from which there is inferred a conclusion about the relation between the two extremes. There are three different relations in which a middle term (m) can stand to the two extremes (A, B): it can be subject to one and predicate to the other (m is A and B is m – the first figure); predicate to both (A is m and B is m – the second figure), or subject to both (m is A and m is B – the third figure). From each of these conjunctions of premisses there follows a valid conclusion about the relations between the extremes (B is A) for some combinations of universal or particular, negative or affirmative statements. The theory of the syllogism explains *which* combinations are valid. Aristotle found four each for the first and second figure and six for the third; medieval logicians added two to each of the first and second figures. For instance, one of the valid patterns in the first figure is 'All m is A, all B is m: all B is A' ('All men are mortal, all philosophers are men: all philosophers are mortal'); in the second figure, no A is m, all B is m: no B is A' ('no angel is mortal, all men are mortal: no man is an angel'); in the third figure, 'some m is not A, every m is B: some B is not A'. ('some men are not philosophers, every man is mortal: some mortal things are not philosophers'). The everyday piece of argument about burglars and stealing from bedrooms might be universalized and formalized as a second figure syllogism: 'All stealing-by-burglars is located-in-bedrooms. Some cash is not located-in-bedrooms: some cash is not stolen by burglars'. Aristotle's scheme was as valuable in showing up invalid patterns of argument as in providing valid ones. Suppose, for instance, the scheme 'all/some-not/some-not' were applied not to the second but to the third figure; there would result the following scheme: 'all m is A, some m is not B: some B is not A', one which every student of the *Analytics* would recognize as invalid – with good reason, since otherwise the following argument would be invalid: 'All bipeds are mortal, some bipeds are not men: some men are not mortal'!

Later medieval thinkers did not construct whole works simply from chains of syllogisms; but syllogistic reasoning was one of the techniques very regularly used to put forward a position. They would find the syllogistic premisses for the conclusion they wished to propose, and then set about proving each of them in turn: once the premisses had been justified, the truth of the conclusion was assured. Sometimes even a premiss of one syllogism was itself proved by being shown to be the conclusion of another syllogism with demonstrably true premisses. The syllogism thus served as a way of breaking up argument into manageable steps, of working from what was obviously true to what was true but less obviously so. One of the great theologians most fond of presenting his arguments syllogistically was Ockham. He uses the syllogism not only to establish positions, but also to confute them. For instance, the first question he asks in his commentary on the *Sentences* is whether evident knowledge of the truths of theology is possible in this life. The first argument (for the opposing view) is immediately put syllogistically (3:4–4:4): evident knowledge of the truths of theology is impossible without distinct knowledge of God; distinct knowledge of God as God is impossible for the *viator* in this life; and so knowledge of the truths of theology must be impossible in this life (a second figure syllogism: all *A* is *m*, no *B* is *m*, therefore no *B* is *A*). There follow in turn arguments to prove the major and the minor premisses. When, at the end of the question, Ockham has to show why the argument is false, its syllogistic form is useful to him. He simply rejects the minor premiss and the argument used to support it (72:13–18).

(2) Topical reasoning

Later medieval scholars were familiar with another method of logical argument besides the syllogism: topical reasoning. Syllogisms are valid or invalid by virtue of their form, whatever terms are substituted for *A*, *B* and *m*. By contrast, the validity of a topical argument depends on its particular content. Many examples of everyday reasoning – which are not immediately analysable into formally valid syllogisms – can be explained by the logic of topics. Consider, for example, the two following remarks:

(1)　'I can't give you coffee with milk because I don't have any milk';

(2)　'He's a member of neither House of Parliament, so he isn't a member of Parliament at all'.

Each derives its argumentative force from an assumption which is so obvious that it seems unnecessary to state it. In (1) it is assumed that where the matter from which something is made is lacking, so is the thing itself; in (2) that, if something does not belong to any of the parts which make a whole, then it does not belong to the whole. Self-evident assumptions like these, which are useful as unstated bases for arguments, were called 'maximal propositions' (*maximae propositiones*). Ancient theoreticians of logic and rhetoric were concerned to list and classify maximal propositions, because they provided a way for writers, orators and advocates to find arguments for their case. Aristotle's treatise on the subject – his *Topics* – was known to western scholars from the mid-twelfth century onwards; and Cicero's *Topics*, along with Boethius's commentary, had been available far earlier. But it was another work by Boethius – the *De Topicis Differentiis* – which, from the eleventh century to the end of the Middle Ages, remained the main authority on this area of logic. Here Boethius sets out and compares the two main schemes of classifying maximal propositions (those of Cicero and Themistius), both of which present them in classes and sub-classes according to their *differentiae*. For example, the maximal proposition which underlies (1) is concerned with causes – in particular, material causes (cf. 1189CD); that which underlies (2) with parts – in particular, parts which divide a whole (cf. 1196D).

Boethius did not explore the wider implications of topical reasoning. It was Abelard, more than any other writer, who examined this type of non-formal argument from the point of view of philosophical logic (see especially his *Dialectica*, Tractatus III). Later medieval logicians took a different approach. They tried to work out how – using the theory of topics – they could convert the non-formal arguments dependent upon implicit maximal propositions into syllogisms that would be formally valid; and these efforts played an important part in the formulation of a comprehensive theory of formal consequences. For students interested primarily in logic as a technique, the topics continued as they had been for Boethius – a way of finding arguments.

Logic and interpretation: the *De Sophisticis Elenchis* and the theory of the properties of terms

(1) The properties of terms: the *De Sophisticis Elenchis* and the origins of the theory

Later medieval thinkers are skilled not only in argument but also interpretation. Authoritative texts provided the basis for each element in the university curriculum, and much effort had to be spent on determining their meaning and resolving their apparent contradictions (see above, Chapter 1). Aristotle's *De Sophisticis Elenchis* and the 'theory of the properties of terms' each provided techniques for this work of interpretation.

The great popularity of the *De Sophisticis Elenchis* from the 1140s onwards might seem strange to the modern observer, who would probably find this treatise on fallacies Aristotle's least exciting logical treatise. Behind its popularity lies, almost certainly, the demands of the *quaestio*-technique. The *De Sophisticis Elenchis* helped the student both to refute seemingly rational but in fact fallacious arguments for the opposing view, and to show why certain inferences which had been drawn from authoritative texts did not in fact follow from them. (For an example, see below, p.45.)

The theory of the properties of terms originated, in part, from the mid-twelfth-century interest in the sophisms to which Aristotle had drawn attention. Since variation in the reference of a word was one of the main causes of sophistical argument, treatises on fallacy contain detailed studies of different types of reference (*appellatio*). For instance, the *Fallacie Parvipontane* from the late twelfth century explains how a word such as 'man' can refer to itself (' "man" is a noun'), to an individual man ('Christopher is a man') or to the species Man. Reference had also been discussed by eleventh- and early twelfth-century logicians, like Anselm and Gilbert of Poitiers, who investigated the theory of meaning. From their discussions a distinction had come to be commonly recognized between what a noun signifies (*significat*) and what it appellates: it signifies the universal, but it appellates the individual things to which it refers.

These two different approaches to the problem of reference merged into a single theory. The theory of the properties of terms examines how words are used as terms in a statement: most important, how substantives refer to different things depending on their context. For instance, in different statements the word man might refer to the species Man; or to all men existing now; or to all men who are, have been and ever will be; or to some group of men such as white men or black men; or to the English word 'man'. The theory of the properties of terms provided a classification of these different types of reference and a method for detecting the fallacies which often occur when an argument involves two statements each with same word used to refer in a different way.

(2) The varieties of supposition

The theory of the properties of terms is fully but unproblematically formulated in a series of textbooks (covering all the branches of logic, old and new, as well as this contemporary branch) from the early thirteenth century. The most influential was Peter of Spain's *Tractatus* (later called *Summule Logicales*), copied in hundreds of manuscripts right up to the end of the Middle Ages. Two other treatises, more detailed and much less widely read, were written around the same time as Peter's: Lambert of Auxerre's *Summa* and William of Sherwood's *Introductiones in Logicam*. Peter, Lambert and William were expositors rather than logical innovators. The main lines of the theory of the properties of terms had previously been worked out in a number of anonymous later twelfth-century textbooks. Even the divergences between William, on the one hand, and Lambert and Peter on the other, seem to represent the differences between an Oxford tradition and a Paris one, visible already in the anonymous treatises.

Terminist logicians (as Peter, Lambert and William are often called) used the word 'supposition' (*suppositio*) for a term's general property of referring to things; 'appellation', in their vocabulary, means the species of supposition where a term correctly refers to something in the present. For example, in the sentence, 'Men who are living should remember people who have died', 'men' appellates its referents, whilst 'people' just supposits for them. The terminists devoted much of their attention to classifying the various different types of supposition a term could have, depending on its context in a sentence. As Table 4 illustrates, the writers were in general agreement about the possible types of supposition (although only William has 'material supposition'), but not about their relation to each other. A noun's supposition can be 'discrete' (*discreta*) – as of a proper name, which always refers to just one thing – or 'common' (*communis*), as of a common noun like 'man'. It can be 'simple' (*simplex*), when the reference is to a universal or 'personal' (*personalis*), where the noun refers to individual things. Personal supposition can be 'determinate' (*determinata*), when the reference is to a single member of the species, or 'confused' (*confusa*) when it is to every member; and confused supposition itself is of two main types: mobile and distributive, and immobile. A word has confused but mobile supposition in a sentence which remains true when the name of any particular member of the class the word refers to is substituted for it ('descent to singulars'): in the sentence 'Every man is an animal', for instance, 'man' has confused but mobile supposition, since it does follow from it that 'Socrates is an animal', 'Plato is an animal' etc. . But the supposition of 'animal' in the same sentence is confused and immobile, since it does not follow that 'Man is a giraffe', 'Man is an octopus' etc. . 'Material' (*materialis*) supposition – a category not in Peter or Lambert – is found when a word refers to itself as a written or grammatical object.

Table 4   **The types of supposition**

Peter of Spain

discrete_____common
(SOCRATES is a man) |

    natural_____accidental
    (MAN taken *per se*: see below) |

        simple_____personal
        (MAN is a species) |

            determinate_____confused
            (A MAN is running) |

                mobile and_____immobile
                distributive   (Every man
                (Every MAN is   is AN
                an animal)   ANIMAL)

Lambert of Auxerre

natural_____accidental

    simple_____personal
                                      |
                                   etc. (as Peter
                                   of Spain)

William of Sherwood

material_____formal
(MAN is a monosyllable) |

    *either*_____*or*
simple___|___personal   common___|___discrete
                |
          etc. (as Peter of Spain)

In addition to classifying the types of supposition, the terminists considered certain ways in which a word's supposition could be 'restricted' or 'ampliated' by other words in the sentence. Restriction narrows down the range of individuals for which a word supposits: for instance, in 'there is a white man', 'white' restricts the supposition of 'man' to men who are white. Similarly, a word's supposition can be restricted by the tense of a verb. Ampliation, by contrast, increases the range of individuals supposited: it can be effected by verbs like 'posit', 'think of', 'can'. For example, when the sentence 'men who think' is changed to 'men who can think', the supposition of 'men' is ampliated.

A discussion in Aquinas's *Summa Theologiae* (1,36,4) shows how the theory of supposition could be used as a tool by thinkers. Aquinas is arguing that the Father and the Son are a single source (*unum principium*) of the Holy Spirit. He frames the following argument for the opposing view (4): If Father and Son are a single source, it must either be a single source which is the Father or a single source which is not the Father; but each alternative produces an unacceptable consequence – from the former it follows that the Son is the Father, from the latter that the Father is not the Father. To answer this objection (ad 4), Aquinas explains that the word *principium* does not have determinate supposition, but confused supposition for two persons together. The opposing argument depends on taking the reference of *principium* as being to a single thing, and is shown to be invalid as soon as this assumption is rejected: it commits, as Aquinas remarks (illustrating the links between sophisms and the theory of the properties of terms), the fallacy of *figura dictionis*.

The most striking and thorough use of the theory of supposition, however, is William of Ockham's. He transforms the technique into an instrument for clarifying and justifying his own, innovative views about meaning and universals (see below, pp. 181–2). After Ockham, the logic of supposition became even more pervasive in the writings of university men, so that when, in his *Utopia*, the humanist Thomas More was ridiculing scholastic education, 'restrictions, ampliations and suppositions' were prime targets for his scorn.

(3) Natural supposition, accidental supposition and signification

One of the distinctions in supposition – that between natural (*naturalis*) and accidental (*accidentalis*) supposition (shared by Peter and Lambert) – has not yet been mentioned, because it is of rather a different sort from the others. Whereas the other divisions help to make the analysis of supposition into a tool for distinguishing sophisms from valid consequences (a tool used in much the same way by the various logicians, for all their incidental differences in presentation), the distinction between natural and accidental supposition relates to a deeper, theoretical question: what precisely is

supposition and how does it differ from signification? It is worth-
while to pause and examine this problem, although it does not
strictly concern supposition as a technique, both because it helps to
clarify the notion of 'natural' supposition and because it illustrates
how questions of philosophical logic cannot be entirely avoided
even by the most technical of logicians.

Earlier scholars used the concepts of appellation and signification
to distinguish between the things to which a noun refers and the
universal which they considered to be its sense (for instance, 'man'
signifies the universal Man but appellates a particular person). This
neat distinction could not be retained (even with a change of
terminology) in a comprehensive theory of supposition, since one
type of supposition (simple supposition) was held to be that where
a word supposited for the universal it signified. What then is the
difference between signification and simple supposition? Much of
the practice of Peter, Lambert and William suggests a clear answer.
A term signifies regardless of its use in a sentence, whereas its
supposition is determined by its context. 'Man' always signifies the
universal Man; but it can supposit for various things (all men, a
single man, white men etc.). In certain sentences (such as 'Man is a
species'), the supposition which the context determines for the
term is what the term signifies. However, the theoretical distinction which Peter (p.80:8–16) and Lambert (p.206) make between
signification and supposition is not the one their practice suggests.
They believe that the two concepts should be used to answer two
different types of question about a word. If I ask, 'How do the
letters M, A, N come to mean man?', my question is about the
signification of the word 'man'; if I ask, 'To what does the word
'man' refer?', I am enquiring about its supposition. I might be
asking about its reference within the context of a particular
sentence. But I might be trying to find its reference outside any
such context; and, for both Peter and Lambert, this would be a type
of supposition: 'natural supposition'. Natural supposition is very
wide: for instance, 'man' naturally supposits for all men past,
present and future (Peter p.81:2–5; Lambert p.208).

William of Sherwood's theory is more consistent with his
practice. He defines signification (p.74:16–18) as the presentation of
the form of something to the intellect and supposition as the
ordering of the understanding of something under something else.
And, at one point (p.76:22–24), he makes context an explicit
condition of supposition when he explains how a word has
signification (as opposed to supposition) before it is arranged with
other words into a sentence. In accord with this approach, he has

no category of 'natural' supposition. He allows that, in addition to
its actual supposition, a term may be said to have supposition
secundum habitum – the capacity to supposit. But, as the very name
which he gives it indicates, supposition *secundum habitum* is deriva-
tive from the actual supposition of various sorts which a term can
have in a sentence and not therefore a type of supposition which a
term is assumed to have by its very nature. William's differences
from his contemporaries are similarly evident in the way he
distinguishes between supposition and appellation. Peter, Lambert
and William all retain the definition of appellation which had been
current since the time of the *Dialectica Monacensis*: a term appellates
individuals which exist at the present. But Peter and Lambert see
appellation as a restriction of a term's natural capacity to supposit
for individuals past, present and future: as Peter puts it, ' "man"
signifies Man and by its nature supposits for both existing and
non-existent men and appellates only existing men' (p.197:12–14;
cf. Lambert p.212). By contrast, William considers that on its own
a term supposits only for existing things (p.85:15–31; cf. p.74:21–
23) – it supposits for what it appellates: but, because of its context, a
term's supposition can vary from its appellation. Although here
William runs the risk of suggesting that terms have some sort of
natural, contextless supposition, by identifying this with appellation he comes close to a recognition which completely escapes
Lambert and Peter: that the theory of supposition concerns the use
of terms in their context within statements, whereas the distinction
between signification and appellation is most usefully regarded as
one between the sense and reference of terms considered in
isolation apart from any context.

Logic and scientific method: the *Posterior Analytics*

Although the *Posterior Analytics* was read and commented from the
1230s onwards, it never properly became part of medieval logical
studies. Whereas the other books in the logical corpus provided
thinkers with the tools for their work – concepts, ways of arguing,
methods of interpretation – the *Posterior Analytics* taught them how
to organize their ideas into a whole. It was a work to be studied
after the more basic elements of logic had been mastered.

The *Posterior Analytics* is a complex work. But, although its
interpretation in the light of Aristotle's own practice is open to
dispute, later medieval scholars took from it certain very definite
notions about the organization of scientific knowledge. For Aristotle, scientific knowledge is of facts which cannot be otherwise than

they are (71b15); its objects are eternal and changeless. Individual things, which come into being, change and decay, cannot therefore be the direct objects of a science; but the genera to which individual objects belong are changeless and can be studied scientifically. Each branch of scientific knowledge (*epistēmē/scientia*) is concerned to reveal, by syllogistic argument, the essential attributes of a genus (75a40). It does so using statements which predicate attributes 'universally' of their subjects – of every member of the widest class for which it can be so predicated (73b25–4a3). A scientific demonstration must therefore be confined to a single genus: members of different genera might share attributes accidentally, but not essentially.

A demonstration needs a beginning; and, if there is not to be an infinite regress, this must be provided by principles which are not themselves demonstrated. Aristotle believes that by 'intuition' (*nous/intellectus*: cf. 99b–100b), certain self-evident (*per se nota*), indemonstrable first principles (*prima principia*) can be known to anyone. Each branch of knowledge, Aristotle says, has its own first principles. A principle such as 'when equals are taken from equals the remainders are equal' might seem to contradict this view, since it is an indemonstrable basis of a number of sciences, among them arithmetic and geometry. But, as Aristotle points out, the geometer intuits this principle of magnitudes alone ('When something of equal size is taken from things of equal size, what are left are of equal size') and the arithmetician intuits it of numbers alone ('If $n = m$ and $a = b$, then $n-a = m-b$') (76a30–b12). Only analogously is the principle common to more than one science. Aristotle does, however, allow that there are certain branches of knowledge which do not have their own first principles but have to rely on those of another, particular *scientia*: the propositions of harmonics, for instance, are proved by arithmetic (76a10–14).

Although the *Posterior Analytics* merely expound a method of clarifying scientific investigation, the book was extremely important for later medieval thinkers because it suggested how all the work of argument and interpretation, based on the tools provided by the earlier stages of logical training, should be put together and divided. Moreover, it provided a set of criteria for deciding whether a particular area of discussion constituted a science: each branch of scientific knowledge had to be a single subject with its own self-evident first principles from which a structure of syllogistic argument could be drawn. In their prologues, medieval scholars were keen to show how the subject they were about to examine satisfied these demands. This wish extended beyond the arts faculty

– where the set-texts each concerned an Aristotelian science – to the theologians. From the middle of the thirteenth century, one of the questions which intrigued masters of theology was related to the *Posterior Analytics*: is theology a science in Aristotle's sense? There was no single or simple answer (see below, pp.80–2). But, whatever conclusions individual theologians reached, their arguments about the scope and methods of theology took place within the context of Aristotle's theory of science.

3 *Philosophy: the ancients, the Arabs and the Jews*

The arts faculty did not merely provide formal training in grammatical and logical techniques. From the mid-thirteenth century onwards, most of Aristotle's non-logical works were also studied as set-texts; even before then, their language and ideas had begun to be copied and adapted by theologians as well as arts masters. Along with Aristotle, a variety of other non-Christian texts – Greek, Arabic and Jewish – gradually became known. In what stages was Aristotle translated, and which other authors were put into Latin at the same time? How soon were these works read and assimilated? What sort of subjects do they investigate? What avenues did they open and what threats did they pose?

Greek, Arabic and Jewish philosophy: the translations

(1) Translations of Aristotle

The non-Christian philosophical material which became available to thinkers in the west from the late twelfth century onwards was of three main sorts: texts by Aristotle himself, works interpreting or commenting them, and writings unconnected with Aristotle. The first category included, by the end of the thirteenth century, very nearly all of Aristotle. In the second category the commentaries of the Arabs Avicenna and Averroes bulked larger than the exegeses of antiquity. The third category included treatises by ancient Neoplatonists, by Arabs and by Jews.

A literate knowledge of Greek or Arabic remained throughout the Middle Ages an unusual skill, rarely possessed by the most sophisticated thinkers. With a few exceptions, medieval scholars had to rely on translations for their knowledge of pagan philosophy. Only when a text had been put into Latin could it begin to circulate and be studied.

Aristotle's logic, except for the *Posterior Analytics*, had been translated in late antiquity by Boethius. In the hundred years from about 1140 almost all his remaining works were translated, by a number of different scholars living in different places. The most prolific was James of Venice, apparently a Greek by birth, education or adoption, who – probably between about 1130 and 1150 – translated from the Greek the *Posterior Analytics, Physics, De Anima, Metaphysics* – at least Books I – IV,4 (up to 1007a30) of which part was revised in the thirteenth century, and some of the *Parva Naturalia*. Among the other twelfth-century translations made from the Greek were the *De Generatione et Corruptione*, Books II and III of the *Nicomachean Ethics* (the *Ethica vetus*) and the *Metaphysics* complete except for Book XI (the *Metaphysica anonyma* or *media*). In the early thirteenth century the whole of the *Ethics* was translated.

Direct translation was not the only way in which Greek philosophy could reach the medieval west. Much of Aristotle was available in Arabic. In areas where Christians and Muslims mingled, like Toledo or Sicily, there were scholars who could translate Aristotle from the Arabic. Gerard of Cremona (d. 1187), who worked in Toledo, made Latin versions of the *Posterior Analytics, Physics, De Caelo, De Generatione et Corruptione* and *Meteorologica* ASI–III. When, a little later, the commentaries of Averroes were translated (see below, p.52), their lemmata (passages of the original quoted before being interpreted) could be used to provide a Latin text of Aristotle: a version of the *Metaphysics* was compiled in this way.

Between about 1240 and 1280, new versions of Aristotle were produced as the result of the work of two men: Robert Grosseteste and William of Moerbeke, both of whom worked from the Greek. William's work made a few new Aristotelian texts available (the most substantial was the *Politics*); but the most important result of his and Robert's activity was to provide clearer and more reliable versions of the books already known. Grosseteste was a distinguished scientist and theologian, and also an important ecclesiastic who had taught himself Greek late in life. Around 1246–7, probably with assistants, Grosseteste prepared a new translation of the complete *Nicomachean Ethics*. Later he translated part of *De Caelo*. William of Moerbeke devoted himself more completely to translation and either revised or made an entirely new version of most of the Aristotelian corpus.

(2) Translations of antique and Arab commentaries on Aristotle

There was a large ancient literature of commentary on Aristotle. At each stage when the philosopher's works were translated, some of his commentators too were put into Latin. Boethius's commentaries, although published as original works, closely followed the Greek exegetes (see above, pp. 35–6). In the twelfth century late antique commentaries on the *Posterior Analytics* and the *De Sophisticis Elenchis* were translated, and a treatise *De Intellectu et Intellecto* by Alexander of Aphrodisias, in which he expounded his version of Aristotle's theory of the intellect. The later thirteenth-century translators were particularly keen to make available ancient exegeses of Aristotle. Robert Grosseteste translated a whole set of Greek commentaries to the *Ethics* along with his version of the work itself; and he probably also translated commentaries on the *Physics* and the *De Caelo*. And William of Moerbeke translated a number of Neoplatonic commentaries on Aristotle, the most influential of which was that on the *De Anima* by Simplicius.

Among the Arab commentators on Aristotle, the greatest were ibn Sīnā (980–1037) – known to the Latins as Avicenna – and ibn Rushd (1126–1198) – known to the Latins as Averroes. Avicenna's *Kitāb Al-Shifā' (Book of Healing)* is not a section-by-section exegesis of the Greek philosopher's texts, but a discursive exposition of his views. The sections on the soul (*De Anima*) and metaphysics, and some of those on logic and natural science, were translated into Latin in the second half of the twelfth century. The names of two Toledan scholars are associated with this activity: that of Gundissalinus, a canon of Toledo, and that of Avendeuth, a Jew. It is not easy to determine the two men's respective roles. They certainly collaborated in the translation of at least one work (the *De Anima*), but each also worked with other collaborators, and possibly on occasion without any assistance. The writings of Averroes on Aristotle were not put into Latin until the thirteenth century. Averroes produced three sorts of Aristotelian commentary: epitomes, 'middle' commentaries, 'great' or 'long' commentaries (see below, p.62). Some of the middle commentaries were translated by Hermannus Alemannus (who worked in Toledo in the mid-thirteenth-century) and by William of Luna. But the most energetic translator of Averroes was Michael Scotus, who worked in Toledo and Sicily. It was probably in Sicily, in the 1220s, that he made Latin versions of four of Averroes 'great' commentaries, including those of the *De Anima* and *Metaphysics* and also translated two 'middle' commentaries and an epitome.

(3) Translations of other ancient, Arabic and Jewish material

Besides Aristotle and his commentators, there were three other sources of non-Christian material which became available in translation: ancient Platonists, Arabs and Jews. Shortly after 1150 Plato's own *Phaedo* and *Meno* were translated direct from the Greek by Henry Aristippus in Sicily; more than a century later, William of Moerbeke made a Latin version of part of the *Parmenides*, along with the commentary by the late Neoplatonist, Proclus. Proclus's *Elements of Theology* was excerpted and adapted in the *Liber de Causis* (see below, pp.58–60), taken from the Arabic by Gerard of Cremona; it was afterwards translated in full from the Greek by William of Moerbeke. Works by Arab thinkers such as al-Kindī, al-Fārābī and al-Ghazālī– (Algazel) were put into Latin at Toledo at much the same time as Avicenna's. They are often connected with Aristotle and his commentators, but are less properly expositions of the Greek philosopher than the writings of Avicenna or Averroes.

There were also, in Arabic, works by Jewish thinkers who had adopted the language of the Islamic lands where they lived. The *Liber de Definitionibus* of Isaac Israeli and the *Fons Vitae* of Solomon ibn Gebirol (Avencebrol) were translated in the twelfth century, the latter by Gundissalinus. Maimonides's *Dux Neutrorum* ('Guide to the Perplexed') was translated, from a Hebrew version, in the early decades of the thirteenth century.

Greek, Arabic and Jewish philosophy: availability and use

Once translated, the work of a Greek or Arab or Jewish thinker was in principle ready to be used in the Latin west. Yet very often there is a considerable gap between the time a translation was made and the moment when it seems to have become generally available, outside the circle of its translator (and there were some translations which never achieved any degree of popularity). Moreover, the fact that a certain book is cited, even frequently, shows that it was available but not necessarily that it was read carefully or studied. A text can be used in many ways which do not involve much effort at understanding it; and a merely quantitative assessment of borrowings can be misleading.

(1) The use of the translations in the twelfth century

The new translations of Aristotelian, Arab and Jewish works had very little impact on the mainstream of intellectual life in the twelfth century. A few, isolated quotations from Aristotle appear in theological works of the 1180s and 1190s. Only the *Liber de Causis* found a serious reader in Alan of Lille, who used it for material and method in his *Regulae Theologicae* (which is perhaps from as early as 1160).

The one writer of the time whose works show wide-ranging knowledge of Avicenna and Jewish thinkers as well as the *Liber de Causis* was a very special case: Gundissalinus, one of the most active Toledan translators. In a series of works he combines passages from Greek and Arabic works with more familiar Latin material. For example, his *De Anima* is mainly extracted for Avicenna, but adds material from Avencebrol and Boethius and has an explicitly Christian conclusion which shows the influence of Cistercian spirituality; the *De Processione Mundi* also combines Avicenna, Avencebrol and Boethius, whilst his *De Divisione Philosophiae* – a short introduction to the various branches of learning – makes extensive use of Al-Fārābī's *De Ortu Scientiarum*, a work on this theme, but also incorporates extracts from Avicenna, from the Jewish philosopher Isaac Israeli and also from Isidore of Seville, Quintilian, Boethius and Cicero. Although these compilations show extensive verbal knowledge of Arab and Jewish philosophers, they evince little understanding of their ideas. Only superficial resemblances link the arguments which Gundissalinus juxtaposes; and he does as much violence to the thoughts of Avicenna and Avencebrol in amalgamating them with each other as in combining them both with Boethius and the Bible.

(2) Aristotle and Avicenna in the universities, 1200–1215

The most frequently used piece of evidence about the study of Aristotle and his commentators in the early thirteenth century is a sentence in Robert of Courçon's instructions to the arts masters of Paris (see above, pp.16–17). Having prescribed for study Aristotle's logic, Priscian's grammar and, optionally, Aristotle's *Ethics*, Robert goes on to list some texts which were not to be *read*: Aristotle's *Metaphysics* and his *Libri Naturales* (on physics, psychology, cosmology and biology), and abridgements (*summae*) of them. A similar prohibition had been imposed by a provincial council of Paris which met at Sens in 1210. Historians have argued that these prohibitions would have been senseless had the *Metaphysics* and *Libri Naturales* not been *read* in the Paris arts faculty at the beginning of the thirteenth century. But it is worth pausing to consider the other evidence about intellectual life in Paris at this time.

One of the few authors who can be reliably placed as a master of arts in early thirteenth-century Paris is John Blund. He is described in a commendatory poem as 'reading' in Paris, and in Oxford, the books of Aristotle which 'the Latins had recently received from the Arabs'. Blund's only surviving work, the *De Anima*, seems to give an idea of what was involved in this 'Aristotelian' teaching. The book is not a line-by-line commentary on Aristotle's *De Anima* but rather a treatise putting forward a coherent body of psychological doctrine. In all the main lines of his thought Blund follows Avicenna. Although he makes some direct references to Aristotle's *Libri Naturales*, these are merely asides, useful additions to an argument derived from elsewhere. Avicenna rather than Aristotle is an important influence in another work which most probably dates from the first decades of the thirteenth century, the *Liber de Causis Primis et Secundis*. A compilation rather than an original composition, the *Liber* combines passages from Avicenna's *Metaphysics* with extracts from the *Liber de Causis* and the *Periphyseon* of John Scottus Eriugena. The sections from the writings of the heretic David of Dinant, which can be reconstructed from Albert the Great's attacks on him provide further evidence that in the early 1200s, when David was a master of arts, Aristotle was quoted piecemeal, with no attempt even to distinguish his arguments from those of the earlier thinkers he set out to refute. Further evidence of this attitude comes from Alexander Nequam's *Sacerdos ad Altare*, written between about 1200 and 1210 when Alexander, after study in Paris and teaching in Oxford, had entered monastic life. Nequam exhorts the student to read Aristotle's *Metaphysics, De Generatione et Corruptione* and *De Anima*, yet he shows no direct knowledge of these works himself: even in one instance where he quotes Aristotle's definition of the soul, he seems to be basing himself on Calcidius.

In the absence of other evidence, it is safest to conclude that, among the masters of arts in early thirteenth-century Paris, Aristotle's *Metaphysics* and 'books of natural philosophy' were admired more than read, frequently referred to, sometimes quoted textually but rarely understood. But Avicenna and the *Liber de Causis* were more fully used. Nor is there reason to believe that Aristotle was more widely studied at this time in Oxford. Although the English scholar, Alfred of Sareshel, was probably working there when, around 1200, he composed a commentary on the *Meteorologica* (and perhaps on other works by Aristotle), Alfred was a translator himself and so cannot be considered representative. No other of his Oxford contemporaries seems to have followed his example.

(3) Aristotle, Avicenna and Averroes in the universities, 1215–1240

It is very difficult to know exactly how much Aristotle and his Arab commentators were studied in the arts faculties of Paris and Oxford between 1215 and 1240. Robert of Courçon's statutes forbade the *reading* of these texts in Paris; and, although in 1231 a commission was appointed by Pope Gregory IX to investigate whether the prohibitions should remain in force, no conclusion seems to have emerged from its deliberations. A manual, prepared between about 1230 and 1240 by an arts master in Paris as an aid for examinations, suggests that most of the new Aristotelian material was known but not very thoroughly studied in the faculty: the *Physics* and *Metaphysics* are indeed discussed, but briefly. The *Posterior Analytics*, however, receives thorough treatment. So, too, does the *Ethics*; and a number of commentaries which survive from this time also illustrate its use.

However, private study of Aristotelian and Arabic texts remained possible. From about 1225 onwards, a number of treatises were written which very clearly reflect the teachings of Averroes. Scholars of this period (by contrast with those of the 1260s and 1270s: see below, pp. 68–9) looked to Averroes as the champion of the doctrine – in opposition to Avicenna's – that the active intellect is contained within the individual human soul (for the notion of 'active intellect', see Part Two, below pp. 99–103). This Averroism also had its exponents in Oxford.

The theologians of the period from 1220 to 1240 seem to have known well some of Avicenna's ideas and they were also influenced by Averroes. Their works also contain – in increasing numbers as the years go on – direct quotations from Aristotle's *Metaphysics* and *Libri Naturales*. But it is questionable to what extent their authors grasped Aristotle's ideas as a whole. For instance, William of Auvergne – one of the best informed and most powerful theological thinkers of the time – attributes to Aristotle doctrines about the soul which are in fact Avicenna's (see below, p.109).

In general, then, the period from 1215 to 1240 can be characterized as one in which knowledge of the Arab commentators of Aristotle, rather than Aristotle himself, became deeper. But this picture is not uniform. William of Auvergne was considerably influenced by the *Posterior Analytics*; and, in England, Robert

Grosseteste commented the *Posterior Analytics* (in about 1228) and then the *Physics* (probably between 1228 and 1231).

(4) The full introduction of the new material in the universities, 1240–1270

Although Robert of Courçon's prohibitions were not revoked, they appear to have lost their effect by the 1240s. When, between 1240 and 1247, Roger Bacon taught arts in Paris, he *read* a wide range of Aristotle, including the *Metaphysics*, *Physics*, *De Generatione et Corruptione*, *De Anima* and other of his scientific works. In 1252, the *De Anima* was included as a set-book in the statutes of the English-German Nation at Paris (*Chartularium* no. 201); and in 1255 the arts faculty as a whole adopted a syllabus which included almost all of Aristotle's works (*Chartularium* no. 246). The *reading* of Aristotle's *Metaphysics* and *Libri Naturales* made possible the assimilation and understanding of the Greek philosopher evident in the writings of medieval thinkers from the 1250s onwards. In the second half of the thirteenth century, therefore, it is right to think of the 'new Aristotle' as being, not merely available, but known in depth and detail, by both arts masters and theologians. And in the 1260s and 1270s, the new or revised translations by William of Moerbeke provided thinkers with a clearer and more accurate text of Aristotle.

There was never the same interest in Platonic texts in the later Middle Ages. The one work which was frequently studied was the *Liber de Causis*, which had been read since the time of Alan of Lille. William of Moerbeke translated a complete text of Proclus's *Elements of Theology*, the work from which the *Liber* was extracted; and some writers, including Aquinas, made use of it (see below, p.79). Although Plato's own *Meno* and *Phaedo* had been translated, they were very little read: thinkers preferred to take their view of Plato's own position from Aristotle's description of it.

The new texts which were assimilated in the 1250s supplemented the older ones but did not replace them. Although scholars became able to distinguish many of Avicenna's views from Aristotle's, Avicenna none the less remained an influential and much studied author. Of the surviving manuscripts of Avicenna in Latin translation, over a hundred were written after about 1250, fewer than thirty before then. Later thirteenth and fourteenth-century scholars read Avicenna along with Aristotle; and they read Aristotle using Averroes who, despite the condemnation of some of his views, remained *the* Commentator in their eyes.

Greek, Arabic and Jewish philosophy: scope and subjects

(1) Greek philosophy

Aristotle's non-logical works offered later medieval scholars a wide-ranging scientific encyclopaedia. From the *Physics* and the *De Generatione et Corruptione* they could learn about the constitution of material things; from the *De Caelo* and *Meteorologica* they found out about the heavens; the zoological writings taught them about animals and the *Nicomachean Ethics* extended the examination to human behaviour: it provided not merely terms for judging human conduct but also concepts for analyzing it. The *De Anima* was concerned with the life-giving principle in plants, animals and man, and it included a discussion of the human intellect and its ways of knowing (see below, pp.95–102).

It is much more difficult to characterize the *Metaphysics*. Aristotle distinguishes its subject matter in a number of different, though related, ways: it is the first principles and causes of things (982b) or, more precisely, the science of being as being (1003a). Later (1026a) he adds that, if besides the substances formed by nature there is an immovable substance, it will be for this 'first philosophy' of being as being to consider it. And Book xii of the *Metaphysics* does indeed include an elaborate discussion of God, the unmoved mover of the universe. The way in which these related subjects are actually investigated is uneven and disorderly. Some parts of the *Metaphysics* summarize and criticize the views of earlier philosophers. A whole book is devoted to a kind of lexicon of philosophical terms. Many sections of the work are aporetic – concerned to explore a question and the difficulties it raises, rather than to advocate a particular theory as a solution. It is possible to list the problems raised and the arguments developed in the *Metaphysics*, but very rarely to isolate a definite position which Aristotle adopted as his own. Whereas the ancient and Arabic tradition of exegesis on Aristotle's other works was used by later medieval scholars to throw light on individual passages and positions, commentary was required in order to make sense of the *Metaphysics* at all. Even when thirteenth- and fourteenth-century thinkers know Aristotle's text of this work well, they tend to view the aims and possibilities of metaphysics in the light of Avicenna's interpretation (see below, pp.59–61).

Among the new translations, the one influential work from the platonic tradition was the *Liber de Causis*. Proclus's *Elements of Theology*, from which the *Liber* was taken, is a highly organized account of the intelligible world according to neoplatonist theory.

But whoever compiled the *Liber* (see below, p.60) took trouble to alter some of the ideas in his original, emphasizing certain Aristotelian positions in ontology and making his work monotheistic in bearing.

(2) Islamic philosophy

(i) *The philosophical tradition in Islam*
The Islamic thought which intrigued and disturbed the theologians of thirteenth-century Paris and Oxford belonged to one particular tradition. In Islam, just as in the Christian world, there developed a scholastic theology (*kalām*) which was concerned both to defend the truths of the Muslim faith and to elaborate them by reason. This work was of very little interest to Christian thinkers since they could not accept the revealed premises on which it was based, and it remained untranslated. By contrast, the Islamic philosophers – from al-Kindī (?801–?866) and al-Fārābī (?879–?950) to Avicenna and Averroes – devoted themselves to understanding and explaining the Greek tradition of philosophy. They did not derive explicit premises or arguments from the beliefs of Islam, although these no doubt influenced their presuppositions and the directions in which they interpreted ancient texts. Among the writings of antiquity, those of Aristotle held for them the predominant place. Whereas scholars in the medieval west came to read Aristotle's non-logical works only in the thirteenth century, most of Aristotle was available even to the earliest of the Islamic philosophers thanks to the work of Syrian translators like Hunain ibn Ishāq (809–873).

Although both Avicenna and Averroes wrote independent works, it was through their expositions of Aristotle that they were known in the Latin world (see above, pp.52 and 53–7). Of the parts of the *Shifā'* available in translation, the two most influential were the *De Anima* (see below, pp. 103–6) and the *Metaphysics*, and it is in the *Metaphysics* that Avicenna's conception of philosophy and his relation to Aristotle can be most clearly seen.

(ii) *Avicenna's* Metaphysics *and Aristotelian philosophy*
Despite his wide knowledge of the texts, and the assistance of an established Arabic tradition of commentary, the Aristotle presented by Avicenna in his *Metaphysics* is hardly recognizable to the modern student of Greek philosophy: in place of the sober investigator of the abstract problems raised by the real world there appears a systematizer determined to map out the intelligible world and its

relations to the deity – a contrast artificially sharpened by textbook accounts which ignore the subtle argumentation underlying even Avicenna's most extravagant conclusions. How can Avicenna have believed that he was expounding Aristotle when his ideas and interests are so very different from those of the Greek philosopher? The explanation is usually thought to lie in the misattribution by Islamic writers of two Neoplatonic works to Aristotle: the *Theology of Aristotle* – a selection of passages from Plotinus's *Enneads* – and the *Liber de Causis* – from Proclus. However, there are historical reasons for denying such a role to these pseudepigrapha. Despite its title, the *Theology of Aristotle* was not universally accepted as a work of Aristotle's (Avicenna was among those who seem to have suspected the attribution). And there is great doubt about when the *Liber de Causis* was composed: quite possibly the Arabic version was put together (by, perhaps, Avendeuth) only just before it was translated into Latin in the mid-twelfth century – after Avicenna's death. Moreover, different as Avicenna's Aristotelianism may be from that of the modern scholar, his metaphysics (and even less his psychology) does not simply adopt the theories of Plotinus and Proclus. Avicenna is doubtless influenced by Neoplatonism, but it is Aristotle's text which he is trying to explain in his *Shifā'*. Avicenna wished to uncover the sense which lay behind Aristotle's difficult treatises. He relied on two preconceptions to guide him in his attempt: one was about the nature of philosophizing and the other about the nature of God. Aristotle almost certainly shared neither of them. But both would almost certainly have been held by medieval thinkers in the Latin west – a fact which is most important in explaining the influence of Avicenna there in the thirteenth century.

Philosophy for Avicenna, as for Aristotle, was an argumentative discipline; but for Avicenna the arguments had to lead in the direction of a theory. He therefore assumed that Aristotle's profound but chaotic *Metaphysics* must have been trying to put forward a single, well-defined position on a clearly identified subject. His task as an expositor was, as he saw it, to draw together the different threads of argument in the ancient philosopher's texts so as to make their direction apparent. He would not have thought that he was adapting or distorting Aristotle, but rather making manifest the underlying structure and intention of his thought.

Aristotle had given a number of different descriptions of the subject-matter of metaphysics, including 'being as being' (see above, p. 58). But Avicenna has a far more fixed view: for him metaphysics is the branch of knowledge which treats the existence and attributes of God. None the less, the Arab philosopher is able to remain more faithful to Aristotle's varied notion of the subject-matter of metaphysics than his emphasis might seem to imply. The subject of a science, says Avicenna (p.4:57–68), must be something which can be assumed to exist – either because its existence is self-evident or because it is proved in another science. But God's existence is not self-evident, and it is one of the tasks of metaphysics, and of no other branch of knowledge to prove it. Being as being is, according to Avicenna as well as Aristotle, the subject of metaphysics. But the study of being is far more intrinsically related to the study of God for the Islamic thinker than it was for his great predecessor. This difference results from Avicenna's un-Aristotelian preconception of God's nature.

In Aristotle's universe God is the final cause. He puts the world into motion because all things move to him as the object of their desire; but things do not depend on him for their existence. Avicenna, by contrast, never conceives God as other than the source of all things. The special concern of his metaphysics is to show not merely that God puts the universe into motion, but that he underlies its very existence. Avicenna accomplishes this task through a theory of the possible and the necessary which is largely his own. Everything, he says (pp. 43–8), is either a possible or a necessary being. Possible beings are such that they may or may not in fact exist, whereas a necessary being is such that it cannot but exist. Possible beings each require a cause which determines whether or not they exist; a necessary being, which by its nature must exist, is uncaused. Avicenna goes on to argue that there must be just one necessary being. This necessary being is Avicenna's God and, without him, the universe of possible beings could not be determined into actual existence. In Book 8 it is shown how the necessary being must also have the other properties of God: it is pure intelligence, perfectly good and perfectly beautiful.

Although Avicenna's conception of God as necessary being determines the direction of his *Metaphysics*, the framework of the book leaves great room to discuss the constitution of material things in an Aristotelian manner. Many of Aristotle's anti-Platonic positions are adopted, including his criticisms of Plato's theory of ideas (Book VII). Even Book 9, where Avicenna describes the emanation from God of a series of Intelligences, is closer to Aristotle in much of its argument than such a description might suggest.

(iii) Algazel and Averroes

The influence of the other Arab works translated in the twelfth century tended to be lost in the general current of Avicennian Aristotelianism. This is true even of the one case where a version was made of a treatise by a dedicated Islamic opponent of Avicenna, *Intentions of the Philosophers* by al-Ghazālī ('Algazel': 1058–1111). This treatise, which had been designed to summarize the doctrines of al-Fārābī and Avicenna only in order to refute them, was treated in the west as a simple introduction to Avicennian thought.

Averroes, although an original thinker and the author of several important independent works, was known in the medieval west only as an interpreter of Aristotle: an exegete of such outstanding value that medieval scholars would refer to him simply as 'the Commentator'. His Aristotelian commentaries were of three sorts: short commentaries, which summarize a work; middle commentaries, which paraphrase and explain; and long or 'great' commentaries. The long commentaries provide a section-by-section analysis of Aristotle's texts. Since Aristotle's meaning is often far from clear, this task of exposition is far from routine. On some questions, different interpretations had been advanced by ancient commentators known to Averroes and by his Arab predecessors: Averroes must therefore discuss the different arguments and put forward his own version of Aristotle's meaning. In some cases, the material is so complicated that Averroes's interpretation itself needs interpreting. One notoriously difficult passage in Aristotle is his discussion of the potential and active intellects in the *De Anima*: the interpretation of it consistently attributed to Averroes from the 1260s onwards, which became the hallmark of what medieval and modern scholars call 'Averroist', is very different from that attributed to him by scholars in the earlier thirteenth-century (see below, pp.68–9 and cf. 106–8). Perhaps Averroes was not himself an Averroist.

(3) Jewish philosophy

Later medieval thinkers also had some access to the philosophical works produced by Jews who lived in Islamic lands. Their writings had much in common with those of the Islamic philosophical tradition: they were written in Arabic; they used the same range of sources; and they sometimes entered into debates which had been conducted between Islamic thinkers. But, for the medieval Christian theologians who used them, the two most influential Jewish philosophical texts – Solomon ibn Gebirol's (Avencebrol's) *Fons Vitae* and the *Dux Neutrorum* ('Guide to the Perplexed') by Maimonides – were importantly different from any of the works by Arab philosophers. The Arab philosophical tradition was seen by medieval theologians as, at its best, a continuation of the ancient Greek way of philosophizing. Its exponents shared (or distortingly emphasized) those elements in Greek thought irreconcilable with the faith; and – even where these ideas were also contrary to Muslim teaching – the Arab philosophers did not examine the contradictions. By contrast, the *Fons Vitae* was accepted as a text completely in accord with Christian teaching (indeed, some scholars – such as William of Auvergne – thought that its author must have been a Christian). Those who objected to it did so on philosophical grounds. And the *Dux Neutrorum* was read especially for its discussions of the relation between reasoning and revelation.

The *Fons Vitae* is, like Avicenna's *Shifā'*, a work which does not explicitly presuppose the revealed truths of a religion. Indeed. Avencebrol is even more scrupulous in eliminating traces of the particular dogmas of Judaism from his book than Avicenna in keeping the tenets of Islam from his interpretation of Aristotle. However, Avencebrol does explicitly assume certain truths which are shared by Judaism, Christianity and Muhammadanism, such as the existence of a single God who created the universe *ex nihilo*. Avencebrol uses a certain amount of Aristotelian vocabulary and techniques, but his thought is in no sense an exposition of Aristotle. It derives almost entirely from Neoplatonic sources, such as the *Theology of Aristotle* (see above, p.60), and from a collection of material in Arabic translation misattributed to the pre-Socratic philosopher Empedocles. Often, when he cannot make clear and coherent the ideas taken and combined from his various sources, Avencebrol resorts to simile and metaphor. None the less, for many a Christian thinker the *Fons Vitae* (rather like Boethius's *Consolation of Philosophy*) seemed to show that it was possible to argue philosophically, making no use of revelation, and yet to arrive at a theory fully in accord with the faith.

Maimonides's understanding of Aristotle is far deeper than Avencebrol's. But the *Dux Neutrorum* is not an Aristotelian philosophical treatise. Rather, it is an exploration of the points of contact and difference between the God of Aristotle and the philosophers, and the God of the Old Testament. Maimonides was both a pious Jew and a thinker committed to rational argument. He deliberately tries to hide parts of his teaching from the reader who is not ready for it; and so it is often not easy to be sure of his true opinions.

Modern interpreters have not reached agreement about the nature of his conclusions in those cases where philosophical argument seemed to him to contradict Jewish teaching. Medieval Christian readers did not share these problems of interpretation. For them, passages in the *Dux Neutrorum* provided useful discussions of problems about the nature of God or of religious faith. For example, Aquinas's arguments about the need for divine revelation are explicitly based on Maimonides (3,1; cf. *Quaestiones de Veritate* 14,10); and the *Dux Neutrorum* played an important part in the development of thirteenth-century creation theology.

Greek, Arabic and Jewish philosophy: challenges and opportunities

The newly-translated Greek, Arabic and Jewish books presented medieval thinkers both with a challenge and a set of opportunities. They were challenged by views, supported by argument, which were plainly incompatible with the faith (such as Avicenna's hierarchy of creating Intelligences and Averroes's insistence on the unity of the potential intellect). Earlier medieval scholars, too, had been confronted by doctrinally unacceptable ideas in some of the works they knew by Plato and his followers. But they were usually able either to detach what was useful to them from its objectionable context, or to show by allegorical explanation that the texts contained truths – acceptable to Christianity or even specifically Christian – hidden by figurative language. The newly translated texts offered a challenge, because they presented unacceptable doctrines as the conclusion of tight, logical reasoning. Their coherence made it very difficult to use individual, acceptable passages in isolation; and their dry, argumentative manner ruled out the possibility of allegorical interpretation. The old methods for using and adapting non-Christian ideas were not adequate to the new material.

The opportunities which the newly translated works offered were of three main sorts. First, there was much in the new books which was not – or not obviously – incompatible with Christianity, and which investigated aspects of man and the universe never treated by Latin writers with such breadth and sophistication: the mechanism of growth and reproduction, the workings of the mind and the senses, the motions of the heavens, the constitution of physical things. Second, the medieval scholars found in the new texts ways of thought which could extend the techniques they learned from logic. They assimilated a series of concepts about being; matter and form; potency, disposition and activity; faculties of the mind, their powers and operation – concepts which could be used in answering different questions and presenting different views from those of their non-Christian originators. Third, some of the new, non-Christian material contained rational, and often highly elaborate, arguments for truths about the existence and attributes of God – truths which every Christian would accept.

In the light of these opportunities, arts masters and theologians came to various conceptions of their subjects' aims, their appropriate methods and the relations which should obtain between them. And, in accord with these conceptions, thirteenth-century thinkers tried to meet the challenge with which, as well its opportunities, the new material had presented them.

4 The aims of arts masters and theologians

Philosophia and the arts faculty

Pupils of the later medieval arts faculties were engaged in studying *philosophia*; if they went on to the theology faculty, they became students of *theologia* or *sacra doctrina.* What is the meaning of this distinction?

Philosophia is a word in medieval Latin which, like the modern English 'philosophy', has a wide and changing range of reference. But, when arts masters and theologians in the thirteenth and fourteenth centuries contrast *philosophia* with *theologia* or *sacra doctrina* they usually have a fairly definite meaning in mind. *Philosophia* is what men can discover by reason and observation, starting from the self-evident principles of each human discipline, without the aid of revelation. Theology, by contrast, although a discipline which requires argumentative reasoning, makes use of the revealed truths provided by Scripture. In the writings of Aristotle and his Greek and Arabic commentators medieval thinkers could find *philosophia*. Aristotle was usually called the *Philosophus* and, in general, the ancient pagan thinkers of Greece and Rome and the exponents of the Arab and Jewish Aristotelian traditions were described as *philosophi*. Although a contemporary Christian thinker would not normally be called a *philosophus* (or at least, not in the sense of the word which contrasted with 'theologian'), those in the arts faculty, where the texts were the works of the *philosophi*, were students or teachers of *philosophia*.

Even in the restricted meaning by which it was contrasted with theology, *philosophia* has a wide range of reference: the term includes every branch of purely rational and experimental knowledge: there is metaphysics or 'first philosophy', as it is sometimes called (see above, pp.58–61); natural philosophy, which includes physics, cosmology, biology and the study of the human soul;

mathematics; logic, which is often seen as a type of *philosophia* in its own right as well as a tool for use by other types; ethics; and many other subjects, varying in description from classification to classification and including certain practical disciplines, such as mechanics and architecture, as well as theoretical ones. Although the courses in arts faculties were rarely as comprehensive as the classifications of *philosophia*, it would be very misleading to describe them as 'philosophy' in the modern sense: besides logic, which was regarded as fundamental, a large part of them was devoted to what we would call science – physics, cosmology, biology – although it was studied by interpreting texts, not experimentally.

The autonomy and superiority of theology as a discipline was accepted almost without question, even by the most independent and self-assured arts masters (cf. Siger of Brabant Commentary on *Metaphysics* VI. Commentum I). The very structure of university education made the study of arts subordinate and preparatory. But this role did not restrict arts masters so much as secure their position. They were able, for the most part, to teach their various disciplines in the terms they learnt from authoritative texts without having to worry about or justify the nature of their pursuit. But some of the ideas with which their authorities presented them were ones which Christians could neither accept – even within a discipline acknowledged as merely preparatory – nor easily explain away or detach. It was in the 1260s and 1270s, when the newly translated texts were first thoroughly absorbed, that this became a serious problem for some arts masters, and the occasion of controversy with theologians and condemnation by the authorities of the church. The controversy provoked some of the most detailed medieval analyses of the relations between faith, reason and the writings of the *philosophi*, and for this reason it is worth looking in detail at the contributions made to it by artists and theologians. But these writings do not provide a reflection of the usual relations between arts masters and theologians. The conflict they record was a passing episode, of little more than ten years; and most of the arts faculty was not involved in it. In general, the extension of the arts syllabus in the mid-thirteenth century to include Aristotelian natural science and metaphysics did not affect its unproblematically propaedeutic role.

When reason seems to contradict the faith

In the later Middle Ages intellectual speculation – as the preceding chapters have illustrated – was based on the reading of authoritative texts, although they were certainly not studied in a servile or merely literal fashion. It is not surprising, therefore, to find the problem of rational arguments which seem to contradict the faith closely linked, in thirteenth-century accounts, to the problem of antique philosophical texts, which seem to contradict the faith. But the two are distinguishable and medieval thinkers directed their efforts towards defining the correct relation between the problems.

Two particular theses are central to the controversy: that the world is eternal, and that the potential intellect (*intellectus possibilis*) is one for all men (that is to say, all men reason by virtue of their contact with a single intellect, rather than from the powers of their own mind – see below, pp.99–101). Both of these theses were clearly incompatible with the faith as understood by thirteenth-century Christians. Scripture, they believed, tells not only that the world was created, but that it had a beginning; and the unity of the possible intellect would make individual immortality in the Christian sense, with the reward of virtue and the punishment of vice, impossible (cf. Aquinas *De Unitate Intellectus* – Prologue). But the relation between the two theses, the teachings of the *philosophi* and the arguments of reason was much less clear.

(1) The unity of the potential intellect

Historians have often regarded the unity of the potential intellect as a position proposed by Averroes in his commentary on Aristotle's *De Anima*. But it would be more accurate to regard the doctrine as a particular interpretation of Averroes's problematic text (see below, pp.106–8). This interpretation is first found around 1250, in the works of theologians such as Albert the Great and St Bonaventure; it replaces an earlier way of reading Averroes, which made him the champion of a united potential and active intellect within the individual human soul (see above, pp.56, 62). Albert and Bonaventure described the view they took to be Averroes's in order to reject it. The attitude of Siger of Brabant, a master in the Paris arts faculty, was different. Although he relied on the theologians for much of his information, he used it in his own way. In his *reading* of Aristotle in about 1265, Siger adopted the 'Averroist' view of the unity of the potential intellect (combining it with aspects of the earlier interpretation of Averroes) and proposed it as the correct interpretation of the *De Anima*. In the record of this teaching which survives – a poor copy of a *quaestio*-commentary on

De Anima Book III – Siger does not qualify this position or comment on its relation to the faith.

Neither the ecclesiastical authorities nor the theologians could permit such teaching. In December 1270 the bishop of Paris, Stephen Tempier condemned, under pain of excommunication, a list of errors which included several pertaining to Siger's view of a unique potential intellect. In the same year, the theologian Thomas Aquinas wrote a treatise *De Unitate Intellectus contra Averroistas* (*On the Unity of the Intellect against the Averroists*). Although Aquinas does not mention Siger by name, he seems to have seen a *reportatio* of his commentary similar to that which survives, but with some more details about Siger's attitude to the faith. In the *De Unitate*, Aquinas sets out to show that Siger's position – which is without doubt contrary to the faith – can also be dismissed on Siger's own ground of philosophical arguments and authorities. Siger's position, he believes, misrepresents Aristotle: Aquinas offers a close study of the text of *De Anima* and the testimony of Greek and Arab commentators to support his view. He also argues that Averroes's position is in itself untenable as a rational explanation of human thought.

Siger wrote a reply to Aquinas – now lost but partly reconstructable – and then, in about 1273, he produced the *De Anima Intellectiva* (AI), another extended treatment of the intellect. In this work (and in others written after 1270, such as his commentaries on the *Metaphysics* (M) and on the *Liber de Causis*) Siger tries to respond to the various types of criticism he had received. Some of the views he expounded had been condemned as heretical; now he is careful to point out that he is just an expositor. His task is to reveal his author, Aristotle's intentions; he does not claim that these always correspond to the truth (AI p.70:11–15; cf. M III, 15 in Maurer, III, 16 in Dunphy edition. In the *De Unitate*, Aquinas also blames his opponent for treating the truth of faith as if it were just one philosophical position among others and speaking as if Christian law were not his own. In the *De Anima Intellectiva* Siger makes it clear that faith is always to be followed where it seems to contradict reason or authority; although he has expounded what Aristotle says, his preference is always for the view of 'the holy Catholic faith' (AI p.88:50–53, cf. p.108:83–87). As the professed expositor of Aristotle, he is therefore particularly anxious to defend himself against Aquinas's charge that he has misrepresented the Aristotelian position, and he argues at length that, whatever the truth of the matter, it is he, rather than Aquinas or Albert the Great, who has discovered the Philosopher's intention. But Siger seems to have been impressed by some of Aquinas's rational objections to his position and he alters some aspects of his interpretation of Aristotle in an attempt to answer them.

Siger returns briefly to the problem of the intellect in his commentary on the *Liber de Causis*, probably the last of his surviving works. He is now willing to reject the unity of the potential intellect as heretical and also irrational, although he believes that Aristotle may have held this position. In general, he does not claim as he had previously done merely to be expressing his author's intentions, but rather to be giving arguments in accord with reason: his solution to each *quaestio* usually begins with a phrase such as 'It is argued by reason. . . ' or 'According to reason it ought to be said . . .'. What is the purpose of these remarks? To emphasize that Siger is not using revealed premisses? Or to suggest that the authoritative antique text and reason are in perfect accord? Or, rather, that he is following reason, not merely expounding a text? This uncertainty reflects a more general uncertainty in Siger's works. He does not – at least not after his earliest pieces – find any difficulty in declaring his allegiance to faith beyond all reasoning and authority; but he seems never to have been successful in defining the relation between the problem of antique texts which seem to contradict revelation, and the problem of reasoning which seems to contradict it.

For Aquinas, by contrast, the relationship between these two problems was clear. At the end of the *De Unitate*, St Thomas attributes to his opponent the statement: 'I conclude of necessity that the intellect is one in number; but I firmly hold the opposite from faith'. He objects to it strongly. Whatever is opposite to a necessary conclusion is logically impossible (*falsum impossibile*), Aquinas explains; and so, according to this position, the faith includes logical impossibilities. But even God could not make what is logically impossible true, and so no Christian can accept this position. In the unpolemical context of his commentary on Boethius's *De Trinitate* ([T] 2,3; see also SG 1,7, ST 1,1,8), Aquinas gives the background to his view. Both faith and reason come from God and, although not all things which are manifest to faith are manifest to reason, 'it is impossible that those things which are divinely passed to us by faith should be contrary to those which are within us by nature'. Any piece of reasoning which is contrary to the faith can (at least in theory) be refuted by reason, without the aid of revelation. But do not the *philosophi*, who argue from reason alone, sometimes contradict the faith? Aquinas anticipates this objection by explaining that whatever the *philosophi* say which is contrary to the faith 'is not philosophy but rather an abuse of philosophy from a failure of reason'. Aquinas believes, then, that reason and faith can never contradict each other; whereas the texts of the *philosophi* can and sometimes do contradict faith when their authors have deserted reason, not when they have followed it. But, as Aquinas shows when he discusses the eternity of the world, this assertion of reason's power must be balanced by an awareness of its limitations.

(2) The eternity of the world

Many believed that it was possible to demonstrate, by rational argument, that the world had not existed for ever. The sixth-century Greek Christian, John Philoponus, put forward a sophisticated set of such reasonings, which were partly taken up in the early 1250s by Bonaventure in his commentary on the *Sentences* (II, 1 pars 1,1,2). But Aristotle and the *philosophi* seemed to hold that the world was eternal. Whilst Aquinas was in no doubt of the revealed truth, that the world has not existed from eternity, he did not find demonstrations such as Bonaventure's convincing. In his various discussions of the subject (for example, SG II,31–8; ST 1,46,1) Aquinas attempts to show that neither the rational arguments which have been against the eternity of the world nor those which have been advanced for it are conclusive. In the *Summa Theologiae* (1,46,2) he goes on to argue that the world's not having always existed cannot in principle be rationally demonstrated. His last discussion of the question is in a brief treatise devoted especially to it, the *De Aeternitate Mundi* (1270). His own position hardened by the attacks from supporters of Bonaventure's view, he argues, not merely – as before – that it is impossible to demonstrate that the world has a beginning, but also that it is in theory possible that the world did not have a beginning although, in fact, from revelation we know that it did.

In his commentary on Boethius's *De Trinitate* (T 2,3) Aquinas makes especially plain the view of faith, reason and the *philosophi* which lies behind these positions. Reason, properly used, can never arrive at what is contrary to the faith; but this does not mean that it will always be able to demonstrate what faith holds. It can demonstrate that a position contrary to the faith is not necessary (because it can counter every argument in defence of the position), but not always that the position is false. Aquinas implies that, although on some subjects the *philosophi* are wanting in their reason, on the question of the world's eternity it is not their reason, but reason itself, which is deficient.

Siger of Brabant's contemporary in the arts faculty, Boethius of Dacia (see below, pp. 133–8), used his monograph *De Aeternitate Mundi* as the occasion to illustrate a very different but no less clearly conceived theory about the relations between the revealed truth, reason and the *philosophi*: he believes that, even on the question of the eternity of the world, where so many have found conflicts, he can show that revelation, reason and the *philosophi* are in accord. In his view, not only does each branch of knowledge have its own principles (an Aristotelian theory: see above, pp.47–8): the conclusions of each branch must also be understood in the light of those principles and qualified by them. For example, whenever a natural philosopher demonstrates a proposition, he must be taken to mean, not that it is true absolutely, but that it is true so far as natural causes and principles are concerned. Just as there is no contradiction between any two propositions such as 'Socrates is white according to x' and 'Socrates is not white', so there is no contradiction between the faith, which asserts that the world has a beginning, and a natural philosopher, who asserts that it has no beginning, because in the philosopher's assertion is implied the qualification 'according to natural causes and principles' (p.351). The same applies to the other branches of *philosophia*. In general, whatever a *philosophus* describes as possible or impossible he asserts so far as it can be investigated by human reason (p.364). Since it is not demonstrable by human reason that the world has a beginning, there is no contradiction between the *philosophi*, who hold – with this implicit qualification – that it is eternal, and faith which – without qualification – denies this. There is a further refinement to Boethius's position. Like Aquinas he thinks that, even according to reason, the eternity of the world (though it cannot be shown to be impossible) is not demonstrable. But he is keen to reconcile, not only faith and reason but also Aristotle, the *Philosophus*; and so he uses a text from the *Topics* as a basis for claiming that Aristotle too believed the eternity of the world to be a topic on which a philosopher must be neutral in position, because it can neither be demonstrated as true or false (p.356; cf. Aquinas's *Commentary on Sentences* II,1,1,5 and contrast his *Commentary on Physics* VIII,2).

(3) The condemnations of 1277

Despite Siger of Brabant's care in qualifying his views after the condemnation of 1270, and despite the nuanced and fundamentally orthodox position which emerges from a careful reading of Boethius of Dacia, there were many in the Church who were disturbed by some of the teaching which, they believed, went on in the Paris arts faculty. In January 1277, Pope John XXI asked Bishop Tempier to investigate the errors being propounded in the university. Tempier set up a commission of theologians; and, on the basis of their hurriedly composed report, on 7 March he condemned two hundred and nineteen erroneous propositions in *philosophia* and theology and threatened those who continued to hold them with excommunication.

It seems clear that – as medieval commentators recognized – the condemnation was directed against arts masters: Siger of Brabant, Boethius of Dacia and others. But the condemned articles by no means provide a faithful reflection of Siger's or Boethius's teaching or that of their colleagues in the arts faculty. The two hundred and nineteen propositions are a heterogeneous collection. Some present doctrines incompatible with Christianity which had been held by Arab expositors of Aristotle. Many of these views are found in surviving texts from the arts faculty – but often they are intended merely as explanations of Aristotle rather than as expressions of the truth (see above, pp.69–70). Some of the articles are directed against an approach to knowledge based entirely on self-evident truths and reason, which leaves no room for revelation. Although the wording of these statements is often close to remarks by Boethius of Dacia, the doctrine they condemn is a distortion of Boethius's thought. Boethius did not assert the primacy of *philosophia* over theology, but rather the separateness of each discipline. Some of the articles condemn extreme opinions (Confession is unnecessary, except for appearance's sake [203], Fornication is not a sin [205]) which no other evidence connects with the arts masters. And a few of the condemned propositions express views which are debatable but not obviously contrary to Christian teaching.

Some of the articles in this last category, such as those which argue that individuation is by matter (46, 110), condemn positions in fact held not only by arts masters but also by Aquinas. It does not seem, however, that Tempier's commission wished to mount a direct attack on the respected theologian who had died three years previously. But eleven days later, Robert Kilwardby, the archbishop of Canterbury, condemned a shorter list of propositions at Oxford, many of which do seem to have been intended to reflect aspects of St Thomas's doctrine.

It is very hard to assess the effects of the condemnations. Historians have often said that they brought about the end of 'radical Aristotelianism' in the Paris arts faculty. But was there ever such a movement? They have also suggested that the emphasis in later thirteenth- and fourteenth-century thought on God's omnipotence derives from the events of 1277. But divine omnipotence is a doctrine universally accepted by Christians: if some mid-thirteenth-century thinkers had perhaps gone too far in accommodating it to Aristotle's view of the universe, they had successors who were capable of detecting their weaknesses without Tempier's prompting. Some of the articles did indeed restrict the scope of theological discussion in a few areas, but on most topics theologians remained as free to disagree with each other as previously. And the condemnation of Thomist positions was strongly contested. Within fifty years Tempier's rulings had been modified to exclude from their scope any of Aquinas's doctrines.

★   ★   ★   ★   ★

In their accounts of thirteenth-century universities, historians often concentrate on controversies and condemnations. They trace the development of thought in the period by examining the conflict between Christian doctrine and the newly-translated ancient, Arab and Jewish writings. Often they identify two main opposing groups: the traditional theologians (and the ecclesiastical authorities), who opposed new ideas derived from non-Christian texts; and the arts masters, who were enthusiastic and uncritical advocates of Averroes's Aristotelianism. Between these groups they place Aquinas and his followers, who, they say, attempted to 'synthesize' Aristotelian with Christian teaching. Such a view is not only over-simplified: its emphasis is misleading. Although aspects of the new translations raised problems and led to discussion, debate and, sometimes, condemnations, for the most part Aristotelian and Arabic natural science and metaphysics were absorbed and developed with no problem apart from the inherent difficulties of understanding them. The arts masters, who from the mid-century used the Aristotelian works as their set-texts, were not antagonists of the theologians but co-operators in a common enterprise in which they accepted their subordinate and preparatory role.

Revealed and philosophical theology

At the very beginning of his *Summa Theologiae* (1,1,1), Aquinas asks whether it is necessary to have any other sort of discipline besides the branches of *philosophia*. The placing of the question is thoroughly logical: before Aquinas gives a *summa* of revealed theology he needs to show that the subject is not otiose. One might argue (arg. 2) that 'every sort of being, even God, is treated by the philosophical disciplines: and for this reason there is a part of philosophy which is called "theology" or "divine science", as Aristotle explains in the sixth book of his *Metaphysics*'. Metaphysics, as devised by Aristotle (and as developed by Avicenna – see above, pp.59–61), could be regarded as a theology: it provides proofs for the existence of God and discusses his attributes. Why, then, is revelation (and so theology based on revelation, as opposed to the theology which is metaphysics) needed at all?

Aquinas has two main answers. First, there is knowledge which is essential to human salvation but beyond the power of human reason to attain. Many of the articles of faith are of this sort: for instance, Aquinas holds that God's triunity cannot be rationally demonstrated and the arguments which can be made for it would not even appear very probable except to a believer (T 1,4). Second, revelation is necessary even of knowledge which reason is capable of gaining. There are only few men who investigate the truth about God by reason; their discoveries take many years and are not without many errors: yet 'the whole salvation of man depends on the truth of this knowledge' (ST 1,1,1).

Since there is an area of knowledge which can be gained either from revelation or by reason alone, it is necessary to define the relations between the two ways of knowing the same things. Every branch of knowledge, Aquinas says (T 5,4) in Aristotelian fashion, has its own principles. There are some principles which are only principles. For instance, unity is the principle of numbers and the point is the principle of lines; but unity and points are not things, and so they can only be discussed as principles in the disciplines (arithmetic and geometry) for which they are principles. But there are some principles which are also things (*naturae completae*), such as the stars. They are treated as principles in the discipline which deals with lower bodies, but as things they are also treated in a separate discipline which has them for its subject. The most general of all principles is being (*ens*), and being which is completely in act can be identified with God. Being is therefore a principle and also a thing. In metaphysics (the theology of the *philosophi*) immaterial and motionless being which is God is treated as a principle; being is also the *subject* of metaphysics, but being which is merely *abstracted* from matter and motion (and not actually independent of them). By contrast, in revealed theology immaterial and motionless being which is God is the subject.

If some of the revealed theologian's subject-matter is outside the range of unaided reason, and the rest is treated by the Christian theologian in a way different from the metaphysician's, it might seem that metaphysics has no part to play in revealed theology. But Aquinas is far from believing this. Revealed theology is indeed a discipline in its own right, with its own principles (see below, pp.80–1); but, as the highest branch of all knowledge, it can also use the principles of every other discipline (T 2,3 ad 7; cf. ST 1,1,5 ad 2; SG II, 4). Philosophical reasoning – which starts from self-evident rather than revealed premisses – can therefore play a part within revealed theology. And the special role of metaphysics is to demonstrate those truths, such as the existence of God, which faith presupposes but which also lie within the range of rational demonstration by the metaphysician (T 2,3).

The idea that the theologian bases much of his discussion on revealed truth, which cannot be demonstrated from self-evident premisses, was shared by Aquinas's contemporaries and medieval successors. But the second element in St Thomas's discussion of the relations between metaphysics and revealed theology – his attitude to the use by theologians of purely rational arguments – was less universally accepted. Medieval theologians did indeed, like Aquinas, consider that metaphysical discussions of God, based on reason alone, had some place in theology, but they did not all agree on how to express the difference between the knowledge of God gained from metaphysics and that gained by theology based on revelation. Aquinas had put it in terms of the relations between the subject of a science and its principles. Later thirteenth- and fourteenth-century writers often described the difference in terms of signification: the language of metaphysics refers to the creator in terms which are common to him and his creation, whereas theology can (at least as a possibility) speak of God in the language proper to him.

In addition to its value in demonstrating the *praeambula* to the faith, Aquinas lists (T 2,3) two further ways in which philosophical reasoning can be used by the theologian: to suggest by likenesses the contents of faith; and to refute supposedly rational arguments which are contrary to the faith (since they will always turn out to be sophistical: see above pp.70–1). Almost every medieval theologian would have agreed with him in allowing at least this second, apologetic use of purely rational arguments; although, by the fourteenth century, the differences between contemporary theologians provided the main subjects of theological debate, and there was little time or enthusiasm for purely rational arguments against unbelievers or heretics.

Aquinas and the schools of ancient thought

St Thomas's three categories of uses for *philosophia* in theology – so useful for later medieval theologians in general – are less than adequate to describe his own prolonged and serious discussions of antique thought both within and outside theological works. They are inadequate, not because he gives a greater or more independent role to *philosophia* than they allow, but because of the strength of Aquinas's commitment to *understanding* ancient thought – and understanding it in the light of faith and revealed theology.

St Thomas began his career at a time when a great quantity of ancient thought (and Arab commentaries on it), translated over the previous hundred years, was first being studied thoroughly and in detail. The ancient writings did not present a single position. Not only were there differences among the ancient and Arab commentators about Aristotle's own views; it was also evident from Aristotle himself, from his exegetes, and from some non-Aristotelian texts that there were other schools of thought in antiquity and that other *philosophi* had answered the same questions quite differently from the *Philosophus* himself. To order and judge this heterogeneous material, Aquinas sought to analyse and understand the differences.

St Thomas's contemporaries were confronted by the same material. But none of them applied to it a similar effort of accurate and detailed comprehension. In his commentaries, Albert the Great syncretized, bringing different sources and positions together into a unified view; and his study of the *philosophi* is not seen in any clearly defined relation to his theological work. Bonaventure, like Aquinas, approaches the *philosophi* by asking what part they can play in his theological enterprise; unlike Aquinas, he sees the divergences between the different ancient philosophers as different types of failure to reach the truth. Bonaventure admires both Plato and Aristotle: but Plato, who had the wisdom to postulate Ideas (which Bonaventure interprets as being in God's mind) lacked Aristotle's solid basis of knowledge about the world; whilst Aristotle, who denied the theory of Ideas, lacked Plato's wisdom.

Aquinas's approach to the different schools of ancient thought was influenced by two main factors. The first is Aristotle's presentation of the history of philosophy. In the *Metaphysics*, especially, Aristotle not only expounds his predecessors' theories and explains why they are unacceptable, he also suggests that they constitute a series of attempts to reach a truth which, finally, he has gained: for Aristotle, the development of philosophy reaches its climax in his own work. The second factor is Aquinas's principle that no truly rational argument can ever reach a conclusion contrary to the faith (see above, pp.70-1): an argument which does so must go against reason in some respect. The truths of faith, which Aquinas and other Christians know from revelation, can therefore be used as a tool for sorting good reasoning from bad. Where a philosopher's conclusions contradict the faith, there must be a flaw in his reasoning. The two factors are combined in Aquinas's view. He believes that Aristotle's theories in most fields capture the truths which his predecessors had been working towards, but missing; and he shows how the strength of Aristotle's reasoning, and the weakness of his forerunners', is evident in the way that Aristotle's conclusions do not contradict the faith on many occasions where theirs do.

The individual conclusions of thinkers, St Thomas considers, are based on their fundamental positions. Where a past thinker's conclusion goes against the truth, he is not just content to demonstrate its falsity. He wishes to explain why it is wrong and how it came to be held. This involves discovering the fundamental position from which it is derived. Sometimes the untenable conclusion will have resulted from a mistake in reasoning from these premisses. But often the reasoning is shown to be impeccable: it is the fundamental position itself which is wrong. Aquinas is interested in three fundamental positions: those of the pre-Socratics, Plato and Aristotle. His knowledge of all three comes mostly from Aristotle. Of these positions, only Aristotle's is right (and accords with the faith). But the other two are seen, not as total departures from reason, but as the result of attempts to reach the complex truth which Aristotle finally discovered. For instance, when he is showing that the soul knows corporeal things through the intellect (ST 1,84,1), Aquinas explains that 'the first philosophers who enquired about the nature of things' thought that everything in the world was bodily and, because all bodies are in motion, they concluded that we could never know the truth about things. Then Plato 'in order to permit us to have certain knowledge of the truth by our intellect' posited the existence of incorporeal Ideas. Aquinas both explains, following Aristotle, why Plato's position is wrong and also how Plato might have fallen into error.

Aquinas's interest in the schools of ancient philosophy is seen throughout the sections of the *Summa Theologiae* on the soul and its knowledge (1,75–7; 84–9), where the different views on each topic are expounded and the defects of all but Aristotle's made clear. At the same time as he was writing the first part of the *Summa* (1267), he also composed a commentary on the *De Anima*. This work is not related to his controversy with Siger, as has sometimes been supposed: nor is it – nor Aquinas's other Aristotelian commentaries – just intended as a doctrinally safe exegesis for the use of arts students. In the commentary on the *De Anima*, and the other Aristotelian commentaries he went on to compose, Aquinas is able both more fully to expound Aristotle's position and to investigate more deeply the reasons why the pre-Socratics and the Platonists are wrong in argument. St Thomas's most impressive piece of doctrinal analysis, however, is a commentary, not on Aristotle, but the *Liber de Causis*. The commentary involves throughout the comparison between the *Liber de Causis* itself, the newly-translated text of Proclus's *Elements of Theology* and the writings of pseudo-Dionysius. Aquinas immediately recognizes that the *Liber* is an adaptation of parts of the *Elements*. His purpose then becomes to discover what sort of adaptation, and he does this by reference to the positions of Plato and his followers on the one hand, and Aristotle on the other. Aquinas believes – and modern scholarship has confirmed his view – that pseudo-Dionysius's Neoplatonism is modified by Aristotelian elements in certain important ways. When he analyses the *Liber*, he tries to show that often, when it alters Proclus, its immediate source, it does so in a way which brings it closer to pseudo-Dionysius; and consequently away from a Platonic and towards an Aristotelian position. In doing so, the *Liber* reaches truths which Proclus, misled by Platonism, had missed. St Thomas's instances of the positions which the *Liber* and pseudo-Dionysius share in contradiction to Proclus are often preceded, not by the phrase 'according to Aristotle' but by one more eloquent of Aquinas's views: 'According to the doctrine of the faith and Aristotle. . .'.

Theology as a discipline and as a science

(1) Theology is an argumentative discipline

When theologians disputed, and when they commented Peter the Lombard's *Sentences*, they were involved in an argumentative activity which required the full resources of their training in logic and in conceptual analysis. Outside the limited area where they, like the *philosophi*, reasoned from purely rational premisses, they continued to reason with equal rigour. Their theological arguments were judged by the same logical standards as the argument of a *philosophus*, except that it was acknowledged that among their premisses were some which rested on revelation. Few theological arguments consisted of deductions purely from revealed premisses. The majority mixed revealed premisses with premisses which derived, by deduction from what was self-evident and from experience. In the most unambiguously theological contexts, therefore, the reader of later thirteenth and fourteenth-century *quaestiones* will find lengthy discussions of topics in logic (such as universals, or signification, or modality); in the theory of mind, the emotions and action; in the theory of mathematics (such as infinity and the continuum); in physics and metaphysics. These topics are introduced for the sake of a theological argument, but the reasoning in them has to stand up both to objections based on revelation and to those based only on reason. The sophisticated conceptual vocabulary developed from Aristotle and his commentators was particularly necessary for theologians in their work; and quotations from Aristotle and the *philosophi* are mixed with citations of Scripture and the Fathers in theological *quaestiones*.

(2) Is theology a science?

Thirteenth- and fourteenth-century theologians tried to understand and explain the nature of their discipline by considering how far it could be accommodated to Aristotle's terms. If theology is an argumentative discipline, at least as strict in its logical and organizational requirements as any of the branches of *philosophia*, can it not be described as a science, in the sense Aristotle defines in the *Posterior Analytics* (see above, pp.47–9)? It certainly meets the requirement that its conclusions be deduced from its principles: but does it have its own self-evident principles, as Aristotle required of each branch of knowledge?

Early in the thirteenth century William of Auxerre had remarked that just as every science has its own principles, so does theology: they are the articles of faith. But, as writers noticed as soon as they tried to draw from this perception a theory about theology as a science, the articles of faith are not self-evident: they are matters of belief.

In the mid-thirteenth century, some leading theologians believed that Aristotle himself provided them with a way out of this difficulty. In the *Posterior Analytics*, Aristotle had allowed that certain sciences did not have their own self-evident principles but borrowed them from a superior branch of knowledge (see above, p.48). Medieval writers called the inferior science in such cases 'subalternate'. Bonaventure seems to have been the first to apply the notion of subalternation to theology. The *Sentences*, he says, are subalternate to Scripture: in Scripture the object of belief (*credibile*) is treated as the object of belief; whereas in the *Sentences* it is treated as the object of understanding (*intelligibile*). Aquinas applies the concept of subalternation to theology in a more Aristotelian way. The articles of faith, he maintains, are not indeed self-evident to men in this life; but they are self-evident to God and souls in bliss. Theology therefore is a subalternate branch of knowledge to the science possessed by God and the blessed in heaven (*scientia Dei et beatorum*). It borrows principles which are not its own, but are self-evident in the higher science to which it is subalternated (ST 1.1,2; T 2.2 ad 5). However, Aquinas qualifies his position by remarking that subalternation of theology to the *scientia Dei et beatorum* is different in type from subalternation between any other sciences, since the superiority of the *scientia Dei* is not of subject but in the manner (*modus*) of knowing.

Many of the theologians in the years after Aquinas were not convinced that his use of subalternation gave its principles the self-evidence necessary for theology to be a science. For instance, Duns Scotus (in the Prologue to his *Ordinatio*) argues that men could, without enjoying the beatific vision, construct theology as a science, but only by virtue of a special revelation which God, given his unlimited power, can grant. Normally, men are limited to using the revelation of Scripture to devise a theology which falls short of this possible science. Ockham, who attacked Scotus's theory of theology on many points, agreed with him about the possibility, for men in this life, of a scientific theology, and the non-scientific nature of theology as men are able, in the normal order of things, to practise it.

The different approaches of thirteenth- and fourteenth-century theologians to the definition of their subject illustrate three general points. First, whether or not they concluded that it was a science in the Aristotelian sense, they thought of theology as rigorously logical in its required methods of reasoning. Second, theologians did not think of their discipline as *philosophia* with certain revealed elements added to it: it was a unified discipline in its own right (although one which could make use of other disciplines). Third, the differences between thinkers such as Aquinas, Scotus and Ockham in their conception of theology are primarily theological differences, not differences about the relation between *philosophia* and faith. The terms in which later medieval theologians envisaged their work are not easily accommodated to the presuppositions and expectations of modern historians of philosophy.

Conclusion to Part One:
what is medieval philosophy?

The history of *philosophy* in the Middle Ages is not a clearly and uncontentiously defined subject. Modern scholars have given various answers to the question 'What is medieval philosophy?', and usually their choice has deeply affected their examination of individual medieval thinkers. Often, when their interpretations of a figure's thought diverge, it is not because they understand his texts differently, but because they disagree about what parts of them constitute his philosophy.

Current approaches to medieval philosophy

(1) The distinction between philosophy and theology: 'separationism'

Although the practice of what became known as scholastic philosophy continued from the end of the Middle Ages until modern times, serious historical interest in medieval philosophy began only in the nineteenth century. Many of the subject's earliest exponents, such as Victor Cousin and Barthélemy Hauréau, were secular thinkers anxious to find a place for the Middle Ages in their scheme of the history of philosophy. They are sometimes known as 'rationalists'. They described, usually in pejorative terms, the influence of religious dogma on medieval thinkers: by failing to rely on reason alone their function as philosophers was compromised. The rationalist approach is less important in itself – since it scarcely survives today (except in a transmuted form: see below, pp.85–7) – than for the reaction it evoked from Catholic historians. It might be expected that the Catholic historians would have stressed the interrelations between rational argument and Christian dogma in the Middle Ages, and presented men like Aquinas and Duns Scotus as theologians; whilst the rationalists would stress the purely rational aspects of their thought. But it was the contrary which took place. Catholic historians reacted to the rationalists by proposing a view which might be called 'separationist': they argued that, at least from the time of Aquinas, medieval thinkers recognized the distinction between theology and philosophy. Aquinas and Scotus were indeed theologians, and it is valuable to study their theology; but they were also philosophers, and their philosophy should be studied separately from their theology.

The separationist view has had, and still has, many followers. What does it involve as presented by a learned and clear-minded modern exponent, such as Fernand van Steenberghen? On the one hand, its adherents claim that the view is based on historical evidence. The modern commentator is allowed to separate philosophy from theology in medieval texts because the medieval authors recognized the disciplines as distinct (as the very use of the word *philosophia* to contrast with *theologia* illustrates). On the other hand, exponents of the view acknowledge that, in order to present the philosophy of a medieval thinker, the modern historian must select and arrange. In the case of Aquinas, the task of selecting is easy. Some of his works are purely philosophical (for instance, his treatises on being and on the unity of the intellect, or his commentaries on Aristotle), whilst even in the theological works the separationists find long passages which, except for the occasional scriptural reference, are pure philosophy. In the case of a thinker like Bonaventure, the task is much more difficult, and the historian must scan his theological works in search of the disparate fragments of his philosophy. Once the philosophical material has been collected, it must be arranged according to the different branches of philosophy (which any complete system of philosophy must include), and among these branches epistemology 'naturally' should be placed first. The philosophical system which has been exposed in this way can be compared and contrasted with any other philosophical system. Separationists tend to see each system as a synthesis of mainly old elements. They talk of medieval philosophical systems in terms of Platonism, Aristotelianism, Augustinism, Avicennism, Averroism and explain how parts from these systems were assembled in various different ways by thirteenth- and fourteenth-century philosophers. But they do not think, for this reason, that medieval philosophy was lacking in originality. On the contrary, they make the distinction between systems which are merely heterogeneous collections of borrowed elements, and those (such as St Thomas's) which combine the elements into a new synthesis.

(2) Christian philosophy

A somewhat different approach, which qualifies and adapts the principles of the separationists, has been developed by Étienne Gilson and practised by many of his followers. Gilson believes that the great Latin thinkers of the later Middle Ages should be described, not simply as philosophers, but as 'Christian philosophers'. Along with the separationists, he holds that it is right to consider the history of medieval philosophy as a separate subject from the history of medieval theology; but it is a philosophy which, none the less, depends on Christian revelation and cannot be understood in abstraction from certain fundamental tenets of the faith. Gilson develops his view of Christian philosophy most strikingly in connection with St Bonaventure, whom he represents as rejecting Aristotelian philosophy in favour of a philosophy which makes Christ its centre. But he sees Aquinas, too, as a (very different kind of) Christian philosopher, one who combined what he knew as a Christian with what Aristotle taught him so as to produce a system beyond the reach of the antique philosophers.

Like the separationists, Gilson and his followers make a selection of material in order to present the philosophy of medieval thinkers. But it is a wider selection: although it omits purely theological topics (such as the relations of the persons of the Trinity, the incarnation and the sacraments), it makes no claim to limit itself to arguments which are based on reason alone. And, when they expound the Christian philosophies of the Middle Ages, they do not rearrange the order of material in their sources in the way favoured by the separationists. For instance, Gilson thinks that St Thomas's doctrine should properly be presented in what Aquinas himself describes (SG II,4) as the theologian's order, starting with his discussion of God. Gilson is as apt to explain medieval thought in terms of systems and syntheses as the separationists; but the syntheses he describes are wider ranging and the elements of ancient systems are subsumed into a Christian view of the world.

(3) The modern analytical approach

Until recently, the study of medieval philosophy was rare in the philosophy faculties of English-speaking countries. Whereas it was often pursued by philosophers in France, Germany, Italy, Spain and Belgium, in England and America the subject remained largely the preserve of historians. But during the last twenty years interest in medieval thought has grown remarkably among philosophers trained in the English and American analytical tradition. They have discovered important similarities between the way they, as professional philosophers, approach their subject now, and the way in which thirteenth- and fourteenth-century thinkers worked. Philosophy now (in the English-speaking countries) is an academic discipline, pursued by a small number of highly trained specialists in university departments. In the later Middle Ages, too, sophisticated abstract thought was conducted by masters of arts and theology in the universities – an intellectual élite which had received a lengthy education. Modern philosophy is often technical in its terminology; logic is regarded as of great importance by its practitioners; and the study of language is seen as an important method for solving its problems. Later medieval thinkers, also, used a complex set of technical terms; their logical training is evident throughout their work; and they were fond of turning to linguistic distinctions in their pursuit of truth. Given this likeness in their methods, it is not surprising – they feel – that later medieval thinkers should turn out to have discussed many of the problems which interest philosophers today in Britain and America – not just in formal and philosophical logic, but in ethics, the philosophy of mind and action and many other areas.

The aims of analytical philosophers who study medieval thought are cogently expressed in a passage from the Introduction to the *Cambridge History of Later Medieval Philosophy*:

> By combining the highest standards of medieval scholarship with a respect for the insights and interests of contemporary philosophers, particularly those working in the analytic tradition, we hope to have presented medieval philosophy in a way that will help to end the era during which it has been studied in a philosophical ghetto, with many of the major students of medieval philosophy unfamiliar or unsympathetic with twentieth-century philosophical developments, and with most contemporary work in philosophy carried out in total ignorance of the achievements of the medievals on the same topics. It is one of our aims to help make the activity of contemporary philosophy intellectually continuous with medieval philosophy to the extent to which it already is so with ancient philosophy.

As this statement of intention suggests, exponents of what might be called the 'modern analytical' approach of thought in the Middle Ages concentrate on the philosophical problems which they believe they share with medieval scholars. They try to translate medieval texts so far as possible into modern terms and analyse them with the same care that they would give to the reasoning of a contemporary philosopher. They are willing to point out flaws or weaknesses in a scholastic author's argument – not from a desire to cavil, but because in doing so they come to grasp his thought more closely. Their approach to texts is usually highly selective: they pick out the sections, chapters or paragraphs which contain arguments they find interesting. Although they are aware of the theological context of much of their material, they do not usually think it of much relevance to the particular philosophical arguments they isolate. Similarly, they do not normally think the origin and literary form of texts (commentary, disputation or monograph; *quaestio* or exposition) a matter of importance to them. Their aim is simply to understand whatever they consider to be of philosophical value in the medieval work.

Historical and philosophical justification for the different approaches

Medieval philosophy is sometimes discussed as if there were a correct approach to identifying and studying it, and as if the correctness of this approach could be determined by historical investigation. Separationists often speak in this way, when they refer to thirteenth-century distinctions between philosophy and theology in order to justify their delimitation of their subject-matter; and, in asserting their different view, the exponents of Christian philosophy are equally apt to adduce historical evidence.

But none of the current approaches to medieval philosophy can in fact be supported simply by an appeal to historical evidence, because this evidence (some of which the preceding chapters have summarized) suggests that the role of theology was far more important than modern interpreters (even Gilson and his followers) allow. Most of the thinkers usually regarded as later medieval philosophers – such as Aquinas, Henry of Ghent, Duns Scotus and William of Ockham – were theologians; most of their writings were theological. Some passages in their theological books – short and few in relation to the whole – do develop arguments based on self-evident premises and experience, and not at all on revelation; but these passages form part of a structure of argument which is theological in aim and presuppositions.

There are, indeed, texts by medieval arts masters (none of whom is as profound or inventive a thinker as the great theologians). And there are a few works by the masters of theology which are, in the medieval sense, philosophical rather than theological – such as Albert the Great's commentaries on Aristotle or Aquinas's *De Unitate Intellectus*. It would be possible to base the study of medieval philosophy on these writings alone. But the subject would become very different from that usually presented: except in logic, the historian would have to deny himself most of the texts which are richest in ideas and argument. Even if he felt that, ignoring their context, he could extract from avowedly theological works just those arguments which involve no revealed premisses the historian would only slightly improve his material. Most important medieval discussions of the philosophy of mind and action, of ethics, free will, time, matter, causality (and some about signification, reference and universals) would remain out of his range, because, however rigorous their reasoning, they depend at some stage on premisses known from faith.

Moreover, if the historian of philosophy restricts himself to philosophical texts in order to make his choice of subject-matter historically justifiable, then he must respect the medieval conception of the range of philosophy. Philosophy – in the sense intended by medieval writers when they contrast it with theology – embraces all the branches of knowledge based on self-evident premisses, experiment and reasoning. It includes much which would now be described as science; and the scientific parts of it are often inextricable from the parts which would now be called philosophical. If the historian of philosophy writes about what medieval scholars considered to be philosophy, he will not produce a history of philosophy in the modern sense. But if he separates medieval philosophy (which often still seems powerful in argument and relevant to questions posed by thinkers today) from medieval science (which is frequently no more than an historical curiosity), then he cannot claim that his choice of subject-matter has an historical basis, since he is making a separation not envisaged by the medieval authors.

The fact that none of the current approaches to medieval philosophy can be justified on purely historical grounds does not, however, mean that none is justifiable. Strong arguments can be advanced in favour of each of the three approaches outlined above: but they are arguments based, not on historical evidence about medieval attitudes to philosophy, but on different conceptions of what philosophy should be. Underlying the separationists' approach is a view of philosophy as a discipline which, by reasoning from self-evident premisses, constructs systems to explain the underlying structure of reality – a structure not revealed by empirical scientific investigation. The advocate of this conception of philosophy has every reason to approach medieval texts by asking whether they furnish elements which would allow such a system to be constructed; and, if it does, to extract and assemble them. Given this view of philosophy, he will have selected his material in the only way possible for him to put forward what the texts contain of importance.

Exponents of Christian philosophy select and arrange in a different way, because in one important respect they have a different conception of philosophy: it is a subject which has been changed in its scope by the coming of Christ. Followers of the modern analytical approach differ from both separationists and advocates of Christian philosophy in their view of philosophy as a subject concerned with logical and linguistic analysis. This is reflected in their choice of material. They also differ in openly avowing that their idea of what is philosophy in medieval texts depends on the nature of philosophy as a discipline today.

A fourth approach: 'historical analysis'

Despite the justifiability of all three approaches, perhaps there is something of value to be learned from a new type of approach which might be called 'historical analysis', since it shares some of its methods with the modern analysts, but gives weight to historical considerations which they, along with the exponents of separationism and Christian philosophy, recognize but largely disregard. Historical analysis aims both to bridge the distance between the interests and assumptions of a modern reader and the writings of later medieval thinkers, and yet to take account of it. It tries to explain the ideas and arguments of medieval thinkers, so far as possible, in terms accessible to readers today, relating them where appropriate to modern problems; and to show exactly what questions each thinker posed himself and why he answered them as he did. In this it resembles 'modern' analysis. But historical analysis also asks about the presuppositions and aims of later medieval thinkers, the scope of their investigations, the methods they used, the texts they read. Only by answering these historical questions, it suggests, can the modern reader begin to grasp what medieval thinkers argued and why they did so.

Historical analysis imposes two special restrictions on its exponents. The first prohibits them from making anachronistic assumptions about the identity of the problems discussed in their texts. Many of the areas discussed by later medieval arts masters and theologians still interest philosophers today: for example, topics in the philosophy of mind and action such as knowledge, memory, emotion and intention or topics in philosophical logic such as signification, self-reference and modality. Modern analysts usually assume that medieval texts on these subjects discuss the same problems which engage contemporary philosophers, although in different (often less adequate) terms. The historical analyst is forbidden such assumptions. He may begin his investigations by noticing that a certain set of problems in medieval writings concerns a similar area to a set of problems tackled by modern philosophers. But only by examining the texts they read and the aims they pursued does the historical analyst discover what exactly were the questions which medieval thinkers posed themselves. Only then is he able to decide whether the questions are in any sense the same as those which philosophers ask today.

The second restriction on the historical analyst concerns the scope of his investigations. Historical analysis is ill-suited as an approach to writing the comprehensive *Histories* of later medieval philosophy which have been favoured by separationists, exponents of Christian philosophy and even by modern analysts. The author of such a *History* has to decide what material constitutes medieval philosophy and, in doing so, he must choose between being unhistorical and allowing his choice to be decided by his own view of what philosophy is, or else presenting a medley of logical, scientific and theological discussions which would not, for the modern reader, provide a history of *philosophy*. The historical analyst avoids this problem if he restricts himself to a single topic (or a set of individual topics). The only claim he need make to justify his choice is that the topic once interested medieval thinkers and that questions in the same general area still interest modern philosophers.

Part Two of this *Introduction* is an historical analysis of one topic – intellectual knowledge – in the treatments of some outstanding later medieval thinkers.

Part Two

5 Intellectual knowledge: the problem and its sources

The problem of intellectual knowledge

The historical analyst is forbidden to assume that the problems treated in his texts are the same as those which face modern philosophers. And so an historical analysis of intellectual knowledge in later medieval thought cannot proceed in what might seem to be the obvious way: *first* defining the problem and *then* examining the terms in which thirteenth- and fourteenth-century thinkers framed it. The problem they tackled cannot be grasped apart from the terms in which they saw it. But two preliminaries can make these terms appear more comprehensible to the modern reader before he meets them in the discussion of individual medieval thinkers: an indication of where and why, in the scheme of studies at a medieval university, intellectual knowledge was discussed; and a survey of the ancient, patristic and Arab sources which helped to shape arts masters' and theologians' view of the problem. The first of these is easily given; the second will occupy most of this chapter.

In the arts faculty, questions about intellectual knowledge were raised principally in discussions of signification and of the soul. Both logicians, commenting Aristotle's *De Interpretatione*, and exponents of the highly abstract 'speculative grammar', popular in the later thirteenth century (see below, pp. 136-9), investigated the relations between objects in the world, words in language and thoughts in the mind. The nature of the soul was examined using Aristotle's *De Anima* as a textbook to be understood with the help of antique and, especially, Arab commentaries. Aristotle's view of intellectual knowledge, and the various different interpretations of it which had been offered, figured prominently in these studies. Arts masters were interested in the nature of intellectual knowledge because the problem was raised by the authoritative texts they used; and they wished to answer questions about it simply to reach the truth of the matter, so far as their reason permitted. In this way, their approach might seem to have much in common with that of modern philosophers. But, in practice, arts masters tended to keep close to their authoritative texts and commentaries. Their most sophisticated remarks on intellectual knowledge show the influence of the contemporaries in the theology faculty, who were responsible for most of the original work on the subject.

But problems about intellectual knowledge were most often tackled by the theologians in two contexts which would startle the philosopher of today. One is the theory of trinitarian relations. In his *De Trinitate*, Augustine had suggested that analogies to the Trinity could be found in man's mind. This theme, concisely reported in Peter the Lombard's *Sentences* (Distinction III, sec. 2), provided the basis for elaborate later medieval investigations of the workings of the human intellect. The other context is the discussion of how rational beings other than men in this life – that is to say, disembodied souls, angels and God – know things: their knowledge must be intellectual (since they have no senses) and the intellectual knowledge which embodied men enjoy is usually examined in relation to it. It is true that some of their works gave theologians the chance to consider separately intellectual knowledge in humans on earth. *Quaestiones* on this topic will be found in disputations, and in Aquinas's two *summae*. Even so, these discussions contributed to a wider theme and a wider theological purpose. When theologians explained how a mental 'word' is generated in the process of intellectual cognition, they were not merely trying to illumine the ways of human thought; and their view of the embodied intellect always belonged to a more general understanding of beings more purely intellectual than men in this life.

Sources: the intellect and its knowledge in ancient thought

(1) Plato and the Platonists

For Plato, the intellect (*nous*) is the highest part of the human soul. Through it man can gain wisdom, which consists in contemplating the Ideas. The Ideas are eternal, immutable, incorporeal entities on which all other things depend for their being. On some occasions Plato talks about them as if they were universals of sorts of thing – such as the Idea of a bed, by which a bed is a bed; but in his fullest account of intellectual knowledge of the Ideas (*Republic* vi–vii), he talks of them as universals of qualities – such as the Idea of the

Good, the Just, the Beautiful. Only some men, after many years of rigorous training, will ever be able to use their intellects to their purpose and grasp the Ideas. Contemplation of the Ideas has usually been described as some sort of non-propositional thinking, a sort of mental seeing. But it has recently been argued that to grasp an Idea is to understand a proposition: it is to know, for instance, what the Good is, or what the Just is. Even if, supposing that this interpretation is correct, the activity of the Platonic intellect in grasping the Ideas is propositional, it is not discursive. Much intellectual discourse – reasoning from one proposition to another – is required in order to reach the stage of contemplating an Idea. But the act of contemplation itself is non-discursive.

Plato's discussion of intellectual knowledge had almost no direct influence on the later Middle Ages. But it had an important indirect influence in two ways. First, it provided the context for Aristotle's examination of the intellect. Second, Plato's views were the starting-point for later Platonists' discussions, some of which were known by later medieval thinkers.

The Platonists tended to stress those aspects of Plato's account of intellectual knowledge which made it different from ordinary human ways of thinking. 'Intelligizing', the primary activity of the intellect, was distinguished by Plotinus from discursive thinking. The late Neoplatonic Christian writer, pseudo-Dionysius, whose works were studied intently in the Middle Ages, attributed to the angels the pure activity of the intellect. Because human thinking is discursive, it cannot, he argues, be considered entirely intellectual. Augustine's remarks on intellect were even more influential on medieval thinkers. He uses the term *intellectus* not to designate a part of the soul but rather the activity of which the human reason (*ratio*) is capable at its highest (an activity, he suggests, which requires divine aid or 'illumination').

(2) Aristotle

Although later medieval scholars read Augustine, pseudo-Dionysius and other Platonist texts, the basis of their treatments of intellectual knowledge was provided by Aristotle – whether partially understood, as by William of Auvergne; understood, accepted but transformed, as by Aquinas or Henry of Ghent; or largely rejected, as by William of Ockham.

(i) *Potency and act, matter and form, soul and body in the* De Anima

Aristotle explains human knowledge in terms of the striking

conception of soul and body which he develops in the *De Anima*. This view, in its turn, depends on Aristotle's distinction between potency and act, and the theory of form and matter which he develops from it. The concepts of potency and act are easiest to grasp in connection with Aristotle's biological interests. Seeds grow into trees; but to say 'this very thing was a seed and is now a tree' would seem strange, since how can the same thing be both tree and seed? Potency and act provide a way of describing such natural change: the seed, Aristotle would say, is *potentially* a tree; the mature tree is actually one. Aristotle also used potency and act to explain the relationship between individuals and the classes to which they belong. By virtue of what is an object something of particular kind – a stone, a stick or a lamp-post? Plato had said that things belonged to their various kinds by participating in incorporeal, eternal and unchangeable Ideas. Aristotle preferred to investigate the particular objects themselves. Each, he argued, could be analysed into matter and form. An object's form is its definition, what makes it one kind of thing rather than another – a stick rather than a stone. The form must be combined with matter to constitute an individual thing (this stick, that stone), but matter without form exists in potency only. Form determines matter as a particular kind of individual thing which exists in act. Uninformed matter, therefore, does not actually exist; nor is there any need to posit a world of disembodied forms.

In Book II of *De Anima* (412a–3a), Aristotle uses his theory of matter and form to define the soul (this is the translation usually adopted for *psuche*, but it is important to adjust the connotations of the English term in the light of Aristotle's discussion). The soul, he says, is 'the form of a natural body which potentially has life'. The relationship between soul and body, he argues, is the same as that between matter and form. Aristotle tries to show why this explanation is not as odd as it might seem by introducing a further distinction. Something can be neither purely in act nor purely in potency, when it has a disposition (what Aristotle usually calls a *hexis* and the scholastics a *habitus*) for an act which it is not at that moment performing. For example, it is possible to distinguish between lacking knowledge, possessing knowledge without exercising it (as in the case of someone asleep), and actually exercising knowledge. A similar distinction, Aristotle believes, can be drawn between a lifeless body, the capacity for the various functions of life (the 'first actualization' of the body as a living thing), and the actual exercise of those functions. The soul, says Aristotle, is the first actualization of the body, its capacity to exercise the functions which make it a living thing. Just as matter can be something in act only if determined by a form, so the living thing is what it is because of its soul. If the eye were a living thing, Aristotle explains, then its soul would be sight, because an eye is defined as something which sees: a sightless 'eye' is no more really an eye than a painted or sculpted one

Aristotle's concept of the soul is such that every living thing must have one, since only those things which have the capacity to live are alive. But he distinguishes several different 'faculties' of the soul – different ways in which something can be alive: nutrition and reproduction; sensation; desire; movement; imagination and intellect. Not all living things have every faculty. Plants have only the first; animals also have at least the sense of touch, and many of them possess the other senses and the other faculties of the soul, except for intellect, which belongs to humans alone.

(ii) Sensation and thought

Aristotle considers that the human soul has two cognitive faculties – faculties capable of acquiring knowledge. His discussion of how humans know things will seem less baffling than it might if a difference between Aristotle and modern thinkers is borne in mind. Nowadays, a distinction would usually be made between a scientific account of human cognition (which might include the physics of sound-waves, the chemistry of odours and the physiology of nerve and brain-cells) and philosophical analysis of it. It would not have occurred to Aristotle or his contemporaries to make such a distinction: Aristotle seems to aim at what would now be considered a scientific explanation but uses methods of argument which are nearer to those of a modern philosopher than those of a modern scientist.

Sensation, according to Aristotle (416b–8a), is a process in which the sentient subject is changed by the object sensed. The faculty of sensation exists only potentially: it is that which has the potentiality to become whatever is sensed. The senses (424a) are receptive to the form of sensible objects without the matter, like wax which receives the impression of a signet ring but not the gold or bronze from which the ring is made. The sense organ and the object it senses are two different things; but the act of sensing and the act of the object sensed are one and the same (425b): the ringing of a bell *is* the act of the sense-faculty which by hearing it is converted from potentiality.

Sensible perception is not the only kind of cognition. On the one hand there is a kind of perception which is like sensation, but takes place in the absence of the object sensed: Aristotle calls this imagination (427b–9a). Imagination belongs to most, though not all, animals. On the other hand, there is a kind of cognition unlike sensible perception – a kind which humans do not share with the animals. Not only can a man see and touch a stone, or call a mental picture of that stone into his imagination after he has seen it, he can also think about the stone, and he can think about stones in general without adverting to the characteristics of any particular stone. A modern thinker would almost certainly discuss this ability in terms of language: he would say that the stone is an object of thought, rather than merely sensation, not because it is somehow perceived by a special faculty of thought, but because it is the subject of mental discourse.

Aristotle sees the matter differently, partly because he is trying to give a scientific account of the workings of the soul and attributes to the intellect a mechanism similar to that he has found in the senses; and partly because he is influenced by Plato's account of the intellect as the faculty which grasps the forms of things (although his conception of forms is very different from Plato's). The intellect – the faculty of the mind which thinks – must, he says (429a), be receptive to the forms of things in the same way as the faculty of sensation: 'the sensitive is to what is sensed as the intellect is to what is thought'. The intellect is in potency to become the same as its object: until it thinks, it has no existence in act; its only characteristic is its capacity to receive. Aristotle distinguishes the workings of the intellect from those of the sensitive faculty in two ways. The sensitive faculty has organs, whereas the intellect has none (429a27). And the object of intellectual knowledge differs from that of sensible knowledge: the intellect perceives the essences of things: not the straight line but straightness; not flesh but what it is to be flesh (ibid.; 429b). The essence of something, Aristotle adds, is like the snubness of a snub-nose: it implies not only a definite form (snubness) but a definite matter (the nose), since snubness is a characteristic of noses alone. When the intellect thinks these essences, its thought is undivided and there can be no falsehood. The intellect can also combine thoughts – for instance 'that man is white' – and then there will be room for falsehood (430a26–b5).

Thought is different from sensible perception; but none the less it cannot take place, Aristotle insists, without the use of sensible images (*phantasmata*): we must contemplate a sensible image at the same time as we engage in intellectual speculation (432a9, cf. 431a17; and especially *De Memoria et Reminiscentia* 449b30–450a14).

Although the matter is by no means clear, this reference to the use of sensible images indicates the non-linguistic nature of Aristotle's account of thought here. In having thoughts and combining them, the mind does not use its own language, but rather the *phantasmata*. Rather than mental speech, Aristotle seems to envisage the attention to and manipulation of mental pictures.

But the *De Anima* was not the only source of Aristotle's philosophy of mind available to later medieval thinkers: they also knew the views he puts forward in the *De Interpretatione*. There Aristotle states that:–

> What are spoken (*ea quae sunt in voce*) are symbols (*notae*) of the affections in the soul, and what are written of those that are spoken. And just as there are not the same written letters for everyone, so there are not the same spoken sounds (*voces*). But the primary things of which these are signs – the affections of the soul – are the same for all; and those of which they [the affections] are likenesses (*similitudines*) – things (*res*) – are also the same. (16a3–9; Boethius's translation – 5:4–9)

Despite the many things which are left unclear, a number of definite positions are adopted. Words do not stand directly for things in the world, but for 'affections of the soul'. These affections are the same for all men, despite the different spoken and written languages they use. If, for example, two people who speak different languages are trying to talk about a dog, they will use a different word; but not only will the thing they are talking about – the dog – be the same for them both, so will the affection of each speaker's soul. And it will be this affection of the soul for which their spoken words stand. Just as truth or falsity are not attributed to individual words (like 'dog') but only to statements made up from them ('The dog is black'), so in the language of the mind affections must be 'compounded' (into positive mental statements – *compositio*) or 'divided' (into negative mental statements – *divisio*) before they become true or false.

(iii) The potential intellect and the active intellect
One of the most puzzling – and most discussed – sections of the *De Anima* is Book III, Chapter 5.

> Since just as in the whole of nature there is something which is matter to each kind of thing (and this is what is potentially all of them), while on the other hand there is something else which is their cause and is productive by producing them all – these being

related as an art to its material – so there must also be these differences in the soul. And there is an intellect which is of this kind by becoming all things, and there is another which is so by producing all things, as a kind of disposition, like light, does; for in a way light too makes colours which are potential into actual colours. And this intellect is distinct, unaffected, and unmixed, being in essence activity.

For that which acts is always superior to that which is affected, and the first principle to the matter. . .and it is not the case that it [sc. the active intellect] sometimes thinks and at other times not. In separation it is just what it is, and this alone is immortal and eternal. (But we do not remember because this is unaffected, whereas the passive intellect is perishable, and without this thinks nothing). [430a10–25 – Hamlyn's translation. Medieval authors, working from Arabic and Latin translations, cannot be presumed to have had *exactly* this text before them. William of Moerbeke's, however, is remarkably close to the modern translation, whilst James of Venice's Latin version is obscure rather than actually misleading. The Arab version used by Averroes, and translated along with his commentary is less accurate – the second sentence distinguishes *three* intellects: one which 'is made everything', one which 'makes all thinking' (*facit ipsum intelligere omne*) and one which 'knows (*intelligit*) all things'.]

The intellect which becomes all things seems to be the intellect which Aristotle talks about elsewhere in the treatise – the faculty which, like the sensitive faculty, exists only potentially until it is informed and which medieval Latin writers therefore called the 'potential intellect' (*intellectus possibilis*). The description of the other, active intellect poses great problems of interpretation, especially given the corrupt state of the end of the passage. Aristotle calls it a disposition and compares it to light. It would be tempting to refer to the treatment of light earlier in the treatise (II vii; 418b–19a) and argue that, just as light is the actuality (*entelecheia*) of what is transparent, so the active intellect is the actuality of what thinks. The active intellect would then bear the same relation to the intellect in potency and the intellect in act as the soul to the lifeless body and the body exercising its vital functions. But it is hard to see how this interpretation could be consistent with the idea that 'in separation [the active intellect] is just what it is'. A more plausible reading (cf. Hamlyn) takes the active intellect as a necessary, but not a sufficient, condition for thinking. In positing its existence,

Aristotle is not trying to explore the mechanism of thinking, but its fundamental conditions.

One of the reasons why ancient and medieval scholars were so interested by Aristotle's fleeting description of the active intellect is its bearing on the problem of the immortality of the human soul. Aristotle considers that the soul is the body's actuality; as such, it cannot be separated from its body and so must perish when the body does. But Aristotle does leave it open that there might be parts of a soul which are *not* the actuality of a body and so might continue to exist in separation from it. His treatment of the passive and active intellects can be taken, depending on how it is interpreted, either as explicitly affirming or explicitly denying that there is in fact such an immortal part in each man's soul. If an active intellect is part of each individual human soul, then every human soul is in part 'immortal and eternal'; but if the active intellect is distinct from individual human souls, then they are left with nothing beyond the vegetative and sensitive faculties but the potential and – as Aristotle says – 'perishable' intellect.

Another reason for medieval interest in Aristotle's comments on active intellect in the *De Anima* is the way they can be linked with certain of his remarks in the *Nicomachean Ethics*. There (e.g. 1140b–1141a) Aristotle sometimes uses the term 'intellect' (*nous*) in a special sense. It is not (as in the *De Anima*) the whole faculty by which humans think, but rather the power by which we apprehend the indemonstrable first principles of the sciences discussed in the *Posterior Analytics* (see above, pp.47–8) – an active power rather than a mere capacity for determination. English translators sometimes render *nous* in this sense 'intuition'.

(iv) How does the Aristotelian view of intellect differ from Plato's?
Aristotle uses the concept of intellectual knowledge to explain the form of being alive which human beings do not share with other animals or plants. When man uses his intellect, he is thinking (rather than just growing or sensing). Human knowledge which is not sensitive is intellectual. But Aristotle's account of intellectual knowledge, though profoundly suggestive, is not completely clear or coherent. In the *Ethics*, the term 'intellect' can be used to designate a very special type of thinking; and the active intellect mentioned in the *De Anima* is necessary for thinking, but does not seem to be what thinks.

Although pseudo-Dionysius and Augustine do not use the term 'intellect' in exactly the same way, for both – and for most other Platonists – intellectual knowledge is not equivalent to all non-sensitive human knowledge. An examination of intellect would not be for them a treatment of more than part – the highest part – of human thought. They do not merely differ from Aristotle in their theories of intellectual knowledge, but in their presumption about what such a theory should try to explain. But the incoherencies in Aristotle's account, and the various antique and Arab interpretations they receive, made later medieval readers less sensitive to the differences in objectives between Aristotle and the Platonists than to the possibilities of combining their theories.

(3) Antique and Arab interpretations of the two intellects

Aristotle's antique commentators made it their task to remove the obscurities in his text by clear distinctions. In doing so they often changed the nature of the problem which was being tackled in the original. In his theory of the intellect, Aristotle attempts to analyse the process of knowing in terms of act, potency and disposition. His main concern is with how the human intellect comes to exist in act by becoming its object; his reference to the intellect which is always in act is merely fleeting. The commentators, however, wished to state exactly the relation between the potential intellect and the active intellect and – since Aristotle's text is vague enough to admit many interpretations – the subject became a matter for lengthy discussion and dispute. Is there an active intellect in each man, or is there merely one active intellect? If so, is it to be identified with God? Among the many thinkers who addressed these questions were Alexander of Aphrodisias and Themistius. Their different answers give some idea of the material which Avicenna, Averroes and the Latin scholastics had before them.

Alexander of Aphrodisias (who worked at the turn of the third century) identified the active intellect (*nous poētikos/intellectus agens*) with God. Individual humans have only a material intellect (*nous hulikos/intellectus materialis*) – an appropriate name for the potential intellect, since matter is pure potency – which will perish with the body. Like Aristotle, but unlike almost all his expositors, Alexander did not assign a role to the active intellect in the process of human cognition. The material intellect, he thought, itself has the power to abstract universals from sensible particulars. As a person exercises this power and is instructed by others, he develops a disposition to engage in intellectual thought – for his intellect to be in act. The active intellect is described as an ultimate source of the intelligibility of things, probably because it has made them such that they can be thought by the intellect.

Themistius (224:1 – 244:6) believes that it is clear from Aristotle's account that each individual soul has an active as well as a potential intellect. Yet he believes that there must be a single active intellect in order to account for the common intellectual conceptions which everybody shares. He therefore suggests that there is one first active intellect which illuminates the active intellect in each human soul. The illuminated individual active intellect illuminates both the potential intellect and the sensible forms, which are intelligible in potency; by doing so, it brings about intellectual knowledge. Themistius says little about what the first active intellect is, except to make it clear that it *cannot* be identified with God.

Sources: two Arab Aristotelians on the intellect

(1) Avicenna

In his *De Anima*, Avicenna hoped – as much as any of the earlier exegetes – to reveal to his readers Aristotle's underlying intentions. But his efforts were affected by the common desire of expositors to clarify and schematize, by the established tradition of commentary and by a set of presuppositions not shared by the Greek philosophers. All these factors led him to see the origins of intellectual knowledge as lying beyond the powers of the individual soul. In order to explain how men come to learn and are able to remember what they know intellectually, Avicenna had therefore to develop a sophisticated view of the internal senses (such as memory and imagination). The result is a treatise which echoes some of Aristotle's ideas, but puts forward a different and more complex theory.

Although the particular subject of his *De Anima* is the soul in conjunction with the body, Avicenna assumes from the beginning that the soul is in fact separable (ɪ p. 22:68–9; cf. ɪɪ p. 132:17–23). Like Aristotle, he considers that it is by having a soul that a living body differs from a dead one. Unlike Aristotle, he does not hold that the soul is merely the capacity for the functions of life of a suitable natural body. His translation of Aristotle's word for this capacity (*entelecheia*) is 'perfection': by talking of the soul as the 'perfection' of the body, rather than its form, Avicenna avoids any suggestion that the soul requires a body as its matter. On the contrary, Avicenna clearly believes that the soul uses the body as its instrument (ɪɪ p. 115:80). His presuppositions come out particularly clearly when he takes it for granted that the soul can leave its body; assumes that the ensouled body has as its form, not the soul itself, but a *forma complexionalis* which is suitable for the soul; and talks of the soul as substituting another form in the body which it has left (I pp.59:46–60:61).

In his discussion of intellectual knowledge, Avicenna does not pause to consider whether the active intellect is part of the human soul or not. He takes it for granted – following many earlier commentators, especially his Arab predecessors such as al-Fārābī – that the active intellect is unique and separate from individual souls. He identifies it, not with the deity, but with the *intelligentia agens*, the lowest of the Intelligences which emanate, as he argues in his *Metaphysics*, from God (see above, pp.60–1). Avicenna rejects entirely Aristotle's idea that the human intellect is converted from potentiality to act by becoming what it thinks (II pp.134:50 – 136:69). It is the *intelligentia agens* which makes the human intellect know in act, by providing it with intelligible forms (II pp.126:29 – 127:35).

It might seem that the theological emphasis, already present in the late antique and earlier Arab expositors, has become even more predominant in Avicenna's account of knowledge. But there are two other aspects to his theory: first, his attempt to show how learning and memory lead to intellectual knowledge; and second, his theory of the internal senses. If intellectual knowledge derives entirely from the *intelligentia agens*, how can human efforts play any part in its acquisition? Avicenna allows that by perceiving singular things through the senses the soul can help itself to gain intellectual knowledge (II pp.102:97–104:21). Universals can be abstracted from singular things; from the constant conjunctions among individuals, universal propositions can be established; and certain relations between universals indicate necessary, self-evident truths. Avicenna has to combine these ideas with his view of the *intelligentia agens*. He tries to do so by turning Aristotle's comparison of the active intellect with the sun to his own use. The *intelligentia agens*, he says, stands in the same relation to our soul as the sun does to our sight: it strips sensible images of their matter and accidents. But it is not these images which inform the intellect. The process of abstraction merely makes the potential intellect ready to receive the appropriate form directly from the *intelligentia agens* (II p.127:36–47).

The knowledge possessed by the *intelligentia agens* and passed to the human intellect is itself simple, not propositional: it does not involve a combination of different elements (II 143:57–144:65 – this passage, however, is misleadingly translated into Latin). Suppose a man is asked a question and knows the answer, but neither replies nor even starts to order the pieces of information in his mind: Avicenna insists (II pp.140:10–142:40) that the knowledge will not merely be in potency, however immediate, but in act. But he also recognizes that human intellectual processes can involve putting such simple knowledge into complex form. The same piece of (simple) intellectual knowledge can be represented by different complex propositions, such as 'every man is an animal' and ' "animal" is predicated of every man' (II pp.138:92–139:5). The process of instruction illustrates the relation between simple and complex knowledge. As the teacher answers his pupil's questions he teaches himself the complex form of knowledge which he possesses simply (II p.142:40–44).

These parts of his theory explain how intellectual knowledge can be discovered and taught, but Avicenna has still to show why, when a person has learned something, he is far more readily able to bring this knowledge to mind than someone who has never learned it. It would be easy to explain this by referring to the memory. But Avicenna argues that intellectual ideas – unlike sensible forms – cannot be stored (II pp.144:74 – 149:43). Learning is not a matter of putting information away in the mind, but of acquiring the ability to join the intellect with the *intelligentia agens*. The educated man is like someone with sick eyes which have been healed: if he looks at something he can see it; if he turns his gaze away, he can still decide to look at it again. The embodied soul does not generally have the power to receive forms from the *intelligentia agens* without preparation; learning brings the capacity to do so (II pp.149:44–56).

In his treatment of the internal senses, Avicenna tries in a different way to explain how humans come to know things in the world and how they think about them. This account aims to be physiological: Avicenna is dealing here with workings of the soul which require corporeal instruments, and each of the internal senses is situated in a part of the brain. Elaborating on the Arab exegetical tradition, he distinguishes five of them (I pp.87:19–90:60; cf. II pp.1:4–11:50). The *fantasia* or *sensus communis* receives all the different forms which are perceived by the external senses. The *imaginatio* stores these forms. The *vis aestimationis* apprehends *intentiones* which are not sensed: for instance, it is by this sense that the sheep judges that a wolf is something to be fled from, whereas it should cherish a lamb (for a full discussion of *intentiones*, see below, pp.139–43). The *vis memorialis* or *reminiscibilis* stores these *intentiones* in the same way as the *imaginatio* stores sensible images. Another internal sense is called the *vis imaginativa* in animals, but the *vis cogitans* in man: it compounds and divides (*componere et dividere*) both sensible forms taken from the *imaginatio* and *intentiones* taken from the *vis memorialis*. Beginning with one of them, it proceeds by nature to another which is contrary or similar or in some way to be compared to the first (II pp.20:76–21:82). As the name Avicenna chooses for it in humans indicates, the *vis cogitans* engages in discursive thought; but the cause of its movement from one image or intention to another is always a singular thing, not a universal.

Avicenna, then, in expounding the *De Anima*, puts forward a rich, but not entirely coherent set of ideas about thought and knowledge. He posits a type of thought which belongs to the internal senses and which is described in terms of mental pictures, which can be combined or divided. The rational part of the soul engages in various processes prior to the acquisition of intellectual knowledge – abstraction, the formulation of necessary and of universal propositions – in which it makes use of sensible perceptions. It also puts the simple knowledge it gains from the *intelligentia agens* into complex form. The distinguishing feature of these complex intellectual processes, both of discovery and exposition, seems to be that they involve language: whereas the internal senses combine and divide mental pictures, the reason combines and divides terms (but Avicenna himself does not bring out this point). But intellectual knowledge properly speaking does not involve propositions. It is simple not complex, and whilst enquiry and education help towards its acquisition, it can neither be discovered nor remembered, but only received from the *intelligentia agens*.

(2) Averroes

The debates about Averroes's interpretation of Aristotle's doctrine of the potential and active intellects were so important a feature of thirteenth-century thought that they have already been mentioned in Part One (see above, pp.62, 64, 68–9). According to the particular interpretation which became current from the 1260s onwards, Averroes argues that the potential (or, as he calls it, material) intellect is one for all men. Both the form and implications of this doctrine seem so strange to modern ears that it is easy to be content with treating Averroes's long commentary on the *De Anima* as an historical curiosity, interesting only because some Latin thinkers accepted it as a correct interpretation of Aristotle whilst others, like Aquinas, were energetic in refuting it. Yet this would be to do grave injustice both to Averroes as a philosopher and to the Latin thinkers who so eagerly read his work. They regarded Averroes, indeed, as a commentator, whose passage by passage exegesis helped them with Aristotle's difficult texts. But had he not also been an original thinker, who tackled problems merely implied by Aristotle's discussion, he would not have commanded the interest – or provoked the hostility – of his cleverest Latin readers. Here just one section from the long commentary on the *De Anima* will be considered. It is one of the passages which lends itself most to the later thirteenth-century interpretation of his views – the 'Averroism' of Aquinas and Siger of Brabant. But it is also one where he considers an important problem which, although not entirely neglected by earlier commentators, had never before received such extended or perceptive treatment in this context. Although the problem is not one which modern philosophers would pose themselves in the same form, it is one they can recognize as related to questions which still occupy them.

It might be argued that thought and sensation differ in their privacy. Another person cannot, except metaphorically, feel my pain; and, although we might both remember the same thing, my mental image is not the same thing as his. But if the two of us are together alone in a room, then do we not share the same piece of knowledge, that there are two people in this room? If we have intellectual knowledge of the same thing, then must not the thing in our understanding be the same? A modern philosopher would be unlikely to accept this way of putting things. He would query the notion of 'a thing in our understanding' and want to clarify the concept of a 'piece of knowledge'. If we both know that there are two people in this room, then we know the same fact. When we are both actually thinking that this is the case, then we are contemplating the same, true proposition. Averroes saw matters differently. He follows Aristotle, or at least, his view of Aristotle. For Aristotle – as Averroes read him – complex intellectual knowledge (of facts) is gained by combining things known simply by the intellect. And the notion of a thing in our understanding (*res intellecta*) is indispensable, since it is by becoming what it perceives that the intellect is converted from potency into act: the intellect in act is the *res intellecta*.

Averroes realizes that there are great difficulties both if the *res intellecta* is said to be the same for different people and if it is said to be different (pp. 411:710–412:721). If it is in every way the same, then if one person knows something, so automatically others must know the same thing. If the *res intellecta* is different, how will learning ever take place? The teacher's knowledge is not a force which can generate another individual of the same species as itself, in the way that fire can. Averroes attempts to overcome these problems, not by abandoning Aristotle's terms, but by a rigorously accurate understanding of them.

Intellect, Aristotle says, is like the senses (p.400:379–393). Sensible knowledge is brought about by two subjects. One is the thing which is sensed: it is what makes the sense-impression true. The other is the capacity of sensation, which makes the sense-impression into a form which exists. There could be no sense-impressions without things to be sensed and senses to receive them. Similarly, a piece of (active) intellectual knowledge has two subjects. One is that which makes it true: this is made up of forms in the imagination, themselves the images of true things. the other is that by which the piece of knowledge is something which exists (*unum entium in mundo*): this is the material intellect.

A piece of intellectual knowledge cannot be called yours or mine unless there is something to link it to us. Averroes suggests (pp.404:501–405:527) that only one of the two subjects which make a piece of knowledge need provide this link. And he urges that it cannot be the material intellect, but rather the forms or *intentiones* in the imagination which do so. This leaves him free to argue that the material intellect is unique and shared by all men. He has a number of exegetical reasons for this position; but it also allows him to resolve the problem about the privacy or publicness of intellectual knowledge. A piece of knowledge which we share is both the same and different: it is one in the subject by which it is something existing, the material intellect; and many in the subject by which it is true, the forms in our imaginations (p.421:724–8).

In line with the tradition of Aristotelian exegesis, Averroes considers that there needs to be an active intellect (*intellectus agens*) as well as the material one. The forms in the imagination are only in potency to move the material intellect; the *intellectus agens* makes them able to do so in act (p.406:556–565). He considers that the active intellect is, like the material intellect, unique; and that both intellects are ungenerated and incorruptible. The material intellect, when brought into act through the intervention of the active intellect, can be called the 'speculative' or the 'made' intellect. As that which receives, the speculative intellect is the material intellect and so is unique and eternal; but with regard to the *intentiones* it receives it is many, generated and corruptible (p.406:569 – 408:623). Averroes uses this part of his theory to explain the way in which certain pieces of knowledge – propositions and concepts which are self-evident to everyone – are, considered in themselves, the same and eternal, even though different people have them at different times. It is enough that, at any given moment, somebody has these pieces of knowledge, for their eternity, in themselves, to be assured.

6 *William of Auvergne*

William's works and their background: Aristotle and Avicenna

William of Auvergne was one of the first Latin thinkers to consider some of the problems raised by the newly-translated Greek and Arabic treatises about intellectual knowledge and to bring to them the special assumptions and concerns of a Christian theologian. After an initial training in arts at Paris, William had gone on to study and then, in the 1220s, to teach theology there; until, in 1228, he was made Bishop of Paris. His main work, the *Magisterium Divinale ac Sapientale* is an encylopaedia of theology, the different parts of which move from a discussion of God (*De Trinitate*), to the created world (*De Universo*) to faith and the Old and New Law, the sacraments and moral theology (*De Fide et Legibus, De Sacramentis, Summa de Vitiis et Virtutibus*). William discusses the intellect and its knowledge most fully in the second part of the *De Universo* (U; written in the 1230s) and another treatise, the *De Anima* (A; from the 1230s or early 1240s).

William did not set out to produce a theory of intellectual knowledge for its own sake. Rather, he was led to discuss the soul by a wish to refute a number of views deriving from the newly translated material which he found – usually for religious reasons – repugnant. His main adversary over the soul's nature and immortality was Alexander of Aphrodisias. Over the intellect, his main opponent was Avicenna, whose views he consistently attributed to Aristotle (despite his own direct acquaintance with Aristotle's *De Anima*). His efforts to dismiss false views encouraged him to refine and justify the ideas he thought were true.

In the *De Universo*, William's discussion of the intellect forms part of his general rejection of Avicenna's Intelligences, creative intermediaries between God and man. The active intellect is the lowest of these, and William wishes to forestall any possible reasoning, based on the nature of human cognition, which would prove the existence of at least this one Intelligence. The *De Anima* gives him the opportunity to work out more fully this theory of the soul and its methods of cognition. Although William is very dependent on Avicenna in his account of the soul which he too treats as the ruler of the body rather than its form, this theory of intellectual knowledge is very different from the Arab philosopher's. It is important and interesting precisely because William does *not* share certain Aristotelian assumptions about knowledge which were common to Avicenna, Averroes and most Latin thinkers from William's time until the early fourteenth century.

The intellect and the world

(1) The intellect does not receive forms but uses signs

For Aristotle, his Greek and Arab exegetes and Latin thinkers later in the thirteenth-century, intellectual cognition is effected by the reception of a form, which determines the potential intellect and converts it from potency to act. The form is the essence or definition of the thing known: that by which it is something of a particular kind – the humanity by which a man is a man and not a horse or a stone. *How* this form is received – whether by abstraction from individuals or directly from the active intellect – is a matter they dispute; but they are all agreed *that* the intellect receives it. Intellectual knowledge is about the world because the forms of things are also the forms which determine the intellect.

For William, by contrast, the intellect knows by using signs for things. To say that something is in the intellect is to say that its sign is there (A p.215a). These signs are not received from things outside, but generated by the intellect itself from natural capacity. Just as a monkey is able to imitate the actions of men, so the intellect is able 'to assimilate itself to things and take up their likenesses or signs' (A p.215b). Although William compares these signs to both pictures and words, he thinks that they are like names in that they need not actually resemble the things which they signify: the sign in the intellect for heat is not, for instance, 'truly and properly' a likeness of it (A p.216a; cf. p.215a). William is so certain that these similitudes in the intellect are in no manner impressions received from things outside the mind that he believes they can even signify things which do not exist (A pp.215b–216a). For William, intellectual knowledge is about the world because it is constituted by signs in the intellect which stand for things outside.

(2) How intellectual knowledge is acquired

How does William think that intellectual knowledge is acquired? There are two different questions to be answered here, although they are not ones which William himself distinguishes clearly. First, what is the origin of the signs in the intellect? And second, what causes the intellect to form its signs in such a way that it can be said to know about the world: what makes it form the right sign at the right time (for instance, the sign for a stone when it recognizes the object present as a stone and wishes to think about it) or the right combination of signs (a true, as opposed to a false mental proposition)?

William is never quite definite in his account of the origin of signs, but one passage does suggest his solution (A p.211a–b). The human soul, he explains, is placed on the 'horizon of two worlds': one is the world of the senses, to which it is very closely joined by the body; but the other world is the creator himself, the exemplar and universal mirror of all things, which is very closely joined and most immediately present to the human intellect. Among the gains from its contact with this higher world, which is God, the intellect is 'inscribed' with signs. This account of the origin of signs automatically explains how intellectual knowledge of self-evident statements is acquired, since the human intellect need only be given the individual signs themselves by God and the validity of the self-evident statements which they form will be apparent (A p.210b). As soon as a man knows the terms of a self-evident statement, he knows the truth of the whole statement. But our knowledge of other kinds of statement cannot be explained in this way. In all cases other than self-evident rules and principles, the gaining of knowledge requires more than the mere acquisition of the signs: they must be brought into relation with the world or with each other or with both.

One sort of intellectual knowledge, in William's view, is the simple cognition of an object in the world. William explains this by excitation. The intellect cannot itself in any way receive sense-impressions; but the senses can excite the intellect to form intelligible signs (A p.215a). The signs themselves originate from God, but it is the senses and the intellect's natural capacity to respond to excitation which cause the right signs to be formed at the right moment.

There are varieties of intellectual knowledge other than the simple cognition of a present object (and other than knowledge of self-evident rules and principles). There is knowledge of the connection between things, in which the intellect connects one sign with another (A p.213b). And there is intellectual recollection, where a fact or an argument is recalled to mind (cf. A p.214b). In these types of knowledge, the intellect itself seems to act, bringing forward the appropriate intelligible signs without stimulation from outside. This creates difficulties for William, since – despite his un-Aristotelian approach – he keeps to the Aristotelian idea that man's intellect is, in itself, in potency. If the intellect itself connected or recalled the signs which constitute knowledge, then it would be both a potentiality and something active – which William considers impossible (A p.214a).

A way out of this problem would be to posit an active intellect. But William consistently rejects its existence. He spends many pages arguing against it on a number of occasions and is most anxious that his own theories should not seem to require it. This is most understandable in the light of his general analysis of intellectual knowledge in terms of signs rather than forms. For commentators in the Aristotelian tradition who make the active intellect play a part in each act of intellectual cognition, its role is to enable a universal *form*, already present in the object perceived, to be present in act in the intellect which perceives it. The active intellect merely facilitates a relation between an object in the world and the potential intellect. If William, however, were to admit an active intellect which, in some types of cognition, provided the potential intellect with the appropriate *signs* of things, then it alone would be responsible for knowledge: there would be no need for experience since the object of knowledge would not be contributing anything (such as a form) to the knower. William finds this implausible: if there is, within each soul, an active intellect to give it knowledge, why is it necessary to learn from teachers or to use effort in finding out things (A p.208b)? William allows that some sorts of knowledge, such as 'prophetic illuminations', do not derive from experience; and he sees that from this an argument might be drawn for the existence of a separate active intellect, providing such illumination from time to time (U p.822bG). But after a long and complex consideration of this problem, William concludes that there is no need to suppose prophetic illuminations come from a single source. They can be given in all sorts of ways, directly or indirectly, plainly or in riddles, through different sorts of messengers or angels (U p.840aG).

Rather than posit an active intellect, William explains the intellect's ability to generate knowledge by a set of dispositions (*habitus*). They are in the potential intellect itself and yet not identical with it, so that the same thing is not both active and passive (A p.214a). Some dispositions are divinely infused, but 'very frequently' dispositions are acquired by experience and learning. The process of learning can be described in terms of gaining dispositions. If one sign comes into the intellect, a disposition causes another, connected sign to follow it. Or a disposition allows a whole connected series of signs to enter the mind. The intellect cannot generate its own dispositions – they must be acquired from God, experience or learning: the concept of disposition is consistent with the passivity of the intellect. Yet these dispositions are capabilities for certain sorts of act which arise from the frequent performance of such acts. The intellect, for William, is not just a mirror which receives the forms reflected in it, but like a special sort of mirror which, through frequency of reflecting, has gained the ability to generate forms without having to have anything to be reflected in it.

The intellectual cognition of singulars

One of the most interesting aspects of William's analysis of intellectual cognition is his treatment of singulars (individual things). Aristotle's theory excluded the possibility of direct intellectual knowledge of singulars. The form by which, on Aristotle's view, each thing is something of a particular kind cannot be peculiar to any one individual. The form of humanity by which Socrates is a man is the same as the form by which Plato is a man. If the intellect knows by receiving such forms, its knowledge must be universal – not of Plato or Socrates, Dobbin or Red Rum, but of men in general and horses in general. This consequence produced a series of problems. On the one hand, there was the need to explain how the intellect could compose statements about particular things. On the other hand, there were a number of peculiar difficulties for Christian thinkers.

William indicates two of the most serious (A p.203a–b). If intellectual knowledge of singulars is impossible, then no soul in heaven will be able to enjoy beatitude, which consists in the contemplation of God, since God is singular and disembodied souls cannot perceive except intellectually. Moreover, since God's knowledge is intellectual, it will be impossible for him to know any particular things: he will be ignorant of individual men, their good and evil acts and their prayers. Later thirteenth-century thinkers would find it very hard to avoid these unacceptable consequences (see below, esp. pp.128–30, 152, 156–7, 177–8). By contrast, William's theory that the intellect knows by signs which it generates itself enables him to insist that it has knowledge both of singulars and universals. For why should the intellect be any less capable of generating signs for individuals than for universals?

William makes it very clear (*De Anima* – A p.204a; the position is less certain in the *De Universo* – cf. U p.822aG) that, in his opinion, people do normally have intellectual knowledge of singular things. There are some objects of cognition about which this must be the case, he says, since they are known and they cannot be known sensibly, such as one's own joys or sorrow. The same is true of the self-conscious awareness that one has some given piece of knowledge. But even singulars which can be known by the senses must also be known intellectually, otherwise the intellect could never correct the information of the senses: one could have no reason, for instance, to deny that the sun's diameter is about one foot, since that is what it seems to the senses to be.

William distinguishes, however, between what intellectual knowledge is, and how it is gained. Men certainly have intellectual knowledge of singulars, but in this life they cannot gain it directly (U p.859aB). In this life, he argues (U p.1057aD), our intellects know singulars by way of the senses. Sensible images are like books in which the intellect reads sensible things. The senses present things with all their variety of sensible accidents: the intellect penetrates beneath these accidents to know the underlying substance (A p.213a). Intellectual perception involves the same process for William whether it is of a non-sensible thing attached to a body – like the soul of a living man – or of a sensible thing. Just as one knows the soul through the external actions of the man, so one knows the substance of something through its sensible accidents.

William recognizes that men's intellects are not restricted to knowing individual things: they can gain a more universal type of knowledge through 'abstraction' or 'spoliation' (*spoliatio*). He compares such knowledge (U p.822aG; A p.213a–b) to looking at a picture from a distance: the spectator can see that a man is being represented but he cannot make out his distinguishing features and so tell which man. In such knowledge, the intellect – as William puts it – fails fully to read the signs brought to it by the senses; and so it is not in a position to reach the individual substance through the sensible accidents. Although William does not think that knowledge of universals reveals the essences of things, he does not deny that it tells something true about the things in the world and their relations; and at one point (A p.213a) he even suggests that the intellectual signs which constitute knowledge of universals are more congruent with the nature of the intellect by being more abstract.

For William, as for most Christian thinkers, an account of the intellect would be incomplete if it were limited to embodied souls. William must consider how disembodied souls, angels and God have intellectual knowledge. It would be implausible for him to suggest that beings without sense-organs gain intellectual knowledge of individuals in the same way as men in this life, starting from the sensible perception of accidents. And so he argues (U p.859aB) that the disembodied intellect has the power to penetrate directly to the individual substances of things – it is like the eye of a lynx. William explains the lesser powers of the intellect in this life by saying that it is 'submerged and buried in the body, and darkened by our original sin'.

Conclusion

William has long been considered a writer who combined ideas taken from Avicenna with a way of thought deriving from Augustine. More recently, his interest in Aristotle and his theory of scientific knowledge has been emphasized. But, important as these philosophical debts may be, William's account of intellectual knowledge differs radically from Aristotle's or Avicenna's because, for him, the intellect thinks by using its own signs for things in the external world, not by manipulating forms which are impressed on it, directly or indirectly, by contact with external objects. William develops his own unusual and coherent analysis of intellectual knowledge and uses it to resolve a number of problems (such as the nature of intellectual cognition of singulars) which a Christian theologian has to face. For many of his successors, whose theories of knowledge were closer to Aristotle's, the same problems would be more difficult.

7 Thomas Aquinas

Aquinas the Aristotelian?

Intellectual knowledge was one of the topics which preoccupied St Thomas. He discusses it in detail in nine of his works: his commentary on the *Sentences* (1252–6), *Quaestiones de Veritate* (quV: 1256–9, *Summa contra Gentiles* II (SG: 1261–4), *Summa Theologiae* I (ST: 1266–9), commentary on the *De Anima* (1267 – see above, p. 79), *Quaestiones de Anima* (qu. A: 1268–9), commentaries on the *Metaphysics* (SM: 1269–1272) and the *De Interpretatione* (SDE: 1270–1) and the *De Unitate Intellectus contra Averroistas* (1270). Although these works range from the beginning to the end of Aquinas's career, the theory they present – some more subtly, some in greater detail, some with a particular emphasis – is remarkably similar. Modern commentators often stress the Aristotelianism of this theory; and – in at least one important respect – with justice.

Aquinas's account of intellectual knowledge is, in certain of its most easily describable features, closer to Aristotle's than any previously given by a Christian thinker. His predecessors had developed two main explanations for the origin of intellectual knowledge – each of them (unlike William of Auvergne's) based on the Aristotelian assumption that the intellect knows by being informed with the forms of things. Both views distinguish between the potential and the active intellect; but in different ways. According to the theory developed by writers such as Alexander of Hales and Robert Grosseteste, and popular among the theologians, the active intellect is God. The human intellect, they believe, cannot gain knowledge simply by using the perceptions of the senses: it also requires the illumination of the active intellect (which is divine illumination), in order to abstract from sensible images what they call 'intelligible species' – the forms by which the intellect is informed. This position accords nicely with Augustine's insistence on man's need for divine illumination of his intellect. The other view – current among arts masters between about 1225 and 1250 and thought by them (though not by Aquinas and his contemporaries) to be Averroes's interpretation – holds that each human being has both his own potential and his own active intellect.

Aquinas follows the second view (more Aristotelian in its emphasis than the first) and insists that each man has his own active intellect. He puts forward his position in a manner which is rigorously and explicitly based on Aristotle. For example, in the *Quaestiones de Veritate* (10.6; cf. ST 1.84.3–5) he identifies the various answers which have been given to the question 'What is the source of (intellectual) knowledge *(scientia)*?' Some have said that it comes entirely from an exterior cause which is separate from matter. They are divided into the Platonists, who hold that we know immaterial Ideas which really exist, and the Avicennists, who consider that our knowledge is given to us by the agent Intelligence. But it has been shown by Aristotle, St Thomas considers, that there are no Platonic Ideas, whilst the Avicennist theory fails to explain the necessary dependency of human knowledge on the senses. Others have said that the source of our knowledge is within us. But these thinkers – among them, it seems, Aquinas would include William of Auvergne – fail to explain why we do not know everything. Aristotle's account of the source of our intellectual knowledge is the only view, St Thomas believes, which escapes these objections: it is the one he will follow (quV 10.6; cf. ST 1.84.6). Our intellectual knowledge originates partly from outside the mind and partly from within it. This two-fold source for knowledge requires a two-fold intellect within each man: a potential intellect which is informed by the forms of things in the external world, and an active intellect which enables this process of information to take place.

Aquinas the theologian and the intellect in man and angels

Despite these obvious and admitted debts, Aquinas did far more than merely follow Aristotle in his account of the intellect. The Aristotelian elements in his discussion belong to a fuller, theological theory, which depends on a hierarchical view of intelligent being. When medieval Christian theologians, such as Aquinas, developed theories of intellectual knowledge, they could not limit themselves to explaining the cognition of the embodied human intellect. Disembodied human souls, angels and God himself cognize intellectually, the theologians held. An analysis of the intellect which applied only to the way humans know things in this life would, in their view, be partial and distorting, attributing to the intellect essentially conditions which are merely the result of the present condition of man. Yet theologians, despite their access to scriptural revelation, are living on earth, not in heaven, and they are forced to take the way in which men on earth think and know as the basis for their view of all intellects. Most medieval thinkers react to this problem by stressing the similarity between our intellects in this life and in a disembodied state, and by extension, their similarity to angelic intellects (and even, in a limited way, to God's) (see below, pp. 149–51, 155–7). Aquinas follows a different course. In his view, the embodied human mind draws its knowledge from a different source and operates in a different way from separate souls and the angels: only in its aim – the truth – is our human knowledge like that of disembodied creatures.

(1) The sources of intellectual knowledge

The source of a being's intellectual knowledge depends, according to Aquinas, on the nature of the being. God's manner of being, Aquinas believes, is knowing intellectually (ST 1,14,1); his sole object of knowledge is himself and, through himself, he knows all things, since he contains likenesses of all other things (ST 1,14,5). When God created the angels he endowed them with the forms (or *species*) which are the sources of their knowledge (quV 8,9; ST 1,55,2). And, once human souls are separated from their bodies, they also draw their knowledge from forms infused by God (quA 15; ST 1,89,1 – see below p. 124). God, the angels and disembodied souls are therefore alike in enjoying an immediate grasp of the immaterial forms on which intellectual knowledge is based. But embodied human souls have no direct contact with immaterial forms. Aquinas insists that the proper object of the human intellect in this life and the source of its knowledge are what he calls the 'quiddities' (*quidditas*) of material things. What does Aquinas mean by a 'quiddity'?

A thing's quiddity is its 'whatness' – that by which it is a man, rather than a dog or a stone. But for St Thomas the meaning of 'quiddity' must be distinguished from that of two apparently similar terms: 'form' (*forma*) or 'substance' (*substantia*). Although he does not think literally of substance as a core surrounded by accidents, or matter as receiving the impression of form, Aquinas does envisage substance and accident, and form and matter as elements from which things are really composed. Quiddity, however, is a term of analysis: a thing's quiddity is in no sense one of its constituents, but rather its definition. As such the quiddity of a material thing is distinguished from its form because the form does not contain matter, whereas matter must be included in its correct definition. The definition can indeed only be reached by abstraction from matter: but what is required is abstraction from particular matter, not from matter in general (ST 1,85,1 ad2). If I wish to reach the quiddity of man, I must abstract from the particular flesh and particular bones of the man standing in front of me. But my definition would be very wrong if it suggested that there could be a man without flesh or bones.

2) The process of cognition: intellect in angels, reason in man

It is not merely by the source of its knowledge that the embodied human intellect differs from higher beings. Its method of knowing is such, Aquinas believes, that – although there is a loose sense of the word 'intellect' in which all human mental activity which is not sensory belongs to it (quV 1,12) – in the strict sense of the word, human cognition in this life cannot be called 'intellectual'. Angels, he says (quV 15,1, ST 1,58,3), are intellectual; humans merely rational. But the complex process of rational thought requires, Aquinas thinks, at least one act which is strictly intellectual. Human rationality, that is to say, can only be understood by relation and contrast to the intellect of the angels.

To demand that the workings of the human mind be understood by reference to what can be surmised about angelic cognition may seem gratuitously mystifying. But Aquinas's position follows from the demands of Aristotle's own analyses, although the framework which allows St Thomas to develop it is that provided by his faith. According to Aristotle's *De Anima*, when the intellect is converted from potency to act by the form of something, its knowledge of the thing is immediate (whatever preparation might have been required by the senses and imagination) and it cannot be false. In all these respects, intellectual cognition is like sensible cognition. But there is a difference. Once a sense has cognized its object, it has reached its cognitive aim. The sensible image can, indeed, be stored in the memory; and Arab thinkers would develop a complex picture of the operations of various inner senses (see above, pp.104–6); but once it has cognized its object, the sensitive faculty can find out no more about the world by any further process. But the aim of the human intellect is not the same as its object. Once determined by a form, the intellect goes on, Aristotle explains, to form propositions by compounding and dividing. The intellect aims to know what is the case; the goal of theoretical knowledge, as Aristotle affirms (*Metaphysics*, 993b21), is the truth. And for Aquinas it is a principle so obvious as almost to be taken for granted that the aim of the intellect is truth (cf. ST 1,16,1).

The human intellect's relation to its goal, as opposed to its object, is neither infallible nor simple. Once the intellect compounds and divides it can err into falsehood; and reasoning is a discursive process which takes time. Would not a being whose intellect reached its aim immediately, just as the senses do, without having to go through a process of discourse from its object, be more properly described as 'intellectual' than man, whose intellect is separated by so many processes from its goal? This is Aquinas's surmise. And he found support for it in another of Aristotle's ideas. Aristotle also has a strict sense of 'intellect' as well as a weaker sense. In the strict sense, Aristotle says that the intellect is the faculty which apprehends the indemonstrable first principles of the sciences (see above, p. 101). And the human intellect has the ability to grasp this knowledge immediately, without any reasoning, and infallibly – the principles are self-evident.

To know intellectually – in the strict sense – is, St Thomas says, to know immediately (*statim*), without mental discourse, and infallibly: ' "intellect" . . . seems to designate simple and absolute cognition – a being is said to *intelligere* because it in some way reads inwardly (*intus legit*) the truth in the very essence of the thing' (quV 15,1). The angels, Aquinas thinks – following pseudo-Dionysius – know in this way. They 'obtain knowledge of the truth immediately in a first and sudden or simple grasp (*statim in prima et subita sive simplici acceptione*), without any motion or mental discourse'. By contrast, men 'can only come to perfect knowledge of the truth by a certain motion, by which they run (*discurrunt*) from one thing to another, so that they can attain knowledge of unknown things from what they know' (quV 15,1). As these passages make clear, the distinction between intellectual and ratiocinative knowledge is not in aim but in the manner of reaching it. Men aim at – with varying degrees of success – and angels reach – immediately and infallibly – knowledge of the truth. Aquinas accepts that, even for angels, such knowledge *is* propositional, in the sense that different concepts are put together; but the angel sees them together in a single regard, just as, when we look at an image in the mirror, we are in the same regard seeing an image of a thing and a thing (I am seeing the reflection of my face, and also the surface of the mirror) (ST 1,58,3 ad1). The angel does not have to engage in a process of putting them together (compounding and dividing), just as it does not have to engage in the process of reasoning from one proposition to another: it 'knows (*intelligit*) the composition and division of terms (*enuntiationum*), just as it knows reasoning in syllogisms: for it knows composite things simply, things which are in motion motionlessly, material things immaterially' (ST 1,58,4). As Aquinas explains (quV 15,1 ad5), reasoning – arguing from one proposition to another – is an activity of man alone; there is no place for reasoning in the activity of an intellectual creature, like an angel, who knows the conclusion of an argument as soon as he knows its premisses. But forming a proposition is an activity which can be rational and intellectual, and it is practised, intellectually, by the angels.

Although humans are rational rather than intellectual creatures, they none the less are capable of two sorts of strictly intellectual act. We can be properly said to *intelligere* 'when we apprehend the quiddity of things (see below, pp. 124–5); or when we know (*intelligimus*) those things which are immediately known (*nota*) when the quiddities of things are known (*notis*) – like the first principles, which we know (*cognoscimus*) when we know (*cognoscimus*) their terms' (quV 1,12). When the mind apprehends a quiddity it reaches its object, but not its aim; when it grasps the indemonstrable first principles, it gains its goal of truth (although in a limited way, because the first principles are only the most general of truths, just the very beginning of scientific knowledge). Aquinas therefore frequently uses our ability to grasp indemonstrable first principles as evidence that we are capable, in a limited way, of properly intellectual action. All our reasoning begins or ends with the knowledge (*intellectus*) of first principles (see below, pp. 124–8). Therefore

> although the human soul's own method of cognition is by way of reasoning, there is however in it some participation of that simple method of cognition which is found in the higher substances – and because of this it is said to have intellectual power. . .At its summit, a lower nature reaches something which is lowest in a higher nature. (quV 15,1; cf. ST 1,79,4)

When a man grasps indemonstrable first principles, his mind is performing the lowest activity of an angelic intellect.

Body, soul and the object of human knowledge

(1) The soul is the form of the body

St Thomas's insistence that the objects of men's intellectual knowledge in this life are quiddites of material things is intimately linked to his account of the relations between body and soul.

Aquinas's Latin predecessors followed the example of Avicenna in using Aristotelian formulas to give a completely un-Aristotelian account of the relations between the soul and the body (for example, see above, p.110). The soul was not for them the form of the body in any sense which Aristotle would have understood, but rather a substance which uses the body as its instrument. Aquinas goes back to Aristotle's idea: for him, the soul is the form which makes the living body what it is. In each man there is an 'intellectual soul' (*anima intellectiva*: here, and throughout this discussion, Aquinas uses 'intellect' and 'intellectual' in the weak sense), which has not only the power of the intellect, but that of sense – which is shared with lower animals – and that of growth – which is shared with lower animals and plants (ST 1,76,3). This soul is not a compound of matter and form: it is the form of the body (ST 1,75,5).

One reason why Aquinas's predecessors had not adopted Aristotle's theory of the soul as the form of the body is that they wished to safeguard its immortality. If man is a composite in which the body is the matter and the soul the form, how can the form endure apart from its matter? Aquinas resolves the apparent difficulty in his position by maintaining that the soul is not just a form. It is also what he describes as 'something subsistent' (*aliquid subsistens*) or 'something subsistent in itself' (*aliquid subsistens per se*) or simply 'this something' (*hoc aliquid*). By all these terms Aquinas means what we might call a thing or a 'thing in its own right' – as opposed to a concept or an accident. The objects in the world – such as stones or chairs – are subsistent things; but something can be subsistent without being, like these, a compound of matter and form. The human soul is something subsistent and also a form without matter. By this definition, St Thomas is able not merely to safeguard the soul's immortality, but also to demonstrate it. Subsistent things which are compounds of matter and form perish (*corrumpi*) if the form is separated from the matter; but a subsistent thing which, like the soul, is simply a form must be imperishable (ST 1,75,6; quA 14).

Aquinas realizes that there is an obvious objection to describing the soul as something subsistent. Is it not, he asks himself (ST 1,75,2 arg. 1), the compound of body and soul which is 'a thing in its own right' (*hoc aliquid*), rather than the soul alone? St Thomas responds (ST 1,75,2 ad 1; cf. quA 1) by admitting that the compound of soul and body is indeed something 'in its own right' but suggesting that, in a weaker sense of the phrase, a thing can be 'in its own right' and yet be part of something else: a hand, for instance, is an identifiable entity in its own right but also part of the human body.

But this answer shows only how it is possible for the human soul to be a subsistent thing, not why it is one. Aquinas finds the proof for the human soul's subsistence as a thing in its ability to think (*intelligere* – in the weak sense). Aquinas calls the activity of which something is naturally capable its 'operation' (*operatio*); and he says that a thing has its own (*propria*) operation – or that it operates *per se* – when it is capable of such activity without the help of anything else. The nutritive and sensitive activities of the soul require a bodily organ: a plant, for instance, cannot grow without a body – roots, leaves, branches – to do the growing; an animal or a man cannot see without eyes or hear without ears. Although a plant's nutritive soul and an animal's sensitive soul each has its operation, neither can be said for this reason to operate *per se* (ST 1,75,3). But thinking (*intelligere*) uses no bodily organ, and so man's intellective soul has its own operation. As such, although a form, it must be also a subsistent thing (ST 1,75,2; quA 1).

Aquinas's view of the intellective soul as the form of the body is one of the main reasons for the intensity of his opposition, on purely rational grounds, to the supposedly Averroist position which makes the potential intellect one for all men. If all individual men share the same potential intellect, then how can they be distinct *as men*? Suppose that they each have their own sensitive soul, this will suffice to make them distinct animals, but not distinct men (cf. SG II,73,6). Sometimes it is suggested that the basis of St Thomas's opposition to 'Averroism' is an empirical observation – 'This individual man thinks (*intelligit*)'. But this observation only gains its point as an objection within a theory which holds that thinking (*intelligere*) is the human soul's own operation, and that the human soul is the form of the body.

(2) The object of human knowledge

The two different aspects of the soul – as form of the body, but also a subsistent thing with its own operation – are reflected in Aquinas's account of human cognition. When the human soul performs its own operation and thinks, it requires nothing bodily –

its operation 'transcends material things' and shows that the being (*esse*) of the soul 'is raised above the body and does not depend on it'. But because the soul of man in this life is the form of a body, it must gain its 'immaterial knowledge' from material things (quA 1). The proper object of the embodied human intellect are the quiddities of *material* things. Immaterial forms – such as the angels or God – are beyond the cognitive grasp of the human intellect in this life (see below, pp.134–5). And the passage from the embodied intellect's object – quiddities – to its aim – the truth – is a long and complex one, where error is possible: human reasoning, not angelic intellection.

Before turning to consider in detail this process of human reasoning, it is important to anticipate a possible misunderstanding of Aquinas's views about the effect on the soul of its embodied state. *As* form of the body, the human intellective soul cannot be fully intellectual (in the strict sense) in its mode of activity. It would misrepresent Aquinas, however, to suggest that he argued that *because* the human soul in this life is the form of the body it is not properly intellectual – as if the body were an impediment which prevented its proper functioning. On the contrary, Aquinas thinks that the human soul is the lowest sort of immaterial substance. It occupies the same, bottom place on the scale of immaterial beings that prime, formless matter holds on the scale of sensible things. Although, as a subsistent thing, it has its own operation, it cannot perform it without being determined to act by intelligible forms which it acquires from things by way of the senses; 'and since the senses operate through bodily organs, the very condition of the soul's nature makes it appropriate for it to be united with a body' (quA 7). So far as the natural order of things is concerned, if the human soul were without a body, it would be incapable of its own operation – intellectual activity in the weaker sense. The way in which disembodied souls know, by infused species, is – Aquinas admits – beyond their original, unaided capacities.

The process of cognition in the human intellective soul

(1) Apprehending a quiddity

According to Aquinas, the intellective soul begins its process of cognition by grasping the quiddity of a material thing. A quiddity is a definition. What St Thomas means by 'I grasp the quiddity of an *x*', then, is better rendered using a noun clause than a simple object. It is not like a mental equivalent of seeing an object, but rather a matter of knowing that, for instance, *x* is a rational, mortal animal – knowing what sort of things *x*s are. But this paraphrase is not entirely accurate. If we say 'I know what *x*s are', we are referring to an intellectual capacity. I use that capacity when I identify an *x* correctly or when I use my knowledge of what *x*s are in order to think about them. But to grasp the quiddity of an *x* is for Aquinas an act and not a disposition. The human intellect can only grasp one quiddity at a time. We can indeed remember quiddities, by storing their intelligible species in our memories (see below, pp.161–2); so that once we have succeeded in abstracting a quiddity we can be said to 'know what *x*s are'. This means, not that we are grasping the quiddity of an *x*, but that we *can* grasp it when we want to without going through another process of abstraction. Should we then paraphrase 'I grasp the quiddity of *x*' as 'I am thinking of what *x* is'? The problem with this version is that it suggests that the mind is forming concepts and even that it is moving from one concept to another, putting them together in mental discourse. Although both these processes form part of Aquinas's account of how men cognize intellectually (in the loose sense), they belong to later stages in the complicated process which Aquinas analyses. And so the most accurate modern paraphrase for 'I grasp the quiddity of *x*' might be this rather clumsy formula: 'It is true that someone knows what *x*s are if and only if he has once performed and has the capacity to perform again the mental action which I am now performing.'

Quiddities are the objects of our intellect; when we grasp a quiddity, Aquinas describes our mind as being informed by an 'intelligible species' – that is to say a form which is not compounded with matter (like the form which makes me a man or that table a table) but rather is that *by which* we know. And Aquinas emphasizes that intelligible species are not *what* we know: if they were, we would only know the contents of our own minds, not the objects in the world (ST 1.85.2).

(2) Forming a definition; compounding and dividing and mental discourse

Most medieval thinkers, following Aristotle, Boethius and Augustine (see above, pp.94, 99), considered that there is a mental language, common to all men. It is this language in which thought takes place, and its words which the words of ordinary written and spoken speech primarily signify. Aquinas is no exception (see e.g. SDE 1,2). His theory of mental words and discourse forms a second stage in his analysis of the process of intellectual cognition in men.

Mental words are not the same as intelligible species. The senses, Aquinas says, can function in two different ways: they can be affected by something presented, or they can form an image of something absent. In the intellect, these two operations – informtion and formation – are combined as stages in a single act. First, the potential intellect is informed with an intelligible species, then it forms what Aquinas calls a mental word or definition (or intention: see below, p.140. These are what written or spoken words signify. The intellect can then go on to compound and divide; and the mental statements it forms in this way are what spoken and written statements signify (ST 1,85,2 ad3).

What exactly does St Thomas mean by a mental 'definition'? Forming a definition precedes compounding and dividing and, as Aquinas frequently insists (see below), truth and falsehood belong to the intellect only when it compounds and divides. Yet when we think of a definition we usually mean a statement of a form like 'An x is a p, q, r' ('A man is a rational, mortal animal'). Aquinas (cf .SM vi,4) seems to envisage a mental definition rather as having the form p, q, r (for instance, 'rational, mortal, animal'). A definition of this sort might be called an 'uncomposed definition', since it is reached before the intellect composes and divides. The notion of an uncomposed definition makes good sense within Aquinas's view of the cognitive process. Suppose a man is standing in front of me. My active intellect abstracts his quiddity, my potential intellect is converted from potency to act and it forms the definition 'rational, mortal, animal': at this stage I have not yet formed any mental statement which could be true or false. Or suppose I have gained the habitual knowledge of the quiddity of man. There is a moment, in Aquinas's view of our mental processes, when I bring this concept – rational, mortal, animal – to mind without having yet constructed a mental proposition with it.

Aquinas grants, following Aristotle, that all things which exist are 'true' and so, when we cognize something sensibly or intellectually, we are cognizing what is true. But to know what is true is not the same as knowing the truth. Truth is a correspondence between a thing and a thought. All natural things are true by virtue of their correspondence to the divine intellect; but truth is also found in the correspondence between things and thoughts in created intellects (ST 1,16,1). For a human intellect to know the truth it is not enough for it to have a thought which does in fact correspond to things in the world: it must know and judge this correspondence, by reflecting back on its own act (quV I,9). The intellect forms such judgements when it composes and divides (ST

1,16,1;2; SDE 1,3). When we form the definition 'rational, mortal, animal' our mind has a likeness of man in it, but it does not know, just by having the likeness, that the definition is a likeness of man. The mind must compose, making the judgement that 'man is a rational, mortal animal'. Then it is in possession of the truth (SM VI,4 n.14). Once truth is possible, so is error; and whilst *per se* a definition which precedes composition and division cannot be false, it can be false accidentally because of its relation to a mental proposition. If I form in my mind the uncomposed definition 'rational, animal, quadruped', this is not in itself true or false, but accidentally it is false because the proposition 'There is a rational, four-footed animal' is false. If I see an ass and form in my mind the uncomposed definition 'rational, mortal animal', then, again, the definition in itself is not true or false, but accidentally it is false because the mental proposition 'an ass is a rational, mortal animal' is false (ST 1,17,3; SM IX,11 n.14).

When the mind has formed a proposition, it is able to begin the mental discourse which Aquinas describes in terms of syllogistic reasoning. This discourse requires the other strictly intellectual act of which men are capable besides apprehending quiddities: grasping the indemonstrable first principles of scientific knowledge. These principles are related to mental discourse as its beginning and end. Aquinas envisages two main methods of rational enquiry – discovery (the *via inveniendi*) and judgement (the *via iudicandi*). When the mind enquires by discovery, it sets out from indemonstrable first principles and builds on their basis a scheme of scientific knowledge using what it has learnt by abstracting quiddities. The first principles are thus the beginning of the *via inveniendi*. When the mind judges, it works back from a definition to the first principles of the science to which it belongs: the first principles are the end of the *via iudicandi* (quV 15,1). Aquinas's concentration on scientific knowledge does not imply that he considers all human thought to follow this syllogistic pattern. But he does take scientific knowledge, as Aristotle understood it, to be the goal of the embodied human intellect, when used speculatively. By reasoning from or to the first principles it can grasp immediately, man's mind laboriously gathers some of the truth about material things which an angel gains effortlessly.

Only some: the qualification is necessary because there is an important difference between what an angel and what a human being ends by knowing. The innate species by which angels know give them knowledge, not just of universals but of singulars too (ST 1,57,2). The scientific knowledge which humans can gain is of universals alone. But men do have some, indirect intellectual knowledge of individuals. In order to understand what Aquinas means by this, it is necessary to look at the part which *phantasmata*, sensible images, play in his view of human intellectual and ratiocinative cognition.

The intellectual cognition of individuals

(1) Thinking and *phantasmata*

Aquinas believes that men cannot think without accompanying *phantasmata* in the sensible part of the soul. He refers to this as the intellect's 'converting itself to *phantasmata*' (*convertendo se ad phantasmata*). If my mind grasps the quiddity of something I am presently sensing in some way, it must do so by abstraction from a sensible image. But even if I wish to think about something of which an example is not sensibly present to me – if I call to mind the intelligible species of a horse when there is no horse here – I must still 'convert my mind to *phantasmata*, summoning up appropriate sensible images for my thoughts'. Aquinas thinks this is a matter of common experience: 'anybody at all can experience this in himself – that when he tries to think about (*intelligere*) something, he forms certain *phantasmata* to serve as examples, in which he as it were inspects (*quasi inspiciat*) what he is attempting to grasp intellectually (*intelligere*)' (ST 1,84,7). And there is a physiological argument for the need to convert one's mind to *phantasmata*. Damage to parts of the brain, Aquinas observes, can impede not only the acquisition of new intellectual knowledge, but also the use of knowledge which has already been acquired. But the intellect itself uses no corporeal organ and so its functionings could not be impaired by brain-damage. The only way to explain the observation is by positing an activity of the sensible part of the soul which must necessarily accompany thought (ST 1,84,7).

It is hard to accept Aquinas's view that our thoughts are always accompanied by sensible images, though no doubt they sometimes are. But proposing it was the only way – as his argument about brain-damage illustrates – in which Aquinas could make a point which we would not only accept, but treat as obvious. Human mental activity – such as thinking, knowing, reasoning (and wishing, hoping, fearing) – is, in some respect, activity of the human body (especially of the brain). We may or may not consider that a description of it in neurophysiological terms would be adequate, but we should be unlikely to deny that there is in theory a close and important relationship between a scientific description of it using the language of the brain ('there are such-and-such chemical changes, electric currents') and a non-scientific description using the language of the mind ('he was engaged in complex reasoning, trying to discover whether. . .'). Aquinas, it seems, would have also have agreed with this position, but his framework of thought was different. For him the intellect is incorporeal; it uses no bodily organ. In order to express his recognition that, in this life, where the intellective soul is the form of the human body, mental activity cannot be separated from physiological activity, Aquinas must insist that thought is accompanied by the activity of the senses.

(2) Indirect intellectual cognition of individuals

The human intellect's ability to cognize individuals indirectly depends on the necessity of conversion to *phantasmata*. For human intellects to know individuals directly is impossible: the intellect is converted from potency to act by the quiddities which the agent intellect grasps. And to grasp a quiddity is, by definition, not to cognize an individual thing in its particular, determinate matter (ST 1,86,1). But, because the human mind thinks *convertendo se ad phantasmata*, it is able, 'as if by a certain reflection', indirectly to consider the *phantasmata* and the individuals from which they derive. The intellect 'apprehends its intelligible thing [that is, a quiddity], it goes back and considers its act [of grasping this quiddity] and the intelligible species which is the starting-point of its operation and the origin of the species. And so it comes to consider *phantasmata* and the singular things, of which they are the *phantasmata*' (quA 20 ad. 1 – 2nd series). If I, for instance, grasp the quiddity of a man, I can then consider that intellectual act, and the intelligible species of man which in that act determines my intellect from potency to act. Then I can consider the *phantasmata* from which the species is abstracted, and so the individual thing or things from which I took the *phantasmata* – either that individual man standing in front of me, or various individual men I have seen at various times.

(3) Direct intellectual cognition of individuals by God

Aquinas found the idea of indirect intellectual cognition of singulars in Aristotle, although he elaborated it in his own way. But there is an important difference between Aquinas's approach to

singulars and Aristotle's. For Aristotle, the highest sort of knowledge is of universals: he would not think it a limitation that
scientific knowledge is not of individuals. A Christian thinker like
Aquinas saw matters differently. Not to know individuals would
be an imperfection in knowledge. It is part of human perfection
that we know individuals, even if we know them indirectly only
through the senses (ST 1.14.11). Higher beings, like the angels and
God, must know individuals too. But their knowledge cannot be
sensible, and our indirect intellectual cognition of individuals is
dependent on the fact that we are bodily as well as spiritual
creatures and that sense-activity is a necessary accompaniment to
our thinking. Since angels know by innate species which derive
from God, the problem about their knowledge of singulars reduces
to that of God's (cf. ST 1,57,2). Some thinkers, Aquinas says,
believe that God knows singulars through their universal causes: 'if
an astrologer knew all the motions of the heavens, he could predict
all future eclipses'. But such knowledge, St Thomas argues, would
not be knowledge of singulars: the astrologer would not know this
particular eclipse here and now, because exactly the same type of
eclipse could happen from the same reasons more than once.

Aquinas explains God's knowledge of singulars by distinguishing between two types of forms or species by which the soul
can know things: those which are taken from things, and those
which are 'factive' of them. If I cognize a house, it will be by a form
taken from it; but when an architect conceives in his mind the form
of a house which he is going to build, the form is factive. Since the
architect creates the form of the house but not its matter, the
knowledge of the house which he gains through the factive form is
only universal. God is in a different position. He creates not only
the form but also the matter of all things. Since things are
individuated by matter, God knows all things individually through
the forms by which he makes them (quA 20; ST 1,14,11).

Conclusion

Many historians present Aquinas's theory of intellectual knowledge
simply as an example of his Aristotelianism. For them, this forms
part of a broader picture of Aquinas as the champion of natural
reason, the thinker who argued philosophically in so many areas
where his predecessors and contemporaries allowed themselves to
be influenced by revelation and the authority of the Church
Fathers. This view is doubly wrong. First, it neglects the extent to
which the Aristotelian elements in St Thomas's discussion belong

to a broader and fuller theory, which depends on a Christian theologian's conception of the grades of intelligent beings: man in this life, disembodied souls, angels and God himself. Second, it too readily follows St Thomas's own assumption that the achievements of natural reason, the domain of philosophy (as opposed to theology) and the theories of Aristotle are coincident.

Aristotle's theory of intellectual knowledge makes so many assumptions unacceptable to the modern philosopher that it is almost irrecoverably obscure. The arguments – and the circumstances of those arguments – which Aristotle devises for it are interesting and important; but the mere repetition by a medieval thinker of Aristotle's reasoning would deserve, at most, a footnote. Aquinas's discussion of the intellect deserves much more. It centres on a question that can be recognized as important even by the modern reader who does not share the religious beliefs which give rise to it. How might the ways of human thought – which seem to be intrinsically linked with the functioning of the brain and the senses – be related to the ways in which an incorporeal being would think? St Thomas's bold solution both underlines the distance and difficulty of the relationship, and yet uses it as a means towards understanding the slow, fallible and distinctively human activity of reasoning.

8 *Modes and intentions: some arts masters on intellectual knowledge*

Modes and intentions: arts masters and theologians

William of Auvergne and Thomas Aquinas were both theologians; the two preceding chapters have argued that their views about intellectual knowledge cannot be understood apart from their specifically Christian presuppositions and aims. But there were, in the medieval universities, a group of teachers who, though Christians, were professionally dedicated to discussing problems by using reason and observation alone and assuming only principles self-evident to all men (not the revealed truths of Christianity). They were the arts masters – some of whom stayed on in an arts faculty long beyond the compulsory two years as regent master ('necessary regency' – see above, p.23). How did their approach to the problem of intellectual knowledge differ from that of theologians?

The obvious place to look for arts masters' views about the intellect might seem to be their commentaries on Aristotle's *De Anima*. But so great was their desire to represent Aristotle's teaching faithfully that the scope for independent thought in this context was usually limited. For instance, the various writings about the *De Anima* by Siger of Brabant – the arts master best known to historians – are interesting, not so much for the doctrines they propound, but for the positions they adopt with regard to supposedly Aristotelian doctrines which theologians would find unacceptable. But arts masters also considered problems about intellectual knowledge in connection with another part of their work. In teaching grammar and logic, they were forced to ask about the relationship between objects in the world, thoughts of them in the mind and the words used to speak about them. Two concepts played an especially important part in medieval approaches to these questions: modes and intentions. When thinkers from the mid-thirteenth century onwards wanted to talk about how one and the same thing exists, is thought and is referred to by a word, they distinguished between modes or ways of being, thinking and signifying (*modi essendi/ intelligendi/ significandi*). When they wished to refer to a concept in the mind, as opposed to the thing thought, they often talked of an 'intention' (*intentio*).

Modes and intentions were discussed by both theologians and arts masters. This chapter will illustrate their differences in approach by a limited comparison: between the treatment of these concepts by an outstanding theologian, Thomas Aquinas, and that given by three important arts masters of the mid to late thirteenth century: Boethius and Martin of Dacia (Denmark) and Radulphus Brito.

Boethius of Dacia was one of the leading masters of arts in the late 1260s and early 1270s. Some contemporaries believed that he was a principal target of the 1277 condemnations – although neither his treatise on the eternity of the world (see above, pp.72–3) nor any other of his surviving works reveals him as a heretical thinker, but merely one who strove to keep separate the domains of each branch of knowledge. Besides the *De Aeternitate Mundi* and a short work on human happiness from the point of view of natural reason (*De Summo Bono*), he wrote a treatise *De Modis Significandi* (MS; c.1269-1270) and *quaestio*-commentaries on a number of Aristotle's works.

Less is known about Martin, another scholar from Denmark. Unlike Boethius of Dacia, after his period as an arts master he went on to study theology. He taught arts during the 1270s and perhaps from even earlier, producing another textbook *De Modis Significandi* (MS) and *quaestio*-commentaries on the *logica vetus*.

Radulphus Brito was an outstanding arts master of a later generation. He taught in the faculty around the turn of the fourteenth century, before going on to study theology, incepting as a master of theology in 1311/1312. Among his non-theological works is a set of *Quaestiones super Priscianum Minorem* (PM) and a wide range of *quaestio*-commentaries on Aristotle, including one on the *De Anima* (A).

Modes

Although modern philosophers debate problems about truth as energetically as their predecessors, they would not think it a problem that thoughts of material things are themselves immaterial. But for medieval philosophers, whose view of the intellect derived from Aristotle, this disparity between what is in the mind and what is outside it seemed a real difficulty which needed resolution. If intellectual knowledge consists in the information of the intellect by an object in the world, then how can that which informs the intellect differ from that which it is supposed to know? By positing a difference between the mode of something's being and the mode of thinking it was possible to resolve this problem.

(1) Aquinas

Aquinas's discussion of the issue is particularly clear. He puts the following argument to himself (ST 1,85,1 arg.1): any intellect is false which thinks of a thing otherwise than as it is (*quicumque . . . intellectus intelligit rem aliter quam sit, est falsus*); if, then, we intellectually cognize (*intelligimus*) material things by abstraction, we will not have true intellectual knowledge, since the forms of material things are not in fact abstracted from particulars. He answers by saying that there will be no falsity in our knowledge if the abstraction is simply a matter of considering one aspect of a thing but not another. Just as we can consider the colour of an apple without the apple, so we can consider the nature of a species without the individuating features of an individual. The phrase *think of a thing otherwise than as it is* can be interpreted in two ways: the *otherwise* can apply to the thing, or to the thinking. In the first case, there would be falsity, but not in the second. 'For there is no falsity if the mode of the thinker in thinking (*modus intelligentis in intelligendo*) is different from the mode of the thing in existing (*modus rei in existendo*): for the thought of the thing (*intellectum*) is in the thinker immaterially, not materially in the manner (*per modum*) of a material thing.'

For Aquinas, a logical point was rarely without connection to a theological one. The modes of being and of thinking provide him not only with the terms to resolve his difficulty about the truthfulness of ordinary thoughts, but also – slightly adapted – with a manner of describing the limitations of human knowledge. Different things, he says (ST 1,12,4; cf. SM II,1,13, quV 8,3), have different modes of being. Bodily things can exist only as individual material things (this man, that house); incorporeal things do not have any matter, but their mode of being is distinguished from God's because, as Aquinas puts it, unlike God they are not their own *esse*. At least some of what St Thomas means by this can be put in linguistic terms: whereas it is coherent, he believes, though false, to say that 'the angel Gabriel does not exist', to say 'God does not exist' is not only false but logically incoherent.

The way in which different beings have knowledge depends, not on the nature of the things they know, but on their own nature: as Aquinas puts it in a phrase he often repeats: 'the thing known is in its knower in the mode of its knower' (*cognitum est in cognoscente secundum modum cognoscentis*). As a corporeal creature, man is fitted to know other corporeal things, although he has the special power to abstract natures which can only exist in matter from the matter in which they exist (see above, pp. 118–19). If, St Thomas says, 'the mode of being of something known exceeds the mode of the nature of the knower, then the knowledge of that thing must be beyond the nature of that knower.' Direct knowledge of separate substances is beyond man's natural grasp, and direct knowledge of God beyond the grasp of the angels: the only being which naturally knows God is God himself.

But Aquinas does not wish to remove all possibility of man's knowing the angels and God. He considers that the souls of the blessed in heaven can be raised above their nature by divine grace so as to see the essence of God (ST 1,12,4;11). Some will be allowed to see it more perfectly than others: what they all see will be the same, but the *modus intelligendi* will differ (ST 1,12,6 ad 2).

St Thomas also believes that men in this life have some imperfect and indirect knowledge of God. In defining it, he develops a notion of *modi significandi*. God unites in himself in a higher form all the perfections which are found in his creatures. When the intellect gains knowledge from created things, it is informed with the likenesses of divine perfections which are in God's creations, such as goodness and wisdom. From these it is able to form a concept of God which is true in the sense that God really does have the perfections which are attributed to him. But the intellect cannot arrive at a definition of God's essence, in the way that it can of man or other bodily things (quP 7,5). Does this mean that, when we describe God, the words we use do not properly apply to God? Our intellect, Aquinas replies (ST 1,13,3), apprehends divine perfections as they are in his creatures and signifies them as such in speech. None the less, with regard to *what* they signify (*id quod significant*) – the perfections such as goodness and life – the words not only apply to God but apply to him more properly than to any of his creatures. But with regard to their *modus significandi* they are not properly said of God, since they have the mode of signifying which is appropriate for created things.

(2) Martin and Boethius of Dacia

For Aquinas, each time he used them, the modes of being, thinking and signifying were a way of discussing the differences between how things are and how they are thought and spoken about by humans. But it was possible to use the modes in a different way, emphasizing their congruity. This was the approach which Martin and Boethius adopted in formulating the theoretical basis of speculative grammar. The modes of being, Martin explains (MS p.4) are 'the properties of a thing according to the thing's being outside the intellect'; the modes of thinking are the same properties of the thing according to its being in the intellect; whilst the modes of signifying are the same properties according to its being signified in speech. Things in the world (MS pp.4–5) have many properties – they are singular or plural, they are passive or active and so on. When the intellect thinks (*intelligit*) something (MS p.5), it conceives it with these sorts of properties; the thing becomes the thing thought and 'what were previously called the "modes of being" of the thing outside are called the "modes of thinking" of the thing thought'. When the intellect wants to signify its concept to another, it imposes words on the thing thought in order to express its concept, just as the inn-keeper puts a circle to signify wine. When words have been imposed, the thing is called the thing signified, and all the properties of the thing, which were first called modes of being and then modes of thinking are now called modes of signifying (*modi significandi*).

As grammarians, Martin and Boethius are especially interested in the *modi significandi*. The thing in thought itself, as represented in speech, is the *significatum speciale*; its properties, 'consignified' in speech, are the *modi significandi* (Martin – MS p.8). Just as things are distinguished by their properties, so the parts of speech (*oratio*) are distinguished by their *modi significandi*. On this basis Martin and Boethius expound a special sort of grammatical theory which became known as speculative grammar. In their analysis a first imposition (*impositio/copulatio*) links a given sound with a given sort of thing; this meaningful, but not yet precisely meaningful sound is called a *dictio*. A *dictio* becomes a part of speech (*pars orationis*) by having *modi significandi*: these distinguish it first as a noun, pronoun, verb, particle, adverb, preposition, conjunction or interjection; and then more precisely with features such as case, number and tense. The *modi significandi* are more than the categories of traditional grammar under a different name, because they involve the explicit attempt to link precise grammatical function with the properties of things in the world.

The analyses worked out by Martin, Boethius and the speculative grammarians (or *modistae*) of the late thirteenth century form an interesting, if somewhat isolated, chapter in the history of grammatical theory. A modern reader might also believe that they are interesting philosophically because – so he imagines – the *modistae* engaged in linguistic analysis, similar in character, though not terminology, to that pursued by some modern philosophers. But they were not. Two fundamental differences separate the theoretical outlook of Martin, Boethius and their medieval successors from modern linguistic philosophers. First, the *modistae* hold to the view of the *De Interpretatione* that thoughts are what words primarily signify, not things (cf. Martin, *Quaestiones* on *De Interpretatione*, 7); and furthermore that sentences cannot be formed in speech without the prior formation of a complex thought (cf. Boethius MS 27). Second, the *modistae* clearly regard the study of the *modi significandi* firmly as the province of the grammarian. It is the philosopher's job to discuss how things are and how they are known; the grammarian's to examine how language corresponds to them (cf. Boethius – MS 2). For this reason Boethius argues that, whoever first imposes words on things must be both a grammarian and a philosopher – a grammarian because he would have to consider the modes of signifying, a philosopher because the task would involve knowledge of the nature of things (MS 12). They do not at all believe, as a modern philosopher might, that the nature of things is to be discovered by looking at the nature of language. On the contrary, from what is known about how things are in reality and in the mind, they find it possible to discuss how they are in speech, which follows thought directly and reality at one remove.

In the discussions with which they introduced their detailed accounts of the *modi significandi*, the speculative grammarians did however consider at least one important abstract question about the nature of thought and language – a question close in subject to one which St Thomas had resolved by reference to 'modes' (see above, pp. 134–5). The properties which something really has, those which it is truly thought to have and those which it is truly said to have are the same; but since things, thoughts and speech are different, how can this be so? The technical formulation of this problem is simple: are the modes of being, thinking and signifying the same or not? Martin (MS p.6) says that they are the same, although they differ accidentally, just as a man who goes from one place to another remains the same man although he differs by the accident of location. Each of the modes are in the thing as their subject; but the modes of thinking are also in the intellect 'as something known in the knower' (*sicut cognitum in cognoscente*) and the modes of signifying in the words (*vox*) as in a sign (p.7).

Boethius of Dacia (MS 27) disagrees with Martin's position: the *modi essendi, intelligendi* and *significandi*, he believes, are similar to one another but different. He argues from the precedence of the mode of being over the mode of thinking, and the mode of thinking over the mode of signifying. Even if something could not be signified in speech in a certain way, it might still be thought that way; even if it could not be thought that way, it might still in reality have those properties. And, contrary to Martin, Boethius holds that the modes are in different subjects: the *modus essendi* in the thing, the *modus intelligendi* in the intellect and the *modus significandi* in the *dictio*. In answer to the objection that it is the same thing which is, is thought of and is signified, Boethius simply answers that a thing, a thing in thought and a thing in speech do differ at least in reason (*saltem in ratione*) although in reality (*realiter*) they are the same. Boethius and Martin, then, each state a position but do not analyse it in much depth.

(3) Radulphus Brito

Radulphus Brito deals with the same problem at considerably greater length. By this time, it was normal to make a distinction between 'active' and 'passive' modes of thinking and signifying (*modi intelligendi/significandi activi/passivi*). The passive mode of signifying, Radulphus explains (PM 18), means a thing's mode of being as consignified in speech; the active mode of signifying is the type of consignification (*ratio consignificandi*) through which a word signifies that mode of being; and similarly for the modes of thinking. The purpose of this distinction seems to have been to accommodate arguments such as Martin advanced for identifying the modes, and arguments such as Boethius's for keeping them apart: the passive modes of signifying and thinking were identical with the mode of being, but the active modes of signifying and thinking were the same as each other but not as the mode of being.

Radulphus himself, however, posits a further distinction: between the modes, active and passive, considered 'formally' (*formaliter*) and 'materially' (*materialiter*). It is difficult to gather Radulphus's meaning for these terms except from the way he uses them. Although they differ materially, formally, he says (PM 22) the active and passive modes of signifying must be the same as each other. One and the same correlation of word and object (*ratio significandi*) makes the word signify the thing, and the thing be signified by the word; and the same must be true of consignification. The active and passive modes of thinking too, though different materially, are formally identical: the cognition by which a thing is thought is the same as that by which the intellect thinks it. In the light of his distinction, Radulphus holds that only materially can the passive modes of signifying and thinking be the same as the mode of being (PM 18); formally the passive modes of signifying and thinking (which are the same as the active modes of signifying and thinking) are similar to each other, but not identical (PM 19), nor are they identical to the mode of being.

What is Radulphus trying to argue in his elaborate fashion? He could be seen as providing a justification for a view like Boethius of Dacia's, that the modes are not identical, by granting that there is just one truistic sense in which they are – it is the same thing which is, is thought of and is referred to in speech. If this interpretation of it is correct, Radulphus's own distinction between taking the modes formally or materially is not supposed to complicate an already overloaded classification, but rather to reveal the artificiality of some of its categories.

Intentions

(1) Avicenna and Aquinas

The Aristotelian view of intellectual knowledge is mainly concerned with the way in which the intellect thinks of (*intelligit*) things. But as well as thinking of things, the mind can think of its own thoughts. By doing so it can form concepts to which nothing in reality corresponds directly. For instance, Aquinas explains (quP 1,1 ad 10; cf. 7,6), the intellect knows that men, horses, dogs and so on are animals (*intelligit naturam animalis in homine, in equo. . .*) and, from this, it knows that 'animal' is a genus. 'Animal' is a term which describes things; 'genus' is a term which describes thoughts about things. As St Thomas says, 'there is no thing in the outside world which is a genus which corresponds to the thought by which the intellect knows what a genus is (*intelligit genus*), but something does correspond to the act of thinking (*intelligentia*) which gives rise to this concept'. Man is an animal; to think of man as an animal is to place him in a genus; and one arrives at the concept of genus itself by thinking of thoughts which place things in genera. The intellect must reflect on itself.

Aquinas calls genera and species 'intentions', of the intellect. A little later they would be called 'second intentions' (following Avicenna – *Metaphysics* 1 p.10:73ff.), a useful distinction, since *intentio* was a term with a wide range of meanings in the later Middle Ages.

First, the word could be used with its original meaning, which was close to that of 'intention' in modern English, to discuss the psychology of action and problems of moral responsibility.

Second, *intentio* could be used loosely to mean thought, meaning or idea – the twelfth-century translators of Avicenna had employed it in this way to translate two Arabic words: *ma'qūl*, 'thought', and *ma'nā* – a vaguer word for thought, concept, meaning or idea.

Third, *intentio* could have the special meaning already noted – a concept to which nothing in reality directly corresponds. This meaning is found sometimes in the Latin Avicenna: for instance, our knowledge of not-being is said to be limited to an *intentio* of it in the mind (*Metaphysics* 1 p.38:14-15). Aquinas's use of the word in this way is not limited to the *De Potentia*: he talks, in the *Summa Theologiae*, of the 'intention of universality' (1,85,2 ad2). Similarly, Martin of Dacia [*Quaestiones* on *Porphyry*, 5] uses *intentionalis* to mean 'in the mind but not in reality'.

Fourth, various other, special meanings were given to *intentio* from time to time. For example, in the *Summa contra Gentiles* (1,53,3–4) – but not elsewhere – St Thomas equates intentions with the definitions of things which the intellect forms in the second stage of its cognitive process, after it has been informed with an intelligible species (see above, pp.126–7).

(2) Radulphus Brito

One of the most thorough and original analyses of second intentions and their relation to other types of thought and to things is provided by Radulphus Brito. Radulphus, in accord with standard later thirteenth-century usage, allows the term *intentio* to mean any sort of thought and distinguishes between 'first intentions' and 'second intentions'. He also makes a further distinction: between 'concrete' first and second intentions (*in concreto*) and 'abstract' ones (*in abstracto*). This distinction represents the difference – which Radulphus is keen should not be forgotten (cf. *Quaestiones* on *Porphyry* 8) – between what is thought of and the thought of it.

In his sophism on second intentions (pp.142-144; cf. quA I.6 – where the discussion is similar but the terminology yet more complicated), he sets out a complete system of first and second intentions in concrete and in abstract. Like Aquinas he postulates three operations of the intellect – (1) simple thought, (2) compounding and dividing (*componere et dividere*) and (3) discursive thought (*discursus*) – although he does not make a distinction between the intelligible species and the mental definition or 'word' (cf. quA III.25; and above pp. 126, 140). Table 5 sets out his scheme, with examples of its application:-

Table 5   **Radulphus Brito on intentions**

First intentions

Operation of intellect	Concrete	Abstract
1) Simple	A man	Thought of man existing as individual apprehended from phantasm
2) Compounding and dividing	The statement that 'every man runs'	Thinking that every man runs
3) Discourse	The argument that 'every man runs, Socrates is a man, therefore Socrates runs'	Arguing that every man runs, Socrates is a man, therefore Socrates runs

Second intentions

1) Simple	The species Man	Thinking of man as common to many
2) Compounding and dividing	A universal affirmative statement	Thinking of 'every man runs' as a universal, affirmative statement
3) Discourse	A syllogism	Thinking of 'every man runs, Socrates is a man, therefore Socrates runs' as a syllogism

Radulphus sets out matters like this because he wishes to revise the common view that second intentions are thoughts about thoughts. From the point of view of what is going on in the mind (*in abstracto*), he believes that the second intentions are, rather, special ways of thinking things. The ordinary way of thinking of man is as a quiddity in individual matter; but it is also possible to think of man as something common to many individuals – that is to say, as a species. Just as ordinary thinking has its concrete aspect – the real man is the concrete aspect of the thought of him – so does this special way of thinking: its concrete equivalent is the species Man. If one thinks of 'thing' (*res*) in this special way, in so far as it is common to many, the concrete equivalent to this thought will be species and genus in general. Species and genus and other second intentions of the first operation of the intellect are not, therefore, the products of thought about thought, but of thinking in a particular way: they are, according to Radulphus's unusual view, in exactly the same position as individual species and genera. He argues (p. 144) that they originate from a thing 'under its mode of being which is common to other things' (*sub modo essendi communi eius*) and the active intellect, but that the potential intellect is not involved as a cause of their knowledge but merely receives knowledge of them. They are therefore (p. 146) real dispositions (*habitus reales*) of things in the world.

The case is different for second intentions of the second and third operations of the intellect. Composition and division, and discursive reasoning take place in the mind. Thinking of a statement as a certain sort of statement or an argument as a certain sort of argument does involve reflection on the workings of the mind: the potential intellect, as well as the active intellect and objects in the world must be posited as the causes of such intentions (pp. 145–146). Statements of syllogisms are objects not in the world but in the mind (cf. p. 147).

Radulphus is not putting forward some kind of quasi-Platonic realism. He does not think that there is a species Man apart from individual men; and even less that something exists which is simply species or genus. It was commonly held that individual species had a basis in the nature of things, although they did not really exist apart from individual things; Radulphus wishes to add that the same is true of the concepts of genus and species themselves. Because of the way that things are grouped in classes, we are able to arrive at a notion of genus and species, just as we are able to arrive at a notion of the individual species Man and the individual genus Animal. But there is nothing in the nature of things which provides a basis for the way we argue, in statements and syllogisms (although the truth of *what* we argue depends on how things in the world are). Logic, which is chiefly concerned with second intentions of the second and third operations of the intellect, is a branch of knowledge to do with thought and not with reality.

Conclusion

Martin of Dacia, Boethius of Dacia and Radulphus Brito spent much more time in the arts faculty than most masters of arts. Their unusual maturity and expertise is reflected in the technical sophistication of their arguments and analyses. The masters are adept at inventing and refining a set of terms. They might, at first sight, simply seem to be positing concept upon concept in a sort of metaphysical fantasy. But this judgement would be unfair, especially to the work of Radulphus Brito: his complex terminology is used to remove unnecessary distinctions rather than to make them. By comparison with the theologians, however, the arts masters seem very limited. They do not provide a different approach to the problem of intellectual knowledge, uninfluenced by revelation; rather, they take their main concepts and arguments from the theologians and, within a narrow area, elaborate and refine them. The great changes in later medieval understanding of the intellect all came from the theologians.

9 Henry of Ghent

A new approach to Henry's discussion of intellectual knowledge

To his contemporaries and immediate successors, Henry of Ghent, a secular master who taught theology in Paris from 1276 to 1292, was a thinker of the greatest importance. Duns Scotus, for instance, recounts his views at length and develops his own theories by arguing against them. But, although modern scholars have begun to acknowledge the importance and originality of Henry's metaphysics, his discussion of intellectual knowledge – which Duns Scotus was particularly keen to discuss – has been less favourably received.

All the teaching which survives and can be certainly attributed to Henry is gathered into two composite works: his *Quaestiones Quodlibetales* (Q) and a *Summa Quaestionum Ordinarium* (S), which is not a unified literary work, like the two *Summae* of St Thomas, but a collection of his ordinary (as opposed to quodlibetal) disputations. Both works are made up of material from various different periods in Henry's career; and there is now good information available as to the chronology of the *quaestiones* they each contain. However, historians have tended to look at Henry's various discussions about the intellect and its knowledge together; and they have concluded that Henry's account of knowledge is a muddled compromise between a theory deriving from Augustine and Avicenna, in which divine illumination is required for human knowledge, and an Aristotelian explanation of intellectual cognition without one of its essential features, the intelligible species.

This chapter will propose a different view. Henry's thought about intellectual knowledge falls into two stages. The first stage consists of those views which he had developed by the beginning of his career and are expounded in the opening articles of his *Summa*.

At this stage Henry had deliberately developed two parallel accounts of how the intellect in this life gains knowledge: one (which might be called his 'Aristotelian' theory) offers an explanation based entirely on man's natural capacities: the other (his 'illuminationist' theory) posits divine intervention. In the second stage of his thinking – which stretches from about 1279 or 1280, the probable date of his fourth quodlibet, to his latest years – Henry does not give up his illuminationist account, but he is far more interested in developing and changing his Aristotelian account so as to dispense with the intelligible species, which had played an important part in his earlier version of it.

The earlier stage

(1) Knowing the truth of things: Henry's Aristotelian account

In his discussion of intellectual knowledge at the beginning of the *Summa*, the question which Henry puts to himself is not 'How do men have a thought of something and what is the relation between the thing and the thought?' but 'How do men gain knowledge of the truth?'. For Henry the truth is a wider concept than for most modern thinkers. A plausible, though by no means universally accepted, modern account of truth would be to say that it is a correspondence of some kind between statements – and by extension thoughts – and facts in the world. A statement is true if it says that things are as they are. Henry does use 'true' and 'truth' in this way (see below, pp. 147, 151). But in addition he has another use for the terms which is less comfortable for the modern reader. 'True' is also used to describe things (as opposed to statements): Henry shared with almost all thinkers in the thirteenth century (cf. above, pp. 119–20) the view that everything which is, is true. And Henry also talks about the 'truth' of things, by which he means, not the correspondence between statements and facts but between things and their exemplars.

Knowing the truth of things has an important place in Henry's theory of intellectual knowledge, according to both his Aristotelian and his illuminationist (see below, pp. 146–7) accounts. He is careful to distinguish it from merely knowing things which are true. Any faculty, sensible or intellectual, which apprehends something as it is in the world outside apprehends what is true in it; but it does not thereby apprehend its truth (S1,2 C). When the intellect knows a thing simply (*simplici intelligentia id quod res est*), it does not reach its truth. The truth of a thing lies in its correspondence to the exemplar, and so it can only be by making a comparison that the intellect grasps it. The truth of a thing, therefore, is reached by the intellect in its second operation, compounding and dividing (S1,2 D: cf. Aquinas, above, pp. 125–7).

What sort of exemplar is the thing compared to, and how is it known? One kind of exemplar, Henry thinks, is the 'universal species existing in the mind, through which knowledge of all its members (*omnium suppositorum*) is gained' (S1,2 E). Henry makes it clear that he means an intelligible species which the mind forms by its own powers through a process of abstraction starting from sensible images and the memory of them (for instance, the form of Man which I abstracted from the sensible images of the many men I have seen). These species can be used by the mind in two ways: either it can treat them merely as images of a particular thing or else it can use them as the way of knowing (*ratio cognoscendi*) something. Only the second of these ways leads to knowledge of the truth of a thing, when the mind forms a concept of a thing which conforms to the universal species it has of it. Such knowledge is exercised when we recognize what species a thing belongs to, or what is the genus of the species. Henry, then, envisages that from experience men build up a knowledge of universal species; they are therefore able to judge correctly that Socrates is a man and Fido is a dog. Such judgements (which are not simple thoughts but involve composition) express knowledge about what Henry calls 'the truth of' Socrates and Fido.

(2) Knowing the absolute truth of things: Henry's illuminationist account

However, the truth of things which can be known in this way, by man's natural capacities, is not, Henry believes, the 'absolute truth' (*sincera veritas*). In common with all the thinkers of his time, even the most Aristotelian (see below, p. 176), Henry thinks that, in the mind of God there are Ideas (*ideales rationes*) of all things. To gain the absolute truth about a thing, the mind must make a comparison with these eternal exemplars. But if someone had the divine Ideas as the object of his knowledge, then he would know the substance of God; and this, Henry considers, is impossible except for souls in glory or those given special grace. None the less, Henry believes that ordinary humans in this life can attain knowledge of truth *through* the divine Ideas, although they cannot do so from their own unaided powers. The mind of God or, as Henry calls it here, the divine light (*lux divina*) is not the object known but the way of knowing (*ratio intelligendi*) it (S1,3 A). Henry elaborates the metaphor of light to explain what he means by this: 'first, the light diffuses itself over the species of things and from them it diffuses itself in the mind, so that it forms a perfect concept (*conceptum*) of the thing itself in the intellect' (S1,3 F).

Knowledge of the truth of a thing is complex knowledge, according to Henry: it must involve composition. The elements which are composed to gain the absolute truth about a thing are, Henry believes (S1,3 G) the intelligible species taken from the thing and the exemplar of the thing in the mind of God. Their combination produces what Henry calls a 'word of truth' (*verbum veritatis*): 'When these two species come together in the mind and from them a single way of knowing (*ratio ad intelligendum*) the thing of which they are the exemplar, the mind is able to conceive the word of perfectly informed truth, which is perfectly in accord with the truth which is in the thing, in no way differing from it'.

(3) Knowing the truth about things

As well as discussing the truth *of* things, Henry considers the notion – more familiar to modern readers – of the truth *about* things. However, this does not play much part in his illumination-ist account of the absolute truth. Henry merely says (S1,2 L) that, in this way, knowledge is gained both of principles and conclusions: perhaps his point is that, by knowing the absolute truth about things, one also knows everything about their relations to one another.

By contrast, in his Aristotelian account Henry works out at some length, although not very thoroughly, an analysis of how by our natural powers we come to know the truth about things (S1,5 B). The potential intellect, informed by the active intellect with the quiddities of things, naturally conceives certain basic concepts, such as being (*ens*), unity and magnitude. It then gains knowledge of self-evident truths (such as 'the whole is greater than its part') by compounding and dividing these concepts. By study and application – and, for most people, by instruction – mental discourse draws from these first truths particular conclusions which make up scientific knowledge.

(4) Truth and certainty: the relations between Henry's Aristotelian and his illuminationist accounts

The preceding sections have suggested that Henry's Aristotelian theory has two elements. The first element explains how men come to know the truths expressed in statements such as 'Socrates is a man'. The second element explains how men gain general knowledge about the world – how, for instance, they come to know that man is a rational, mortal animal. Henry is willing to grant (S2,1 B) that the general knowledge derived in this way is certain, in the sense that it is free from all error (although he sometimes undercuts this with a note of reserve – as at S1,3 G), but he adds that there is a second sort of certainty which is only gained by looking – in the indirect way described in his illuminationist account – at the eternal exemplar of something. But even this certainty is not complete certainty: that can only be had by making the uncreated exemplar the object of knowledge – a possibility open only to those in heaven.

What, then, is the relationship between Henry's illuminationist and his Aristotelian theories? The truths known by illumination certainly include all the truths which can be discovered in the Aristotelian way: the mind requires the intelligible species as well as knowledge of the divine exemplar, according to the illuminationist account; and when the combination of these two elements provides the truth of a thing, this leads automatically to knowledge of the truth about things which, by the Aristotelian account, would have to be discovered by mental discourse based on self-evident first principles. But Henry claims more than this for illumination. It is not just another way of knowing what man could, with more difficulty, know by his natural powers: illumination yields a different and greater truth – *sincera veritas* – and a higher degree of certainty. Why does he think that ordinary scientific knowledge is uncertain? It would be very wrong to imagine that Henry entertains doubts, of a Cartesian sort, about the reliability of the senses and what the mind discovers using them. When he points to the superior truth gained by illumination, Henry is probably thinking, as a theologian, about the limitations of Aristotelian science. Aristotle bases his scientific investigations on the assumption that the species and genera are unchanging and eternal. By discovering, from intellectual perception of the intelligible species, what species and genera things belong to, and how these classes relate to each other, Aristotle gains what he believes to be scientific knowledge – knowledge of things which are unchanging. For a Christian theologian, however, things – and so their species and genera – are God's creation, and the world they make will not last for ever. And the condemnations of 1277, which Henry would play a part in framing (see above, pp.72–4), stress God's power to alter his creation at will. Knowledge about things gained according to Henry's Aristotelian account can therefore only be provisional, but in so far as a man can know what is in God's mind, he knows absolutely what is the case.

The later account

Henry did not abandon his illuminationist account in his later years. In a quodlibet of 1286 (Q9,15) he presents the theory in much the same terms as he had done previously, although he makes one interesting addition to it. Previously he had insisted that knowledge by illumination was granted by God to whomever he wished, but he had not considered whether this happened frequently or only rarely. Now he explains that, in his fallen state, man experiences such illumination seldom. But, from the truths he learns in this way, a person can build up mental dispositions: although the illumination is fleeting, the knowledge it provides remains.

But, apart from a few occasional passages like this about illumination, most of Henry's energies in his later discussions of cognition are given to altering and developing his Aristotelian account.

(1) The abandonment of impressed intelligible species

Henry is unhappy with the principle – essential to Aristotle's account and adopted by Henry in his earlier Aristotelian theory – that the intellect must be acted upon by an intelligible species in order to know something in act. A reason for the unhappiness is Henry's need, as a theologian, to discuss intellectual cognition in separated souls (and God and the angels) as well as among humans in this life. Aquinas had responded to this requirement by emphasizing the closeness of the union as form and matter between soul and body, and so the difference in the means of cognition available to the embodied and the disembodied intellects; even so, he thought that the beatific vision could only be enjoyed by a separated soul which had been raised by divine grace beyond its natural capacities (see above, pp.124, 135). By contrast Henry, like many at the end of the thirteenth century, wishes to stress the similarities between the soul in this life and the soul in bliss. One outcome of the wish is his illuminationist account of how we know, even in this life, the absolute truth; but another is the revision of his earlier Aristotelian theory of intellectual cognition in line with the more perfect model of the disembodied intellect.

Souls in glory enjoy the beatific vision of the essence of God: is an intelligible species necessary for this act? Some believe, Henry says (Q4,7 P–X), that every created intellect is in potency and needs something to determine it into action. The pre-Socratics had thought that the things known by the mind were actually in themselves inside it; but a refinement of this crude view supposes that the intellect is determined into act by the intelligible species of what it knows. And some insist that this is also the case in the beatific vision. But a vision would not be beatific unless God were actually present in it; and so even they have to admit that besides the intelligible species there is also required the presence of God. It is therefore unnecessary, Henry can argue, to posit intelligible species in the beatific vision and, he adds, in any case no intelligible species could possibly be adequate to allow the intellect to know the divine essence.

The activity of embodied intellects is distinguished by Henry from the beatific vision by the nature of the knower and the thing known (Q4.7A). God can be in the glorified intellect in essence: such simplicity is impossible for the embodied intellect in its cognition of material things. None the less, the revised Aristotelian account of ordinary intellectual knowledge which Henry advances accords with his theory of the beatific vision; and it incorporates just the complications necessary to allow an imperfect knower to have knowledge of an imperfect object. Henry is as keen here, as in the beatific vision, to exclude what would normally be regarded as intelligible species – immaterial species in the intellect, which bring about knowledge by determining it. He allows, however, that images (*phantasmata*) in the imagination are necessary for the embodied intellect. And, because he believes that the truth is discovered only in complex thought, he considers that an act of intellectual cognition leads to the production of a complex mental 'word'.

Henry has one difficulty in putting forward this scheme. He wants to remain faithful to Aristotle or, at least, for his theory not to seem incompatible with Aristotle's. Intelligible species are too prominent a feature of Aristotle's theory for him to dispense with them openly and absolutely. Instead, he proposes a distinction, absent from his earlier theory, which enables him to talk as if he accepted the role of intelligible species in cognition whilst in fact eliminating from his account the concept which Aristotelians used this term to designate. There are, he says, 'impressed intelligible species' (*species intelligibles impressae/impressivae*) and 'expressed intelligible species' (*species intelligibles expressae/expressivae*). Impressed intelligible species are indeed impressed by objects in the external world, but in Henry's account they are not – despite their name – 'intelligible': sometimes (e.g. Q4,7 S) they are simply equated with the sensible species – the image or impression present to the sight, hearing, smell, touch or taste – and sometimes with the capacity which enables the memory to bring the species to mind (e.g. Q5,14 K.) (If I know something intellectually, Henry wishes to say, I must either actually be perceiving it with my senses, or remembering a sense-impression of it, or at least I must have the capacity to bring a sense-impression to my memory: cf. Q4,7 V–X). Expressed intelligible species, by contrast, are indeed intelligible; but they are concepts produced by the intellect itself at the end of a cognitive act: they are generated by the intellect itself, not imposed on it by an external object (Q 5,14 K; cf. 14,6 – discussed below).

(2) The process of intellectual cognition in Henry's revised theory

According to Henry's revised theory, an act of intellectual cognition has two stages (Q14,6 E). In the first, the intellect gains knowledge of a thing's *esse universale* – a confused universal knowledge, which does not in itself provide a definition of the thing known. For this knowledge the possible intellect requires a sensible image (*phantasma*) of the thing in the memory and the light of the active intellect which strips the phantasm of its individuating features. Henry does not think of the *esse universale* as an intelligible species by which the potential intellect is informed, but merely that about which it knows: the potential intellect is determined, rather, by the thing itself. He therefore likes to speak of the universal as being in the sensible image (although the image is of an individual). He even refers at one point (S58,2 ad3) to a 'universal sensible image' – which seems a contradiction in terms, until it becomes clear that he means an individual phantasm, stripped of its individuating features by the active intellect, but still a sensible image.

When the intellect knows a thing's *esse universale*, the second stage of cognition begins. The intellect compounds and divides: it recognizes the most general genus to which the thing belongs and then, by adding differentiae, eventually arrives at its most specific species and so is able to define it. Henry calls what is defined the *quod quid est* of the thing as opposed to its confused *esse universale*; the concept in which the intellect forms the definition is the mental word. In another discussion (Q4.8 N) Henry returns to the point he made at the beginning of his *Summa*, that knowledge should be of truth. This is gained, he says, when the intellect, compounding and dividing, arrives at a definition of the *quod quid est*; and when the intellect, through syllogistic reasoning, discovers the causes of things. Here it is particularly clear how Henry's later theory is based on his earlier Aristotelian one. In one respect it is even closer to Aristotle. It drops the earlier theory's strange identification of knowing the truth of a thing with recognizing its species (possibly included there to provide a parallel with the illuminationist theory) and recognizes simply the two sorts of truths which the *Posterior Analytics* allows to scientific reasoning.

(3) The intellectual cognition of singulars

Henry's revised Aristotelian theory allows him to give his own answer to the problem about how the intellect knows individuals (Q4,21 L–M). Like other Christian thinkers of his time, Henry believes that the intellect *must* in some way know individuals. His question is: how? Like Aquinas, the only cognition of individuals which Henry allows the intellect in this life is indirect, obtained by the Aristotelian method of reflection on sensible images (*phantasmata*: see above, pp.98–9, 128–30). Sensible images, however, occupy a different place in Henry's theory than in other Aristotelian accounts, since they are the only sort of impressed species which he admits. They are directly involved in the act of intellection, which ends with the intellect's production of its expressed species or word. And so reflection on *phantasmata* does not, as for Aquinas, involve a complicated process of self-consciousness, but merely attention to the impressed sensible species which is the counterpart to the mental word. For instance, suppose that I look at John and, in doing so, form in my intellect the concept of Man: I can gain (indirect) intellectual knowledge of John by attending to the relation between my sense-impression of John and the concept of Man I have just formed. Henry adds that there is another way of intellectually knowing singulars, which is like seeing them – but this is open only to God, angels and perhaps to glorified souls. Here he touches – though he is not the first to do so – on a topic which would soon become very important (see below, pp.156–7).

Conclusion

Historians have been right to recognize the effects of late thirteenth-century theological movements on Henry's theory of knowledge. But they did not lead him to a muddled combination of Augustinian and Aristotelian elements. On the contrary, he tried to rethink St Thomas's theory of the intelligible word in terms which would answer his particular problems: in the earlier stage of his thought, the need to show how men could to some extent know the absolute truth as well as Aristotelian scientific truth, which he could regard with less trust than his immediate predecessors; in the later stage, the need to make the manner of intellectual cognition in this life less distant from that in the life to come than Aquinas had posited it. Like St Thomas himself, but in a different way, Henry was led by his function as a theologian not so much to adapt Aristotle's view of the intellect as to re-think it.

10 *Duns Scotus: intuition and memory*

Scotus and Scotism

Duns Scotus did not enjoy a long life (he was born around 1265 and died in 1308), and his thought must be gathered from few, though lengthy, works of certain authenticity. Scotus *read* the *Sentences* in Oxford, Cambridge and Paris: the *ordinatio* (O) of his commentary which he prepared and revised is of the greatest importance in understanding his thought. *Reportationes* from one or another of these *readings* are also available for parts of the work: less reliable than the *ordinatio*, they can give an idea of the way in which Scotus developed his thought. A set of quodlibets (Q) from late in his career provide a clear and concise guide to his views, whilst the aptly-titled *Quaestiones Subtilissimae* on the *Metaphysics* (M) are a difficult though reliable source. Many Scotists have been led to misrepresent Scotus by a number of inauthentic or doubtful works traditionally attributed to him, such as a commentary on the *De Anima*, which contains a doctrine of the soul very different from that found in his certain writings, and a treatise *De Rerum Principio*, now known to be by Vitalis of Furno.

But Scotism is also untrue to Scotus in a more fundamental way. Even less than that of other great medieval thinkers is Scotus's thought adequately represented as a system – a set of conclusions which can be summarized and learnt apart from the context of argument in which they arise. Scotus worked at a time when every intellectual issue was far more complicated by differing views than it had been even a few decades before in St Thomas's lifetime. His intellectual temperament was well suited to the situation. Scotus likes to consider an issue from every available point of view. He often develops arguments against his own view with great complexity – greater than that which their own advocates had used – and is concerned to explain exactly where they are wrong; and one of his favourite techniques is to refine a position, by argument and counter-argument and ever more careful definition of his terms – though often the position will not be the one which he will ultimately advocate. By eliminating their context and the work of conceptual analysis which lies behind them, a systematic summary of Scotus's conclusions will make them seem wilfully technical and elaborate, and quite removed from any problem a modern thinker might recognize. Scotus's strength lies in his hesitations, qualifications, even his apparent self-contradictions; here, rather than by the character of his fundamental positions, he emerges as an analytical thinker of rare ability and not merely the representative of confluent currents of thought or the founder of a school.

In order to give some idea of Scotus's way of thinking, this chapter will concentrate on just one aspect of his discussion of intellectual knowledge – his theory of intuitive cognition, and its connection with his analysis of memory. These topics fit into a wider examination of the intellect, in which he considers Henry of Ghent's arguments about intelligible species and rejects them. Here this wider context can only be very briefly sketched.

Intelligible species and the dignity of the soul

Scotus believes – with some justification (see above, pp.149–51) – that Henry of Ghent wished to eliminate intelligible species entirely from his account of intellectual cognition. In the first book of his *ordinatio* (3 pars 3.1), he examines very thoroughly Henry's arguments and the related ones of Godfrey of Fontaines. He does not agree that either thinker succeeds in showing that intellectual knowledge can be explained without positing intelligible species. Sensible images (*phantasmata*) alone are not adequate, he argues, to represent universality; but our intellect knows universals (nn. 352–365); and, if an object is merely present in a sensible image, then it is not thereby present to the intellect (nn. 366–9).

Henry and Godfrey were concerned, like many theologians at the end of the thirteenth century, to safeguard the dignity of the intellect: to show it as something which functions in itself, rather than just being acted upon by the world. Scotus shares this concern, but he thinks that it can be accommodated within a theory of intelligible species, once the respective parts played by the object and the intellect in an act of cognition are carefully examined (O 1,3 pars 2,2). To suggest that the object is the only cause of cognition would greatly vilify the intellect (n.488, cf. n.429). But if the intellect were the only cause, then there would be no reason why it should not always be actively thinking – and this is not so (n.489, cf. n.414). The intellect *and* the object together, therefore, form the cause of the knowledge which we gain (n.494). Two causes which produce a single effect can have various relations. They may each, singly, be capable – at least in their perfect form – of producing the effect (for instance, two men dragging a body); or they may both be necessary, but one has to be moved by the other (I can only hit a ball a long way if I use a stick, but the stick cannot act without me); or they may both be necessary, and both have some power to act by themselves, although one has the power to act more perfectly than the other (Duns Scotus gives the example of a mother and father producing a child) (nn.495–6). Since the intellect and the object, even if perfect, require each other for cognition, the relation cannot be of the first sort; and neither the intellect nor the object requires the other to be able to act, as in the second type of relation. And so the intellect and the object are related in the third way, as a father and a mother are in procreation (nn. 497–8). By this explanation, Scotus preserves much of the terminology and some of the concepts of the Aristotelian theory of knowledge, whilst propounding a very different view of the workings of the intellect from that of earlier thinkers, such as Aquinas.

Singulars, the formal distinction and intuitive cognition

(1) Intuition and the problem of the intellectual cognition of singulars

One feature of Aristotle's theory of intellectual knowledge had caused medieval thinkers disquiet longer standing and no less deep than its apparent threat to the dignity of the human soul. Aristotle had allowed intellectual knowledge to be of universals alone; but this view seems wrong on grounds both of experience and revelation. We think about particular things as well as universals; and Christians believe that blessedness in heaven will be the enjoyment of the intellectual vision of God – a singular not a universal (there are other theological reasons too: see above, pp.113–14). The objections on the grounds of experience might be met by developing Aristotle's own suggestions about the indirect intellectual cognition of singulars: many medieval thinkers choose this course (see above, pp.129–30, 152). But the theological objections were less easy to tackle, and they became particularly prominent from the end of the thirteenth century, when the interests of theologians began to centre on the nature of the intellect absolutely rather than its power as a faculty of the embodied human soul.

One way of solving the problem was to posit, in addition to ordinary intellectual knowledge of universals, a special type of intellectual knowledge of singulars. Henry of Ghent allowed the disembodied intellect – but not the intellect in this life – a vision of individuals (see above, pp. 150, 152). Scotus, too, distinguishes from ordinary universal knowledge a special sort of intellectual cognition, which he sometimes describes as being like vision and sometimes calls 'intuitive', using a word which had been applied previously to the soul's knowledge of its own acts by Matthew of Aquasparta and Vitalis of Furno. Scotus uses the distinction to solve a problem about the cognition of individuals which is similar to that faced by other thinkers: similar, but *not* the same.

(2) Formal distinctions and intellectual cognition

Scotus believes, like most of his contemporaries, that the world consists of singulars (individual things). The intellect, however, can make certain 'formal' distinctions – distinctions which are merely ones of reason in the objects of knowledge, although they are real in the intellect itself. It is thus possible formally to distinguish something's nature, its existence and its singularity. A thing's nature is the sort of thing it is (a man, a dog, a table); its existence is the fact that it is not just a possible but an actual entity; its singularity is the fact that it is not one and the same as any other thing of the same sort. Although in every case the thing which, along with the intellect, gives rise to a cognition will be a singular thing, each of its formally distinct aspects will need to be known in a different way.

A thing's nature is the object of ordinary, non-intuitive ('abstractive') intellectual cognition (at one point, indeed, Scotus calls it 'quidditative intellection' (M vii, 15 n.4)).

To know a thing's singularity would mean being able to distinguish that thing from another of the same species without any accidental differences (M vii, 15 n.5). A little reflection shows that this is not within man's power in this life. Suppose – to elaborate on Scotus's example – that I am shown two exactly similar objects, such as two brand new copies of the same book; and, whilst my back is turned, one of them is selected and presented to me: could I tell which? Surely not. A thing's singularity is not absolutely unknowable – it can certainly be grasped by an angel's intellect – but Scotus can without problem deny it to humans in this life (M vii, 15 nn.5–7; O iv, 45,3 n.21).

A thing's existence, however, raises for Scotus the same sort of problems as singulars do for some of his contemporaries. They would be inclined to ask how it is that we can know contingent statements to be true if we cannot have intellectual knowledge of singulars. Given Scotus's analysis, the problem becomes one of explaining how we know such statements to be true unless we can intellectually know things as existing. It seems undeniable, for instance, that I can judge the truth of the statement, 'There are now more than two chairs in my room', but I can only do this by knowing the chairs as existing here and now, not by knowledge of their nature. And there is also a problem for Scotus about the beatific vision, not because what is perceived is single, but because the way in which the blessed see God must be as existing, otherwise someone could be beatified by an object which did not exist (Q XIII n.8). It is to overcome such difficulties that Scotus distinguishes between intuitive and abstractive cognition.

(3) Intuitive and abstractive cognition in Scotus

Scotus makes his distinction clear by describing its more readily comprehensible parallel in sensible knowledge. There are two sorts of sensible cognition, he argues (Q XIII n.8): one which 'reaches the object in its own, actual existence' – as in the case of any sensation of something in the world (for instance, the sight of a patch of colour); another which is 'not of the existing object in itself – either because the object does not exist, or because at least that cognition is not of the object as it actually exists' (I can call up the image of a colour when it does not exist, just as when it does). 'A similar distinction,' Scotus adds, 'can be shown to exist in the case of intellectual cognition.' There are two ways in which the intellect can know a simple object (simple, as opposed to a statement or an argument): one – abstractive – is indifferent to the object's existence or non-existence, and to its presence or non-presence; the other – intuitive – is 'just of the present object as present and the existing object as existing' (*praecise sit obiecti praesentis ut praesentis et existentis ut existentis*) (Q VI nn. 7–8).

(4) Can our intellect cognize intuitively in this life?

There are a number of passages which suggest that Scotus (like Henry of Ghent: see above, p.152) intends to limit the enjoyment of intuitive intellectual knowledge to disembodied or incorporeal intellects. He says (Q VI, n.8) that, whereas we have frequent experience of abstractive intellectual cognition, our experience of intuitive intellectual knowledge lacks the same certainty; and he goes on to argue that intuitive knowledge is indeed within the absolute powers of the human intellect, because in glory we shall be equal to the angels. Very often the evidence used to show that the intellect can know intuitively does not relate to humans in this life: on one occasion, it refers to angels (Q vi n.8), on another to beatification (Q xiii n.8 – see above, p.159). And when reference is made – as it is in both these instances – to the nobility of the intellect, which should be able to do at least all that the senses can, there is no reason why this should apply to it in its embodied state. Moreover, intuitive intellectual knowledge is usually discussed in an overall context which is not that of human life on earth: the beatific vision (Q vi), angelic cognition (O ii,3,9 nn.6–7), Christ's knowledge (O iii,14,3 nn.4–9), knowledge and memory in disembodied souls (O iv,45,2–3 – but see below).

However, there are at least two passages where Scotus appears unmistakably to attribute intellectual intuition to humans in this life. In one (M vii,15, n.6) he refers to 'a type of knowledge which is called "vision", which can be of the existing nature without a vision of its singularity' (. . . *aliquam intellectionem, quae dicitur visio, quae potest esse naturae existentis sine visione singularitatis . . .*), and then adds that this type of knowledge must be posited 'otherwise there could be no memory in the intellect of what is past, for that is only of what has been the subject of intellectual "vision" '. The second passage (O iv,45,3 n.17) is more detailed. Scotus begins by 'supposing' that the intellect can 'intuitively know what the senses know – because a more perfect and higher cognitive faculty in the same thing knows what the inferior does – and also that it knows sensations (*sensationes*)'. He continues:-

> Both are proved by the fact that [the intellect] knows true
> contingent propositions, and syllogizes from them. For it is the
> property of the intellect to form propositions and make
> syllogisms; but their truth is about objects as known intuitively,
> that is according to their existence, in the same way as they are
> known by the senses (*sub ratione scilicet existentiae, sub qua
> cognoscuntur a sensu*).

Both these passages are concerned with memory: the first of them refers to it explicitly, the second forms part of an extended discussion of the subject. By examining Scotus's complex theory of memory it is possible better to understand the sense and reasoning which underlies his apparently conflicting pronouncements on intuitive knowledge in the embodied intellect. But Scotus's approach to the concept of memory is itself explicable only in the light of ancient and previous medieval treatment.

Memory

(1) Aristotle's *De Memoria et Reminiscentia* and Aquinas's commentary

When later medieval scholars discussed memory they often turned to the brief treatise Aristotle had dedicated to the subject, *De Memoria et Reminiscentia*. Aristotle begins by trying to distinguish remembering from other sorts of cognitive activity. Memory, he says, is only of what is past (449b15). He goes on to explain that, in remembering something, it is not enough just to call to mind the thing remembered, we must also perceive that we saw or heard or learned the thing at some previous time (450a19–21, cf. 449b20–23). For Aristotle, then, the mere exercise of habitual knowledge does not constitute remembering. If, when I see a Latin word I write down its English equivalent, which I know, I am not engaged in remembering, but simply knowing, unless I am also aware that at sometime in the past I learnt the meaning of this Latin word. Aristotle does not elaborate on the nature of this awareness, but he seems to envisage just a general perception that one is exercising knowledge previously acquired. I am not, for example, required to call to mind the exact time and circumstances under which I first learnt the Latin word, merely to be conscious of having learnt it in the past. Aristotle believes (cf.449b30–450a21) that this awareness belongs to the sensitive faculty, not the intellect: some animals without intellect nonetheless have memory, and to perceive time involves the use of a mental picture (*phantasma*), which will belong to the imagination. When objects of intellectual knowledge are remembered, it is the *phantasmata* which accompany them – as they must accompany all thought – which allow them to be memories, since they permit the awareness of the time-lapse between the original learning and the present thought. Memory, therefore, may belong accidentally to the intellect, but primarily it is a function of the sensitive faculty (450a13–15).

When Aristotle says, then, that memory is of the past, he may simply be referring to the concomitant awareness of having thought, learned or sensed something previously. In his commentary on the *De Memoria et Reminiscentia*, Aquinas interpreted him in this way. 'It is not the Philosopher's intention,' he explains, 'to say that memory cannot be of things in the present, but only of those which have been in the past. . . . but to say that memory is of past things so far as our apprehension is concerned (*quantum ad nostram apprehensionem*), that is, that we previously sensed or thought – no matter whether the things considered in themselves are present or not' (I, n11). Nevertheless, some statements in Aristotle's treatise suggest that he did require the object of memory itself to be past, even though this position would hardly be compatible with his view that objects of mathematical and scientific knowledge – which are neither past, present nor future – can be remembered (452a3, 451a29). Some modern commentators have interpreted Aristotle in this way; and, although Aquinas did not, he recognizes a strict concept of memory in which the object remembered must itself be past.

(2) Aquinas on memory in the *Summa Theologiae*

For medieval scholars, it was particularly important to consider whether memory belongs to the intellect. A disembodied soul retains only its intellectual faculties. If, then, souls in the after-life are to have any memory of what they knew or sensed on earth, it will have to be intellectual. In this treatment of the topic in his *Summa Theologiae* (1,79,6), Aquinas is mainly concerned to contrast two concepts of memory, one looser and one stricter than that he would expound in his commentary on Aristotle. Memory in a weak sense means preserving the species of things which are not being apprehended in act (for example, someone could be said to have an intellectual memory of horse if he were able to call to mind the intelligible species of horse in the absence of any real horse). Aquinas believes that in this sense the intellect certainly has memory. He has to defend this view, which he plausibly considers Aristotle to have shared, against Avicenna, for whom intelligible species were preserved only in the agent Intelligence (see above, pp. 104–6). In a strong sense, however, memory according to Aquinas must be of an object which is past, as past (*praeteritum ut praeteritum*). But only individuals are past (or present or future). And, although the intellect can only know the quiddity of man or horse through an individual man or horse, the quiddity itself is timeless. The intellect cannot therefore have memory in the strong sense. Aquinas is not perturbed by this conclusion, since he feels that he can meet his theological requirements by crediting separated souls with memory in the weak sense alone (ST 1,89,6; cf. quV 19,1).

However, these outlines of his argument do not represent all that

Aquinas had to say on the subject.In his reply to an objection (ST 1 79,6 ad2), he considers an intermediate concept of memory, which has a certain pastness but belongs to the intellect. If an act of sensible cognition is past, then so must its object be; but even though the object of an act of intellectual cognition is timeless, the act itself takes place at a given moment. Since the intellect can know its own acts (*intelligit suum intelligere*), it can remember, for instance, its thinking yesterday of the quiddity of man; and so there will be pastness in this memory in respect of the act remembered though not the object remembered. Here Aquinas's train of reasoning is close to that which he would draw from the *De Memoria et Reminiscentia* but differs from it in an important way. For Aristotle's general awareness that one has already thought something, Aquinas substitutes thinking of another *particular* act of thought. He is therefore able to argue that, in this intermediate sense, memory does belong to the intellect.

(3) Scotus on memory

Duns Scotus's discussion of memory is found in two questions of his *Ordinatio* (IV, 45,1/3). Both deal primarily with memory in separated souls, but in the second Scotus enters into a thorough analysis of memory in general. The first question asks whether separated souls can bring to mind the quiddities which they knew (habitually) when embodied. This is a query about memory in Aquinas's weak sense; and Scotus has no hesitation at all in allowing it to the intellect. Granted that there are intelligible species (a point he has already argued – see above, pp. 155–6), there is no reason why the soul cannot retain them or why disjunction from the body should interfere with this. The second question asks whether separated souls can remember past things which they knew when joined to their bodies. When Scotus explains what he means here by 'remember', his way of thinking derives from the *De Memoria et Reminiscentia* and, even more closely, from Aquinas's intermediate concept of memory; but he proposes a more special-ized view of what it is to remember than either Aristotle or Aquinas.

According to Scotus (n.6), an act of memory must have two objects: the proximate object is one of the rememberer's own sensible or intellectual acts (such as seeing, hearing, thinking, learning, wishing); the remote object is the object of this original act (what he saw or heard or thought at the time). The remote object cannot itself be present in the act of memory and yet, when it is recalled, it must be in some way present; and so, Scotus argues, it must be present as a species (n.5). This species is imprinted, he says, by the act of perception, which is the proximate object of a memory (n.6). An example of memory for Scotus is 'I remember my past seeing/knowing that you were sitting down' (n.4). (The Latin – *recordor me vidisse vel nosse te sedisse* – should be translated in this way to show that it is the act of seeing or knowing which is remembered as proximate object). Various types of memory in a wider, and more usual, sense of the word would not come within his concept of it: for instance, 'I remember that face', 'I remember that the Battle of Hastings took place in 1066', 'I remember that you saw him sitting down'.

(i) Sensitive memory, phantasmata and recollection
Scotus asks of his specialized concept of memory, first, whether it can belong to the sensitive faculty and, second, whether it can belong to the intellect. The first question turns out to be the less interesting, but it is handled with characteristic thoroughness. Scotus sets out a series of arguments to show that there is no memory in the senses (nn.7–11) and then 'in accord with Aristotle's views' he answers them (n.12). He proceeds to a lengthy preliminary investigation of the possibility of intellectual memory, setting out authoritative positions for and against it (nn. 13–14) and then providing his own suggestions about how to interpret these pronouncements, without as yet giving his own final view (nn.15–16). He has two main concerns in this section. First – in a manner close to Aquinas in the *Summa Theologiae* – he makes it clear that intellectual memory need not have a past remote object, although its proximate object must be past (cf. also n.18). Second, he refutes the argument that, because memory, in Aristotle's view, involves sensible images (*phantasmata*), it cannot belong to the intellect: Aristotle, he replies, says that all thought requires sensible images, but that is not a reason for denying that thinking takes place in the intellect.

Scotus elaborates on the role of images in his discussion of recollection (*reminiscentia* – cf. also nn.13–14, 18). When I remember something, I bring it back into my mind without effort; recollection, for Scotus, is remembering which requires mental discourse or some external stimulus before the thing remembered can be successfully brought to mind. For example, I may have forgotten what someone looks like, but recognize him when I see him again; or I might be able to recollect what a particular painting looks like by picturing where it hangs in a gallery, or remember a particular argument by recalling those which I read in the same book. In recollection there must be an element of discontinuity as well as one of continuity; continuity to make recovery possible, discontinuity to make it a matter of effort or outside stimulus. According to Scotus, the intellect is an immaterial and immutable faculty and so, when an intelligible species is imprinted in it, it will remain there indelibly. In recollection, therefore, an intelligible species can only provide the element of continuity; and so it will be the *phantasma* which is lost and then recovered.

(ii) Intellectual memory: the problem of interpreting Scotus
Scotus begins the exposition of his theory of intellectual memory by declaring that the intellect does indeed possess memory, granted that it can know intuitively as well as abstractively. There follows the passage already quoted (see above, p.159), which is Scotus's most explicit defence of intuitive cognition in the embodied intellect. On the basis of it and what Scotus has said earlier in the *quaestio*, it might be expected that he would go on to propose the following theory: 'A memory is produced by a species which its proximate object, an act of cognition, leaves. Sensible memory must be the result of a sensible species; intellectual memory the result of an intelligible species. If there is to be intellectual memory of the past – which must therefore be of particular things as existing (not as natures) – this can only be the result of an intuitive intellectual cognition of them. Scotus refers (n.20) to 'an intuitive [intellectual] cognition which accompanies every perfect sensitive one'. He must, therefore, think that every time the senses perceive something which exists and is present, the intellect also cognizes it intuitively. The intuitive act of knowing leaves an intelligible species which is the basis for the intellectual memory. Whatever we sense we also intuitively cognize in the intellect.'

This interpretation is plausible and attractive, and it has been developed with skill and subtlety by Father Bérubé, the most detailed and sophisticated expositor of Scotus's theory of intuition. But it does not seem reconcileable with what Scotus actually goes on to say about the way in which intuition is used in memory. Scotus's view of intuition is nearer to that of predecessors like Matthew of Aquasparta and Vitalis of Furno than Bérubé allows, but worked out in connection with memory with even greater subtlety than he suggests. The intellect, Scotus writes, can cognize (and the context makes it clear that he means: intuitively cognize) the proximate act of the sensible memory and remember it after it has passed; it can also remember many proximate objects which the sensible memory cannot – every past wish and thought (*intellectio*). Scotus goes on to comment that some memories are proper to the intellect, not only by virtue of their proximate object (as in the case of wishes and thoughts in general), but by virtue of their remote object too, when this is a fact of the sort expressed by a necessary proposition (for instance, 'I remember my past learning that a triangle has three sides'). There is, he adds (n.18), another category of memory, which by virtue of its proximate object belongs to the intellect but can also belong to the senses:-

> For instance, if the intellect intuitively knows that I am seeing a white thing, then afterwards the intellect remembers my past seeing a white thing. This proximate object and this remote one can indeed be the object not just of sensible but also intellectual memory, and they are, whenever from such a memory a proposition is drawn (*fit collatio ex tali recordatione*) which leads, by syllogistic argument, to something else.

Intuitive intellectual cognition is indeed central to Scotus's theory of the memory: but its role is to know the proximate object of a memory – the rememberer's sensible or intellectual act – not the remote object. It now becomes clear exactly what Scotus meant when he talked about the imprinted species which memory requires. He was careful to emphasize that it was the proximate object, not the remote object, which effected this imprint: the species by which I know something is not the same as that which I need to remember my act of knowing it. The species, he said (n.6), is imprinted by the proximate object when it is present and in act: it could not be imprinted by an object 'when it does not exist (*quando non est*) or when it is not present in itself'. The conditions under which the proximate object imprints its species are, then, the conditions of intuitive cognition – presence and existence. An act of intuitive cognition imprints the species necessary for memory or – to put it in a way which follows more closely Scotus's path of reasoning – it is because we remember past acts and need species to do so that we can be sure of our power to know intuitively, since only such cognition would produce the necessary species. When the proximate object is an act of the intellect, our intellect intuitively knows it and effects an intelligible species; when the proximate object is an act of the senses, our senses intuitively know it and effect a sensible species, but our intellect also intuitively knows it and effects an intelligible species. The acts of our senses are as present to our intellects as to our senses themselves.

(iii) Intellectual memory: clarification and summary of Scotus's theory
Scotus ends his account of the types of intellectual memory by
noting three restrictions to the concept: (1) the intellect does not
have memory in so far as it merely knows abstractively; (2)
intellectual memory does not require the remote object to be past as
well as the proximate one; (3) the intellect is not 'primarily and at
root' (*primarie et radicaliter*) sufficient for remembering.

Each of these resumes or clarifies a point which he has already
suggested:

(1) Memory must have an act of the rememberer's senses or
intellect as its proximate object: the intellect cognizes this act
intuitively. Even, then, if the proximate object of a memory is itself
an act of abstractive cognition, it must be intuitively known in
order to be remembered. If I simply call to mind the fact that a
triangle has three sides, that is not in Scotus's view remembering; if
I remember my past learning that a triangle has three sides, this is
because I intuitively cognized my original act of learning.

(2) Scotus is willing to say, 'I *remember* my past learning that a
triangle has three sides', although the remote object of this memory
is not in the past. Some sorts of intellectual memories do have
proximate and remote objects which are past: intuitively I knew
that I was seeing that white thing (which is now destroyed), and so
I can remember intellectually my past seeing it.

(3) Scotus has already said (n. 16) that 'so far as its primacy or
root (*quantum ad primitatem vel radicem*), or sufficiency to come to act
from itself, memory in us is not just in our intellect but also in our
senses'. His point there, which is now reiterated, is that intellectual
memory, like all human thought, requires sensible images. Just as I
cannot think that a triangle has three sides without using *phantasmata*, so I cannot remember my having thought it without *phantasmata*. Scotus goes on to stress the part of sensible images in
memory when he answers his original question, which was about
memory in disembodied souls. He accepts (n. 20) that 'the species
in the intellectual memory alone is not sufficient to allow the
embodied soul to remember something'. But in a disembodied
state the powers of our soul will be differently ordered and then –
only then – will they be able to think, and so to remember
intellectually, without *phantasmata*.

All that Scotus says about sensible and intellectual memory and
recollection – the need for species, for intuitive cognition and for
phantasmata – can be put together to form a complicated but
coherent scheme.

Table 6 **Scotus's analysis of memory**

	Remote object	Proximate object	Type of species needed	Also needed
A Sensible memory	A material thing (this book)	My past sensing of the thing (my past seeing this book)	Sensible (from sensible intuition of proximate object)	–
B Intellectual memory of a thing in embodied soul	A material thing (this book)	My past sensing of the thing (my past seeing this book)	Intelligible (from intellectual intuition of proximate object)	Sensible species [in RECOLLECTION this is found only with effort or by stimulus]
C Intellectual memory of facts etc. in embodied soul	A fact, a desired state of affairs, a quiddity (a triangle has three sides)	My past intellectual act with regard to the remote object (my past learning that a triangle has three sides)	Intelligible (from intellectual intuition of proximate object)	Sensible species [*as above* for RECOLLECTION]
D/E Intellectual memory of things/ facts etc. in disembodied soul	EXACTLY AS IN B/C EXCEPT NO SENSIBLE SPECIES REQUIRED			

Scotus's concept of memory might be criticized for being too narrow. Certainly, there are many aspects of what is normally called memory which he does not deal with in this discussion, because he would regard them as belonging to habitual knowledge. But Scotus has analysed a concept which it is not hard to recognize as distinctive and interesting. Memory in his sense plays an important role, not equalled by habitual knowledge, in establishing the different identities of persons. If one of the things which makes me the person I am is the knowledge which, in general, I can call upon, the part of this knowledge which concerns my own past acts is specially pertinent: both memory of my past thoughts, wishes, hopes, doubts and so on, and memory of where, when and how I gained a piece of knowledge which, in itself, is common to many. We might well say that a man who retained all his habitual knowledge but lost entirely his memory of the past, in Scotus's sense, 'had lost his identity'. We would be speaking metaphorically, since we would recognize a physical continuity between the man in the past and the man now. But when Scotus broached the subject of memory he was concerned with the ability of disembodied souls to retain the memories they had collected before death. Behind this question there is a theological problem of fundamental importance. In what sense is the disembodied soul the same as the soul in the living man, when its powers are so different? If it is true that I will live after death, then when I die a disembodied soul must be *mine*. Scotus's theory of memory shows one way in which this difficult area might be grasped.

Scotus's theory of intuitive knowledge in the light of his theory of memory

Scotus's theory of memory also suggests how he envisaged intuitive intellectual knowledge and why some of his pronouncements on it seem to disagree with one another. Each aspect of a thing – its nature, its existence, its singularity – must, he thinks, absolutely be knowable. Our ordinary intellectual knowledge, which we are in no doubt of having, is of natures; singularity is not known in this life. Existence is known by the senses; it also must be known at least by disembodied intellects; and it seems as though it must be known by our intellects in this life, or we could not know the truth of contingent propositions. But how can our intellects know existence, when they cannot be moved directly by what is outside them but only through intelligible species? The analysis of memory provides the answer. There are theological and experiential grounds for believing that our intellect cognizes intuitively the acts of our senses: if this were not so, then disembodied souls could not remember their sensible acts whilst alive, nor could anyone think about the past sensible acts he remembers. If our intellects know the acts of our senses as present and existing, then they also know about what our senses apprehend as present and existing. The intellectual grasp of contingent facts which is explained in this way may seem to be indirect; but how could it be conceived more directly? When Scotus talks of knowing (abstractively) the nature of a thing, he means knowing what sort of thing it is. When he talks of knowing (intuitively) the existence of a thing, he means knowing that it exists and is present here and now. It would be unhelpfully mystifying to suggest that the embodied human intellect could, without the senses, gain such knowledge; its immediate cognition of the act of sensible perception, as existing and present, provides the certainty which Scotus never called into question but constantly strived to explain.

Conclusion

Duns Scotus's theory of memory and intuitive knowledge presents, in a particularly striking way, an important feature of much later medieval theology: it cannot be understood apart from the specifically theological questions which it is designed to tackle, yet it also analyses concepts which modern philosophers will recognize as important and difficult. Scotus's dissatisfaction with the Aristotelian view of intellectual knowledge is provoked both by problems (of concern only to a theologian) about memory in disembodied souls, and the problems about cognition and memory in humans in this life. Scotus differs from Aristotle by recognizing the great importance of the mind's ability to know and remember both its own acts and those of the senses. Even our knowledge of logical and mathematical truths or of truths beyond our own experience has a history, since there was a moment when we acquired that knowledge – a moment which we may even remember. Scotus's discussion of memory and intuition involves a reconsideration of personal individuality and identity which, alone, is enough to suggest that Scotus's celebrated 'subtlety' is not a euphemism for triviality or muddle-headedness.

11 *William of Ockham*

Ockham the innovator

William of Ockham's career is divided in two by his flight from Avignon to Munich in 1328, in the company of Michael of Cesena, Minister General of the Franciscan order, to which he belonged. From then until his death, probably in 1349, he mainly devoted himself to political writing directed against the papacy on behalf of the imperial cause. Up until the time he was summoned to Avignon in 1324 and perhaps during his years there, William had pursued the career of a theologian. He lectured on the *Sentences* in Oxford between 1317 and 1319 and then went to teach at the *studium generale* in London, without incepting as a master (see above, p.24). His commentary on the first book of the *Sentences* exists in an *ordinatio* (O) which he probably compiled while he was in London; that on the other three is preserved in a *reportatio* (R). These texts contain the most comprehensive exposition of William's ideas, but they are complemented by some slightly later writings, all of them from before 1328: among them, commentaries on Porphyry's *Isagoge*, Aristotle's *De Interpretatione* (H) and *Physics*, a set of quodlibets (Q) and a full, mature exposition of his logic, the *Summa Totius Logicae* (SL) (although doubts about the authenticity of the quodlibets and the *Summa* have recently been expressed by some scholars).

Ockham was an innovator. Whereas Scotus proposed original solutions to his problems without fundamentally altering the conceptual framework he inherited, Ockham rejected many assumptions which had been shared for a century and a half. Although he was careful to record and examine the views of his predecessors, he often found their shortcomings such that they could not be maintained by piecemeal revision. Rather, he decided to examine the basic problems afresh, approaching them from different directions and elaborating a new set of concepts and terms for them. Ockham's original thought in one area is often inextricably linked to his reasoning on different but related topics. His theory of intellectual cognition is a case in point.

As the preceding chapters have illustrated, his predecessors each held different views on intellectual cognition; but with the possible exception of William of Auvergne's, they all have more in common with one another than with Ockham's. All are versions – though much modified and much extended – of the Aristotelian view; Ockham's, despite incidental debts, is not. His rejection of the Aristotelian theory is intimately connected with his views on universals, and it would be inexplicable without reference to them. This might seem to lend credence to the approach of some expositors, which makes Ockham's anti-realism the source of all his other novel positions. But thinkers do not, as a rule, formulate a position on one issue in isolation and then base on it all that is distinctive in their reasoning. Especially if, like Ockham, they are radically reformulating accepted problems and solutions, they try to develop a coherent view on different but related topics. Ockham's theory of knowledge does, indeed, make sense only in the light of an anti-realist rejection of the way in which the mind and the world outside had previously been held to be related. But his anti-realism would be untenable were it not complemented by a theory of knowledge which establishes a new set of relations between the world and the language of the mind. It is for convenience of exposition, rather than as a reflection of an essential priority, that this chapter will begin by considering Ockham's negative views – his refusal to accept that universals are based in reality and the consequent attack on the Aristotelian notion of intelligible species – and then go on to his own constructive discussion of intellectual cognition.

Ockham on universals and intelligible species

(1) What was Ockham's anti-realism?

Ockham argues that every thing in the world is singular, and only mental concepts or words can be universal. In doing so he is often described as breaking with the realism of all his thirteenth and early fourteenth-century predecessors. But this description, although not in itself wrong, can easily mislead about the nature of Ockham's differences with thinkers such as Aquinas and Scotus. The most unambiguously realistic position is Platonic realism, which holds that universals really exist in separation from individual things. In the later Middle Ages this view was widely believed to be contrary to both faith and reason: Ockham does not even trouble to attack it in his extended discussion of universals (O 1,2). Another, more qualified realist position is known as 'essential essence realism'. According to this theory, the species exists in each of its individual members, which are numerically differentiated by their accidents (cf. above, pp. 36–7). Ockham does indeed set out and then reject this view (O 1,2,4), but to do so he elaborates in an unusually sustained and thorough way a traditional line of attack, which would have been accepted by most other thirteenth- and early fourteenth-century thinkers. Ockham's most distinguished predecessors may in some sense have been realists, but only in a sophisticated and highly qualified way. The difference between Ockham's position and theirs is best captured by the final question Ockham poses on universals. Is the universal in any way based on any thing (*a parte rei*) outside the soul? (O 1,2,7). They would have answered 'yes'; he argues 'no'.

It is not immediately obvious how to understand the difference represented by these replies. If Ockham's opponents are said to hold, unlike him, that the universal exists within individuals, then how is their view supposed to differ from essential essence realism, which they agreed with him in rejecting? If Ockham is thought to believe that there is no basis in reality for considering anything a member of one species rather than another – that when I call Socrates a man and Fido a dog I am expressing truths only about the contents of my mind and not at all about the world – then his position seems completely inadequate to explain human discourse. Rather, the difference between Ockham and his predecessors is about the basis of the very system of species and genera. For both it is a conceptual system for understanding the world; but for Ockham it is merely a possible system, for the others it is a system which must be used to obtain a full understanding of reality. Ockham's predecessors believe that things in the world are such that, if they are to be properly described, they must be classified into species and genera; whereas Ockham believes that the human mind is such that it can classify individuals into species and genera. The two positions are similar, in a more limited field, to two contrasting views held by modern philosophers (though there are some important differences – see below, pp. 181–2). Modern realists believe that the underlying structure of human language is in some way determined by the underlying structure of reality; anti-realists argue that, on the contrary, it is human language which provides the ultimate structures for the reality it describes. Realists and anti-realists agree, nevertheless, that, once accepted, a human language can be used to talk about the world: many statements are true or false because of the nature of things outside the mind. Similarly, Ockham and his opponents would agree that, granted the conceptual apparatus of genera and species, it is a fact about the world, and not just about the mind, that Fido is a dog and Socrates a man.

(2) Ockham's views on distinctions

Ockham proposes his own position on universals only after giving detailed arguments to show that those of his predecessors are wrong. The basis of his attack on their sophisticated and highly qualified realism is his view of distinctions. His opponents proposed their sophisticated realism by using various types of distinction. By limiting the types of distinction which could meaningfully be made, Ockham made it impossible for their positions to be stated without self-contradiction. Ockham believed that two things could be distinct as things, 'really' distinct (or really identical, in which case they would be not two things, but the same one); and, similarly, that two mental concepts (*rationes*) could be distinct by reason (or not, and so be one concept); and that a thing is distinct from a mental concept (O 1,2,3; p. 78:4–16). He would not accept that one thing could be distinguished by reason, rather than really, from another thing; nor would he accept a refinement of this view, which posits between two things, not a distinction of reason but a 'formal' distinction.

(i) Arguments against the distinction of things by reason
When a thing is described as different by reason from itself or from something else, what – asks Ockham – is meant? There seem to be just two possible meanings. The first (pp.75: 12ff.) is that diverse mental concepts (*rationes*) have been constructed in connection with the thing or things. For instance, if John is a married philosopher, I might entertain in connection with him the concept of philosopher and the concept of married man. Could I not then say that John the philosopher is distinguished by reason from John the married man? Ockham would not agree that I could. The intellect, he would argue, does indeed fabricate various different concepts, such as 'married man' and 'philosopher', which differ from each other not as things – because they are concepts – but by reason. And a combined concept-and-thing (for instance, the concept 'married

man' + the thing, John) can be said to differ 'in some way by reason' from the same thing combined with a different concept (for instance, the concept 'philosopher' + the thing, John). But we do not need to say that a *thing* can differ by reason from itself or from something else according to this interpretation of the distinction.

A different interpretation of the distinction is possible: it might mean (pp.76:18ff) that the same thing is conceived by the intellect in two different ways. But what does this interpretation amount to? Either it is the same as the first interpretation (I can form the conceptions philosopher and married man in connection with John); or it means that the thing is the same but the ways of conceiving it are many (I can accurately describe John as a philosopher, a married man, a taxpayer) – in which any distinction is limited to the ways of conceiving; or it means that thing is really multiple – in which case there are two different things, distinguished in reality and not just by reason.

(ii) Arguments against formal distinctions
Anticipating the type of objection which Ockham would make, Scotus and his followers had introduced another type of distinction, which they called 'formal' (see above, pp.157–8). Where the intellect can distinguish two things which are not distinct as things – such as an object's nature and its existence or singularity – then the mental concepts are distinct and the things themselves are *formally* distinct. A formal distinction is neither real nor of reason, but just what distingushes two really identical things which can be differently conceived by the intellect. Ockham's argument against distinctions of reason in things would not, therefore, apply to it. Ockham must therefore show that the notion of formal distinction is itself incoherent. He does so (O 1,2,1. pp.14:8ff) by a syllogistic argument which he considers equally valid against the notion of formal distinction wherever it is posited:

Major premiss: It is possible to affirm contradictory things of whatever are in any way distinct or non-identical: that is to say, if *a* and *b* are in any way distinct, then there must be at least two predicates *x* and *y* such that it is true that *a* is *x* and *b* is *y* but it is impossible that anything could be both *x* and *y*. (For instance, if the blue book on my desk and the book I was given for Christmas are not one and the same, then I must be able to find at least one true description of one which is incompatible with at least one true description of the other: such as that the blue book has two hundred pages, whilst my Christmas present has more than three hundred).

Minor premiss: Contradictory things can only be affirmed of

distinct things (in the world), or distinct mental concepts (*rationes* –
entities in the mind), or of a thing and a mental concept.

Ockham proves the major premiss by a purely logical deduction.
To say that *a* and *b* are in some way not identical means that *a* is not
the same as *b* in every way. But *a* is the same as *a* in every way.
'The same as *a*' and 'Not the same as *a*' are contradictory predicates
and, as shown, the former can be asserted of *a* and the latter of *b*.
Ockham argues the minor premiss by pointing out that all contradictories have equal repugnancy to one another. By this he means
that it is equally true that 'a man is not not-a-man' as that, for
instance, 'God is not not-God'. If, then, it can be shown with
regard to one pair of contradictories that they can only be affirmed
of distinct things, distinct mental concepts or of a thing and a
concept, then this must be true of every pair of contradictories.
And it can indeed be shown, Ockham continues, with regard to the
contradictories 'is' and 'is not': if *a* is and *b* is not, then *a* and *b* must
be distinct things, or distinct mental concepts or a thing and a
mental concept.

Ockham's strategy, in this drawn-out reasoning, is to analyse
identity and difference in terms of contradiction and non-
contradiction. The proponents of the formal distinction are as sure
as Ockham that a proposition which asserts a contradiction is not
true, and Ockham wishes to show that their position leads logically
to conclusions which they themselves would recognize as false. In
this way he makes evident the incoherence of the notion of formal
distinctions. Another, simpler way of showing this is to point to
one of its consequences. It makes it impossible ever to demonstrate
real differences between things: suppose I argue that a man and an
ass are really distinct, because the former is rational and the latter
not, someone could always reply that the conclusion does not
follow, since a formal distinction would be sufficient. The only
case in which Ockham thinks that it makes sense to talk of a formal
distinction is in discussing God (pp. 19:3ff): the persons of the
Trinity are formally distinct because each is really the same and yet
really different, because God – unlike any created thing – 'is many
things really distinct and each of them'.

(3) Ockham's attack on sophisticated realism

Ockham is now in a position to state his objections to the
sophisticated realism of his predecessors. First, he deals specifically
with Scotus's view, which depends on the notion of formal
distinction. According to Scotus, each thing has a nature, by which

it is the sort of thing it is. It is an individual thing by virtue of its singularity, which is formally but not really distinct from its nature. In itself the nature is neither singular nor universal (an Avicennian position), but it is universal in the intellect which knows it. Ockham (O 1,2,6) tackles this position by referring back to his general attack on the formal distinction (pp.173:11–177:8 – an additional discussion – 177:9 ff. – restates Ockham's refusal to allow the formal distinction to operate as its proponents intended, whilst allowing the distinction itself for the sake of argument).

In the next *quaestio* (O 1,2,7) Ockham tackles sophisticated realism more generally. He proposes two arguments, each related to his view of distinctions, against the position that species are in any way based on any thing outside the soul. The first (pp.235:16–236:9) starts from the fact, admitted by all, that universality and singularity are opposites and so what is singular and what is universal must be distinct. In what way distinct? Formal distinction has been rejected; and Ockham has already been shown that they are not distinguished as thing and thing. They must therefore be distinguished as concept and thing. But the singular is not (just) a concept and so the universal must be. The second argument (pp.236:9ff.) puts the same point more simply from a different angle. In the light of Ockham's views about the formal distinction, the only way to avoid essential essence realism yet base the universal on things will be to hold that the univeral and the singular are really the same. But they cannot be, since the universal is predicable of many and the singular is not.

Ockham's view about ideas in the mind of God is connected with his anti-realism, but as a consequence rather than a cause. Medieval theologians had commonly held (for example, cf. Aquinas ST 1,15,1–3; and above, pp.77, 146) that in God's mind there were exemplary ideas of all things. But they were careful to stress (cf. Aquinas ST 1,15,3 ad4; 1,22,2) that these were not just ideas of species but also of individuals: it is a consequence of God's supreme power that his providence must extend to every single thing. Positing ideas in the divine mind did not, therefore, entail the modified Platonism which it had done for some of its early proponents. It allowed for universals merely the basis in reality which they were otherwise conceded. Ockham (O 1,35,5) allows that there are ideas in God's mind but argues that they are there only 'objectively': the ideas are none other than the things themselves which God knows. Since Ockham has elsewhere established that every thing is singular, it follows that there can be no universal ideas in God's mind. However, a human craftsman is capable of having a universal concept in his mind of something he is making (an architect, for instance, has a general notion of a house) and God can know whatever is known by a created intellect. Ockham is therefore willing to allow that, as well as ideas for particular things in God's mind (which are the things themselves), there are ideas of more than one thing, universal ideas, but these are not in God's mind but in the minds of created artificers, such as humans, although God can indeed know them (pp.505:19–506:24).

(4) Ockham's attack on the concept of impressed intelligible species

In the light of Ockham's anti-realism, the notion of (impressed) intelligible species is unacceptable. Intelligible species are universal, as opposed to sensible species which are particular. Their universality does not itself cause problems from Ockham's point of view, since Ockham is perfectly willing to accept that a mental concept can be universal. But intelligible species in the Aristotelian theory are not merely any sort of universal mental concept, but those which are impressed by the things cognized: they are distinguished from the definition or 'word' or expressed intelligible species which the mind itself produces to complete its cognitive act. They must therefore be impressed by the things in their aspect of universality; but if the things themselves, as things, are in absolutely no way universal, how can they impress a universal species?

Ockham works out these consequences with regard to a position like that of St Thomas (O 1,3,6, esp. pp.488:17–489:20). In order to allow intellectual knowledge to be about things and not just about our minds, Aquinas had argued that the intelligible species is not that which is known, but that by which it is known. That which is known by the intellect is not the individual, but the universal abstracted from the individual (an *abstractum*, as Ockham calls it). In Ockham's view, however, this distinction cannot be maintained. Both the *abstractum* and the intelligible species must be mental concepts because, if the *abstractum* were a real thing, it could not be universal; and like the intelligible species, the *abstractum* must precede the act of knowing, since it is its object. How, then, are the two different? Those who hold that the intelligible species 'represents' the abstracted universal, Ockham continues, would have by the same token to hold that a sensible species will also represent the universal. Given that there is nothing universal about things themselves, representing the universal can only mean being exactly like similar individuals, and so would be the sensible species of one of them. It does no good to suggest that the sensible species is like just one of the individuals, but the intelligible species is like all of them: so long as the individuals are exactly the same, whatever is like one must be equally like the others.

Once even sophisticated realism is dismissed, no amount of elaboration and qualification will save the now redundant apparatus of the Aristotelian theory of intellectual knowledge. Ockham can invoke the principle of parsimony which has become particularly associated with him (although it is in fact based on an Aristotelian maxim, widely known in the later Middle Ages): '. . . plurality is never to be posited except where necessary. But whatever can be explained by positing an [intelligible] species can equally well be explained without it. Such a species should not therefore be posited' (O 1,27,2 p.205:15–18; cf. R II, 12/13 p.256:7–9).

The language of the mind

For Ockham's Aristotelian predecessors, the relationship between the things and thoughts was causal. From things come (by way of *phantasmata* and abstraction) intelligible species, which inform and determine the potential intellect. The intellect is then able to produce its 'word' and form propositions about what it has cognized. This stage of the intellectual process is often described in terms of a mental language; but the relationship between this language and the world is not usually described in terms of signification or supposition: thought in mental language is about things in the world because, through the complicated apparatus of sensible and intelligible species, things in the world have caused the thoughts about them. (This is true even for thinkers who did not posit impressed intelligible species, like Henry of Ghent; for them the *phantasmata* perform the role of intelligible species.)

Ockham rejected this view of the relations between thoughts and things. By proposing an alternative, he is able to show how the Aristotelian system of intellectual cognition, incoherent in his opinion, is dispensable. And, in any case, the traditional view is incompatible with his anti-realism. We think about things universally as well as individually; but how can things, which are all singular and have nothing of universality about them, *cause* universal thoughts?

(1) Thoughts and things: Ockham's earlier theory

Early in his career, starting from a basis provided by scholars such as Henry of Harclay and Hervaeus Natalis, Ockham developed one alternative theory about the relations between thoughts and things, which he later put aside – not as necesarily wrong, but as less convincing than a new and simpler theory he had devised (cf. SL p.43:34–9). According to Ockham's earlier theory (H [Proem] 7/10; O 1,2,8) thoughts (*passiones animae* – the individual components from which a mental proposition is made) are related to things by a sort of representation: thoughts resemble the things they are thoughts of, and so they are able to stand for them. When the intellect thinks it makes what might be called images (*idola*) or fictive things (*ficta*), which are neither 'true qualities of the mind or things really existing subjectively in the mind, but only certain cognitions of the soul (*cognita ab anima*), such that their being is identical with their being thought of (*esse eorum non est aliud quam ipsa cognosci*)'. When the intellect apprehends an individual thing it makes a fictive thing which is like the real thing, but does not really exist anywhere. The fictive thing can supposit in a mental proposition for the real from which it is feigned and which it resembles. A fictive thing can also serve in a mental proposition when the object of thought is not an individual thing in the world, but what is common to a number of individual things – a universal. A fictive thing can be considered universal 'because it bears an equal relation (*respicit aequaliter*) to all the things from which it is abstracted by its manner of being formed or feigned'.

In his earlier theory, then, Ockham felt the need to posit some sort of mental entity to take the place of intelligible species and mental words in the Aristotelian account. The *ficta* are not, like intelligible species, caused by things in the world: the mind feigns them, but it must make them like the individual thing, or like what is common to a number of individual things, in order to stand for these in a mental proposition. As Ockham himself notes later (H 7; pp.360:30–361:45), it is hard to see exactly what these entities are, or in what way – as purely mental concepts – they could be like the things they supposedly represent. However, in the earlier theory there is already to be found the main feature of the later account: the use of supposition rather than a causal relation to link things with thoughts of them. Ockham's progress – spurred by the criticisms he received from his pupil, Chatton – consists in freeing it from unnecessary complications.

(2) Thoughts and things: Ockham's later theory

The *ficta*, Ockham had said, supposit in mental propositions for things in the world. Why not retain the notion of supposition, but do without the fictive things, feigned to resemble real ones? This is Ockham's approach in his later theory (H 6; cf. O 1,2,8 pp.289:11–292:2). Thoughts are simply acts of thinking (*actus intelligendi*): they therefore exist 'really and subjectively in the soul as true qualities of it' – a thought informs the mind in the same way as whiteness informs a white wall or heat informs fire. In spoken and written language there are some signs which, by convention, supposit for only one individual, such as 'Socrates'; and there are some which can supposit for many different individuals, such as 'man'. Similarly, Ockham argues, when the intellect apprehends an individual thing, it produces in itself a cognition which, by nature, supposits only for that individual thing; but the intellect can also have thoughts which supposit equally for all individuals of a certain class.

It might seem to follow from this that a mental proposition will be a series, or a simultaneous set, of acts of intellectual cognition. But, although Ockham considers the possibility that more than one act is involved in a mental proposition, he seems finally (H 6; pp.357:168–358:195) to prefer a different view. He distinguishes apprehending a proposition from knowing it (cf. below, pp. 182–3). To apprehend a proposition is simply to form it: apprehending it is not something we do to a mental proposition – it *is* the proposition (*actus apprehendi magis erit ipsa propositio quam ipsius propositionis*). The mental proposition 'man is an animal', Ockham continues, is 'the intellectual cognitive act (*actus intelligendi*) by which every man and also every animal is apprehended confusedly, and also that man and animal are the same in number, because the former is denoted by the latter'. Although more than one thing is thought of in this mental proposition, it is not therefore composite but a single intellectual act. Knowing a proposition, however, is a different act from apprehending it, but one which can occur simultaneously with it.

In presenting his later theory Ockham does occasionally talk of cognitions being like things in the world. For instance, he describes (H 6; p.355:89–95) the cognition by which all men are thought of confusedly as being 'by some sort of resemblance (*aliquo modo assimilationis*) more like a man than an ass, and not more like this man than that one'. But even here Ockham does not use the pictorial terminology of his earlier theory. In general, in his later theory, thought is presented as parallel with spoken and written language and its relations to the world are regarded in a similar way: 'for every word in spoken language (*vox significativa*) . . . a thought (*intellectio*) can or does correspond, which has naturally the same mode of signifying in respect of the same thing as the spoken utterance does by convention' (H 6, p.357:153–7).

(3) The relations between things, spoken language and mental language

In his *Summa Logicae* Ockham develops some consequences of this attitude to the relations between spoken language, thoughts and things. There was a long tradition, Ockham recognizes, according to which spoken words are the signs of thoughts. But Ockham insists (SL [1], 1), in line with his theory, that 'the spoken words are imposed to signify the same things as are signified by the mental concepts'; and he claims that the authorities, such as Aristotle, Augustine and Boethius, usually invoked to support the standard view, in fact held the same opinion as himself.

One of the complications of Ockham's view is that some thoughts will have to supposit, not for things at all, but for other thoughts. There is no problem about a mental proposition such as 'Socrates is a man'. Here, Ockham would say, both 'Socrates' and 'man' refer to Socrates; but 'Socrates' is a mental sign which can only refer to the one individual, Socrates, whereas 'man' is a mental sign which can refer to many men. Ockham's theory of second intentions (SL 12) is introduced to explain the supposition of more problematic mental propositions such as 'man is a species'. First intentions are mental terms (like 'Socrates' or 'man') which are used to signify things in the world; second intentions are mental terms which are used to signify other mental terms (like 'species' or 'differentia'). When we think 'man is a species', we are not thinking something about any real man or men, but about the mental term 'man': we are saying to ourselves that, unlike the mental term 'Socrates' it can supposit for many individuals, not just one.

As a logician, Ockham deals primarily with conventional spoken and written language, but he needs to discuss it in terms which take account of his view of its relations to mental language. He classifies spoken and written nouns in two ways: as terms of first and second imposition, and as names (*nomina*) of first and second intention. Spoken/written terms of second imposition (SL 11–12) are those which signify other spoken/written terms; the rest are of the first imposition. *Nomina* of the first and second intention are not the same as first and second intentions, because they are spoken/written terms, not mental ones. *Nomina* of the second intention are those which signify mental concepts and not things; the rest are of the first intention. The classification becomes complicated because a word like 'genus' is a grammatical and also a logical term: it is a *nomen* of the second intention and of the second imposition. Ockham refines his scheme by allowing strict and broad definitions of its various categories.

Ockham also modifies the meaning of the different types of supposition in line with his views (SL 64). Personal supposition had usually been defined (see above, pp.42–5) a suppositing for a thing. Ockham says rather that a word supposits personally when it stands for what it signifies, whether that is a real thing, a mental term or a spoken/written term. When a word of second imposition stands for another word ('every NOUN is a part of speech') or a word of second intention stands for a mental term ('every SPECIES is a universal'), its supposition is personal. Simple supposition had usually been defined as when a word supposits for that which it signifies. Ockham says, however, that a word supposits simply when it stands for a mental term but does not signify it (*non tenetur significative*): for example, in 'Man is a species', 'man' supposits for a mental term (because this is all a species is), but it does not signify it: rather, both the spoken/written word and the mental term man signify the same thing. It can easily be seen from these comments that, whilst the concept of supposition is of central importance to Ockham in his account of thoughts and things, the detailed theory of the properties of terms, as he inherited it, does not provide him with any of his characteristic doctrines. On the contrary, he had to modify it to suit his purposes.

Knowing the truth

(1) Evident knowledge and intellectual intuition

Ockham's account of mental language and how it relates to the world cannot alone provide an explanation of intellectual know-ledge. Only some mental propositions constitute knowledge. In order for me to *know* a proposition *p*, it must be the case that *p* is true and that I assent to it (where assenting is understood to refer to a disposition rather than an act, just as knowing is itself disposi-tional). And I would also be said to *know* something if *p* were false and I dissented from it. If I assent to *p* but *p* is false, then I will be said, not to know something, but to hold a mistaken belief; if I do not assent to *p*, whether or not it is true, then I cannot be said to know it, though there are all sorts of other mental attitudes which I might have towards it – such as hoping, wishing, doubting, entertaining, or analysing. Ockham (O 1,Prol,1 pp.16:1–17:12) distinguishes 'apprehending' a proposition – forming and merely entertaining it – from judging a proposition – forming it and assenting to it or dissenting from it. In order to explain intellectual knowledge, Ockham must show what is required for us, not just to apprehend propositions, but to judge them correctly. There are many propositions to which we assent (or from which we dissent), which we do in fact judge correctly and so may be said to know; but for which the correctness of our judgement is not a necessary consequence of the manner and conditions of our making it. Such knowledge might be called 'not fully grounded'. For instance, I say that I know my friend has arrived, when he telephones from the station, or that I know there is a famine in Ethiopia, because I read of it in the newspaper. If it turns out that my friend was playing a practical joke and that the reports in the newspaper were unfounded, then I should have to admit that I did not know these things, but they were mistaken beliefs. It would be possible to investigate the conditions which make it probable that my judgements in such cases would be incorrect (Is my friend reliable? Does the newspaper have good reporters?), but never to set out those which ensure their correctness. Since Ockham wishes to examine the conditions for correct judgement, he must confine himself to fully grounded or, as he calls it, evident knowledge.

One sort of knowledge (cf. O 1,Prol,1 pp5:19ff, R 11,12/13 pp.256:10–257:20) is easily seen to be fully grounded: knowledge of self-evident truths. If a proposition is self-evidently true, I need only know its terms to be able to judge correctly that it is true. But Ockham believes that we also have evident knowledge of certain contingent propositions. If a white thing is placed in front of me, I am able to know evidently the proposition 'this thing is white'. Ockham wishes to define evident knowledge of this sort also by the relation between knowing a true proposition and knowing its terms. Any sort of proposition is known evidently, he says, when knowledge of its terms is sufficient, directly or indirectly, to bring about knowledge of it. By knowledge of its terms Ockham does not mean, in the case of a contingent proposition, mere apprehension of the individual mental concepts from which it is constructed, but rather some type of knowledge of the individual things for which the terms stand. But what type? Ockham calls it 'intuitive' and defines it by reference to evident knowledge. Intuitive knowledge is that by which we can evidently know a contingent proposition; every other sort of cognition is abstractive. Ockham believes, then, that if a white body is placed before me, I can intuitively know the body and its whiteness and this intuitive knowledge is the ground for my being able immediately to assent to the propositions, 'The body exists', 'The white thing exists', and 'The body is white'. The cognitions by which I apprehend and assent to these propositions are not, however, themselves intuitive: the object of intuitive knowledge must always be simple; it cannot be a proposition.

From this account, it might seem that intuitive knowledge is some sort of sensible, rather than intellectual, perception. If a modern thinker were to accept the idea that contingent propositions could be evidently known, he would indeed probably consider an act of direct sensory perception as providing their ground. The difference between my not fully grounded knowledge that my friend is in Cambridge, when he telephones from the station, and my evident knowledge now that he is here when he is standing in front of me is that now I can see him and touch him. Ockham would not agree. There is indeed intuitive sensible knowledge, but there is also intuitive intellectual knowledge, and it is on an intuitive act of the intellect that evident knowledge of contingent propositions must be based: 'no act of the senses is the immediate proximate cause, partial or total, of any intellectual act of judgement' (O I,Pr,I p.22:4–6). Whereas acts of abstractive cognition are easily recognizable as types of thought, it is very hard to know how to describe an act of intellectual intuitive cognition, except by repeating the very terms of Ockham's presentation.

(2) God's absolute power and the intuition of non-existents

There is one aspect of Ockham's discussion of intellectual intuition which can make it seem even more mysterious. For Scotus, intuitive knowledge was of what exists as existing (see above, pp.157–8); it would be self-contradictory, on his theory, to talk of intuitively knowing what does not exist. Ockham (O I,Pr,I p.33:15ff.) rejects this position, partly because he wishes to emphasize that, in theory, any intellectual cognition which makes possible evident knowledge of a contingent truth is intuitive, and partly because of his view of God's 'absolute power'.

God's absolute power (*potentia absoluta*) is distinguished by Ockham from his ordained power (*potentia ordinata*). There are not, as Ockham explains elsewhere (Q 6,1), really two powers in God. But 'to be able to do something' (*posse aliquid*) can be understood in two ways. In one way it contains the qualification 'according to the laws ordained and instituted by God': what God 'is able to do' *in this sense* is what he is said to do by his *potentia ordinata*. But 'to be able' can also be understood as 'able to do whatever does not contain a contradiction': what God 'is able to do' *in this sense* is what God is said to be able to do by his *potentia absoluta*.

In his clearest account of the intuitive cognition of non-existent things (R II,12/13, pp.258:11–261:5), Ockham explains that, *naturally* (according to God's ordained power), intuitive cognition is only possible when the object 'exists and is present in sufficient closeness'. But through God's absolute power either part of this condition can be altered. God might give me an intuitive cognition of an object which is too far away to be cognized intuitively by me naturally. Or he might allow me to know that something is not when it is not. In each case, the intuitive cognition is the ground for knowing evidently a contingent truth; it would be self-contradictory, in Ockham's view, to say that intuitive knowledge ever provided the ground for belief in a falsehood.

(3) Intuitive knowledge and memory

Just as Scotus worked out his theory of intuitive and abstractive knowledge in connection with memory, so Ockham's very different account of a wider concept of remembering (R II,12/13 pp.261:6ff; he treats a concept of memory closer to Scotus's later in his *Reportatio* – IV,12) gives him the chance to develop his ideas on the relationship between the different sorts of intellectual cognition. If yesterday I intellectually intuited an object *x*, then today I know evidently, not that *x* exists, but that *x* existed yesterday: I have only to form the proposition '*x* existed yesterday' to be able to assent to it. What is the ground of this assent? Ockham wishes to explain this type of memory, like all others, by dispositions and not by species. But there is a problem. When acts produce a disposition, the disposition is to perform acts of the same sort. An intuitive cognition is of something which is when it is. If it produced a disposition it would be to a similar act of knowing that something is when it is – I would 'remember' not that *x* existed yesterday but that *x* exists now. Experience confirms that no such dispositions are created by intuitive cognitions. From knowing that something existed I do not gain the knowledge that it now exists. The ground of my assenting today to the proposition '*x* existed yesterday' must be what Ockham calls an act of imperfect intuitive cognition, which is a sort of abstractive cognition (because it is not of what is when it is). Ockham considers seriously the possibility that perfect intuitive cognitions do in fact generate dispositions to acts of a different sort – acts of imperfect intuitive cognition. But he prefers to posit a simple abstractive cognition accompanying each act of intellectual intuition, which provides the ground for remembering. He admits that no one has experienced such abstractive cognitions, simultaneous with an intuitive one, but feels none the less that his reasoning shows that they take place.

Ockham arrives, therefore, at a complex scheme of intellectual cognition and remembering. Suppose that I have before me now a white object x:

[1]   I have an intuitive intellectual cognition of x and
[2]   of the white which inheres in it (w).
        (1) and (2) partially cause and are accompanied simultaneously by
[3]   an abstractive cognition of x and
[4]   its whiteness. (3) and (4) each create dispositions (3*) and (4*) to similar acts.
[5]   If I form the proposition p, 'x is white', then (1) and (2) allow me immediately to
[6]   judge that p is true.

        N.B. [5] and [6] are not necessary for stages [7] –[10] to take place.

Then tomorrow:-
[7]   I have an imperfect intuitive cognition of x by virtue of (3*) and
[8]   of w by virtue of (4*).
[9]   If I form the proposition q, 'x was white yesterday', then (7) and (8) allow me immediately to
[10]   judge that q is true.

What exactly does Ockham mean in this scheme by an intuitive intellectual cognition and by the simple abstractive cognition which, he says, must accompany it? Putting aside the possibilities of supernatural intervention, an intellectual intuition is some sort of awareness in the mind of a thing's present existence. In the example above, [1] might be described as the thought 'x, now'. The accompanying abstractive cognition [3] might be described as the thought 'x at time t' where t is the time of the cognition. It is the specification of time (which need not be very precise) by the abstractive cognition which allows it to generate a disposition to remember that such-and-such *was* the case at such-and-such a time.

Conclusion

(1) Ockham and theology

This chapter has been concerned with the rational arguments and analyses which Ockham used to attack the views of his predecessors on intellectual knowledge and present his own theory. This should not be taken to suggest that Ockham was in any sense more of a philosopher and less of a theologian than his predecessors. On the contrary, Ockham was a theologian by profession: the questions he poses himself were determined by theological considerations, their answers directed towards theological ends. But these ends were the same for him as for thinkers with whom he completely disagrees. Although Ockham's theology may seem to differ radically from that of thirteenth-century thinkers like Aquinas, especially by its stress on God's *potentia absoluta*, the omnipotence of God is a doctrine which every Christian thinker in the Middle Ages accepted. Ockham makes the distinction between God's ordained and his absolute power, not because he has discovered an article of faith ignored by his predecessors, but in order to give a more satisfactory analysis of the body of revealed doctrine shared by all the Christian thinkers of his century and the century before. Similarly, Ockham's innovatory theory of intellectual knowledge – the main subject of this chapter – is developed within the context of his theology. But it is based on a series of rational arguments and analyses designed to show that, from the premisses (some self-evident, some revealed) which Ockham shared with his predecessors, his conclusions follow but not theirs.

(2) Ockham's successors

Until quite recently Ockham was regarded by most historians in negative terms, as a thinker who destroyed the philosophical systems of Aquinas and Duns Scotus. While this view prevailed, little interest was taken by scholars in Ockham's successors. It was assumed that they were exponents of a decadent school of thought where trivial distinctions and pointless logical subtleties predominated. Now that Ockham is recognized as a constructive as well as a critical innovator, more attention is being paid to the thinkers of the mid- and late-fourteenth century and much of their work is being revealed as inventive and sophisticated. It was difficult for trained logicians or theologians to escape the influence of Ockham's terminology or to avoid considering his arguments; but they were not mere exponents of 'Ockhamism'.

Medieval thinkers from the 1320s onwards can be divided into those who by and large followed Ockham's anti-realism ('nominalists') and those who rejected it. But nominalists such as Ockham's pupil, Adam Wodeham (d. 1358), Robert Holcot (d. 1349) – Wodeham's dominican contemporary at Oxford – and John Buridan – who taught in the Paris arts faculty for a long period from the 1320s onwards – each developed very different views. Among the 'realists' were Walter Chatton (d. 1344), who adopted some of Scotus's positions; Walter Burley (d. 1344/5), whose teaching career began before and ended after Ockham's and who used the theory of supposition in a quite different, but no less sophisticated manner than Ockham's; John of Ripa, who worked in mid-fourteenth-century Paris and extended Scotus's theological methods; and John Wyclif (d. 1384), long celebrated as a reformer but now increasingly for his contribution to logic. It would be easy to add to this list (and to the list of important nominalists). The writer of an *Introduction* to *late* medieval philosophy would suffer from no shortage of material; but he would be presenting to the public an area about which serious and thorough historical work has only recently begun.

Conclusion to Part Two

The seven preceding chapters have followed the approach to thinkers of the past which was described at the end of Part One as 'historical analysis'. Their purpose has not only been to introduce the reader to later medieval thought by examining an important theme in some detail, but also to indicate two more general points – points which may seem contradictory but turn out, in fact, to complement each other. The treatment of intellectual knowledge by writers such as William of Auvergne, Aquinas, Henry of Ghent, Duns Scotus and William of Ockham illustrates both the enormous distance in concepts and concerns between the modern philosopher and medieval thinkers; yet also the fundamental similarities between many of their interests. And it suggests that only by recognizing and understanding the distance does it become possible to grasp and appreciate the similarities.

The way to recognize and understand this distance is to examine the factors which produce it: the texts used by thinkers, their methods of study, their aims and presuppositions. Later medieval discussions of the intellect show in the clearest way the extent to which an ancient text (and its various commentaries) could mould the treatment of a whole area of thought for generations. From the 1240s to the 1320s, most thinkers – whatever their differences – analysed intellectual cognition in accord with Aristotle's *De Anima*, as the information of the mind by the form of a thing in the external world; and even William of Auvergne and William of Ockham, who rejected this analysis, had to put their own ideas forward using Aristotelian terms. The close analogy which Aristotle draws between sensing a thing (my fingers sense the heat of the fire by becoming hot) and thinking a thing (my intellect thinks of a fire by becoming a fire-in-thought) is hard for modern readers to accept, and it constitutes one of the main reasons why medieval discussions of intellectual knowledge, which assume the analogy, can seem so strange. When a thinker (such as William of Ockham) is willing to abandon the Aristotelian model, his view of the mind seems remarkably familiar and modern.

Aristotle's *De Anima* and the other popular ancient, patristic and Arab accounts of the intellect were treated, as authoritative texts, with a combination of reverence and independence made possible and necessary by the methods and aims of the medieval universities. Medieval teaching was organized around authoritative texts and it favoured the *quaestio*-technique – a procedure designed to show how authorities, although apparently at variance, were really in concord. This method at once elevated and qualified the importance of received ideas: problems were posed by counterpoising past solutions to them; but the choice of problems was left to the individual medieval thinker, and the very contrariety of the authoritative views was a goad to his powers of analysis and an encouragement to his skills at accommodating interpretation. For instance, the passages in the *De Anima* which suggest that the human soul entirely perishes with the body were found to yield a different meaning; the Aristotelian view of the human intellect as acted-upon was soon complemented by a theory, derived from Augustine and others, of the mind's powers to generate its own language; and Aristotle's restriction of the objects of intellectual knowledge to universals was quickly circumvented. In the arts faculty, however, the balance was often in favour of respect to the ancients. Independence in speculation was usually the preserve of the theologians, both because they were more mature and highly trained, and because a good deal of the ancient and Arab texts was incompatible with their doctrinal aims and presuppositions.

But it is these very theological presuppositions and aims which are the clearest of all the features distancing later medieval thought from the modern reader. Most of the important thinkers of the thirteenth and fourteenth centuries were theologians; most of their important works were treatises of theology. Not only did theologians like Aquinas, Henry of Ghent, Duns Scotus and Ockham presuppose the articles of faith: the main aim of their work was to understand them better and elaborate their consequences. For instance, the view that thought is engaged in by disembodied souls, the angels and God – as well as by humans in this life – was not just the point of departure for these theologians: they were interested in the human mind mostly in so far as its workings helped them to understand the more-than-human minds which were the main concerns of their discipline. Or again: the theologians did not merely take it for granted that God is triune – often their most complex explorations of the human soul were carried out simply in order to penetrate the mystery of the Trinity.

When, without taking account of all these reasons why it is distant from him, a modern reader begins to read a medieval discussion of intellectual knowledge, he will probably find that an initial feeling of familiarity with the questions and ways of arguing is gradually replaced by disappointment and bewilderment. Although the problems had seemed recognizable, the procedures logically rigorous, on closer acquaintance with the text he finds a set of presuppositions and concepts he cannot share, and methods he cannot understand. But once he has gauged the distance and appreciated the reasons behind it, the reader will begin to understand how, if he (or a modern philosopher) shared the training, assumptions and aims of thirteenth- and fourteenth-century scholars, he would approach the problems which interest him now by posing the sorts of questions which medieval thinkers asked and answering them using the techniques which they favoured. There is a danger that this recognition might be patronizing – 'If only medieval scholars had not been limited by their education and culture, they might have been as wise as ourselves!'. Such self-satisfaction is countered by the reflection that modern philosophers, just as much as medieval theologians, are the products of a particular sort of education and operate within the framework of particular profession or occupation; they base themselves – as they must – on presuppositions they cannot prove; they use some methods rather than others; and they have various aims many of which they take for granted. And these are not limitations from which a thinker might, at least in theory, escape. They are the very conditions of disciplined thought.

Abbreviations

AHDLMA	*Archives de l'histoire doctrinale et littéraire du moyen âge*
AL	*Aristoteles Latinus* (Bruges/Paris; Desclée de Brouwer – except where otherwise stated)
AvL	*Avicenna Latinus* (Louvain/Leiden; Editions Orientalistes, then Peeters/Brill)
BCAO	P. Boehner *Collected Articles on Ockham*, ed. E. Buytaert (FIP: 1958)
BE	*Bibliographische Einführungen in das Studium der Philosophie* [series] (Bern; Francke)
BT	*Bibliothèque thomiste* [series] (1921–1927: Le Saulchoir, Kain; revue des sciences philosophiques et théologiques. 1930– : Paris; Vrin)
BFSMA	*Bibliotheca Franciscana Scholastica Medii Aevi* (Grottaferrata: Collegio di S. Bonaventura; Padri Editori di Quaracchi)
BGPM	*Beiträge zur Geschichte der Philosophie des Mittelalters* [series] (Münster; Aschendorff)
CCAA	*Corpus Commentariorum Averrois in Aristotelem* (Cambridge, Mass.; Mediaeval Academy of America)
CHLMP	*Cambridge History of Later Medieval Philosophy*, ed. N. Kretzmann, A. Kenny and J. Pinborg (Cambridge UP, 1982)
CIMAGL	*Cahiers de l'institut du moyen-âge grec et latin*
CLCAG	*Corpus Latinum Commentariorum in Aristotelem Graecorum* (Louvain UP and Béatrice Nauwelaerts, then Leiden; Brill)
CPD	*Corpus Philosophorum Danicorum Medii Aevi*

	(Copenhagen; Gad)
CPMA	*Corpus Platonicum Medii Aevi* (London; Warburg Institute)
DTC	*Dictionnaire de théologie catholique* (Paris; Letouzey, 1923–1950)
FIP	Franciscan Institute Publications (St Bonaventure, New York/Louvain/ Paderborn; the Franciscan Institute/ Nauwelaerts/Schöningh)
FS	*Franciscan Studies*
GAA	M. Grabmann *Gesammelte Akademieabhandlungen*, introduced by M. Schmaus. 2 vols (Paderborn, Munich, Vienna, Zurich; Schöningh, 1979)
MG	M. Grabmann *Mittelalterliche Geistesleben* 3 vols. (Munich; Hüber, 1926, 1936, 1956)
MM	*Miscellanea Medievalia* (Berlin, New York [from 1971]; Gruyter)
MPL	J. Migne *Patrologia Latina*
MS	*Mediaeval Studies*
MedSem	J. Pinborg *Medieval Semantics. Selected Studies on Medieval Logic and Grammar*, ed. S. Ebbesen (London; Variorum, 1984)
PBel	*Les Philosophes belges. Textes et études* [series] (Louvain; Institut Supérieur d'Études de Philosophie – until 1904 also Paris; Picard)
PIMS	*Pontifical Institute of Mediaeval Studies, Toronto. Studies and texts* [series]
PM	*Philosophes médiévaux* [series] (Louvain; publications universitaires/ co-published by various other companies)
RSPT	*Revue des sciences philosophiques et théologiques*
SBAW	*Sitzungsberichten der bayerischen Akademie der Wissenschaften*, Philosophisch–theologische und historische Klasse
SBon	*Spicilegium bonaventurianum* [series] (Grottaferrata: Collegio di S. Bonaventura; Padri Editori di Quaracchi)
SSL	*Spicilegium sacrum lovaniense. Etudes et documents* [series] (Louvain; spicilegium sacrum lovaniense)
UP	University Press

Bibliography

This bibliography is divided into three:

Section I, part (i) is a list of editions of some of the more important Greek and Arabic philosophical works available in Latin translation in the Middle Ages.

Section I, part (ii) is a list of editions of primary works cited in this *Introduction*, modern translations of them (where available) and of a selected number of important texts, available in modern editions and/or translations, not discussed in the text. In no sense is it supposed to be a complete guide to the printed material available.

Section II is a select list of secondary works which have a direct bearing on the matters discussed in the chapters and a few other secondary works which might help to introduce the reader to authors and areas not discussed here. It is broadly arranged according to the chapters of this *Introduction*, but the sub-divisions do not necessarily accord with the sub-divisions in my text. Cross-references in the bibliography are to the other parts of the bibliography: Section I, parts i and ii (I-i, I-ii), and to the sub-divisions of Section II (II.0.1–II.11.2). In cross-references *within* Section II the II is omitted.

The **abbreviations** used for some series and periodicals are listed at the end of this Bibliography.

SECTION I: PRIMARY SOURCES

Part (i): Latin translations used by medieval thinkers

(Except where stated, the editions listed are Latin translations used in the Middle Ages. Arab names are given in their usual Latin versions.)

Author/work	Edition
ALEXANDER of APHRODISIAS	Théry *Autour du décret* . . . II (below II.5.2), pp.74–82

De intellectu
ALEXANDER   ed. S. Ebbesen in *Commentators and Commentaries*
Commentary on *De*   . . . (below, ii.2.5), ii
Sophisticis Elenchis
ALFARABIUS
De Ortu Scientiarum   C. Bäumker (BGPM: 1916)
De Intellectu   Gilson 'Les sources gréco-arabes. . .'
   (below ii.3.2), pp.108–26, followed by a French
   translation of the Latin text
ALGAZEL   Sections on metaphysics and physics: ed. J.
Intentions of the   Muckle (*Algazel's Metaphysics*) (Toronto; St
Philosophers   Michael's college, 1933). Complete text: Venice;
   Lichtenstein, 1506 (*Logica et Philosophia Algazelis*
   Arabis. . .).
AMMONIUS   ed. G. Verbeke (CLCAG: 1961, vol. ii)
Commentary on the
De Interpretatione
ARISTOTLE   A complete edition of the various medieval Latin
Works   translations of Aristotle is being undertaken in the
   series AL. Volumes already available include, in
   addition to those mentioned individually below,
   versions of the *Physics, De Mundo, Rhetoric,*
   Politics and *Poetics*
Logic   ed. L. Minio-Paluello and others (AL: 1961–1975,
   vols, i–vi)
Metaphysics   Translations by James of Venice and *translatio*
   vetus, ed. G. Vuillemin-Diem (AL: 1970, vol.
   xxv. 1–1a); *translatio media*, ed G. Vuillemin-
   Diem (AL: 1976, vol. xxv–2)
Nicomachean Ethics   The various translations are ed. by R. Gauthier
   (AL: 1972–4, vol. xxvi, 1–3 – five fascicles)
De Anima   The version translated from the Arabic can be
   found in the lemmata to Averroes's long
   commentary, ed. Crawford (below). William of
   Moerbeke's translation is used, with some
   variations, by Aquinas for his commentary and is
   found in editions of it (below, Section i–ii)
AVENCEBROL   ed. C. Bäumker (BGPM: 1895). Extracts from
Fons Vitae   the original text are translated into French in S.
   Munk *Mélanges de philosophie juive et arabe* (Paris;
   Franck, 1859); the whole of Bk. iii is translated
   into French by F. Brunner (Paris; Vrin, 1950); and
   there is an abridged English translation by H.
   Wedeck (London; Owen, 1962)
AVERROES   For many of the commentaries, not yet included
Commentaries on   in the CCAA series, the Venetian Renaissance
Aristotle   editions of Aristotle remain the only printed text.

Aristotelis Opera cum Averrois Commentariis
(Venice; 1562–74) has been photographically
reprinted (Frankfurt; Minerva, 1962), but the
1560 edition contains a wider range of the
commentaries.

Long commentary on
De Anima
ed. F. Crawford (CCAA: 1953)

Long commentary on
Metaphysics
Complete text: Venice, 1562–74 ed., vol. VIII; Bk.
II – ed. G. Darms (Freiburg, Switzerland; Paulus,
1966); Bk. v – ed. R. Ponzalli (Berne; Francke,
1971); Bk. IX – ed. B. Burke (Berne; Francke,
1969)

Destructio Destructionis
Philosophiae Algazelis
An English translation of the early sixteenth-
century Latin translation is available, ed. B.
Zedler (Milwaukee, Wisconsin; Marquette UP,
1967)

AVICENNA
De Anima
ed. S. van Riet, 2 vols.:– I (Books I–III) (AvL:
1972), II (Books IV–V) (AvL: 1968). A French
translation of the Arabic text is available: J. Bakoš
Psychologie d'Ibn Sina (Avicenne) d'après son oeuvre
Aš-Šifā, 2 vols. (Prague; L'Académie
Tchécoslovaque des Sciences, 1956)

Metaphysics
ed. S. van Riet (*Liber de Philosophia prima sive*
scientia divina), 3 vols.: I (Books I–IV) (AvL: 1977),
II (Books V–X) (AvL: 1980), III (Indices) (AvL:
1983)

COSTA BEN
LUCA
De Differentia Anime
Spiritus
ed C. Barach in his *Bibliotheca Philosophorum*
Mediae Aetatis II (Innsbruch; Wagner, 1878),
pp.120–139

ISAAC ISRAELI
Liber de Definicionibus
ed. J. Muckle, AHDLMA, II, 1937–8, pp.299–
340

JOHN
DAMASCENUS
De Fide Orthodoxa
Dialectica
two translations ed. E. Buytaert (FIP: 1955)
ed. O. Colligan (FIP: 1953)
ed. G. Verbeke (CLCAG, 1966, vol. III).

JOHN
PHILOPONUS
Commentary on *De*
Anima III

LIBER DE CAUSIS
see PROCLUS

MAIMONIDES
Guide for the Perplexed
An English translation of the original is available,
ed. S. Pines (Chicago UP, 1963)

PLATO
Timaeus
ed. J. Waszink (CPMA: 1975 – 2nd ed.)
Meno
ed. V. Kordeuter and C. Labowsky (CPMA:

	1940)
Phaedo	ed. L. Minio-Paluello (CPMA: 1950)
PROCLUS	ed. C. Vansteenkiste, *Tijdschrift voor Filosofie*, 13,
Elements of Theology	1951, pp.,263–302, 491–531
Liber de Causis	ed. A. Pattin (Louvain; Tijdschrift voor Filosofie,
(adapted extracts	undated)
from the *Elements*)	
pseudo-	The various Latin translations of his works are
DIONYSIUS	collected in *Dionysiaca*, 2 vols ([Bruges]; Desclée
	de Brouwer, 1937)
SIMPLICIUS	ed. A. Pattin, 2 vols (CLCAG: 1971, 1975, vol.
Commentary on the	v/1 and 2)
Categories	
THEMISTIUS	ed. G. Verbeke (CLCAG: 1973, vol. 1)
Commentary on *De*	
Anima	

Part (ii): Medieval Latin texts

ANTHOLOGIES	Anthologies of translated texts include: R. McKeon *Selections from medieval philosophers*, 2 vols (New York; Scribner's Sons, 1929, 1930); J. Wippel and A. Wolter *Medieval Philosophy from St Augustine to Nicholas of Cusa* (New York/London; Free Press/Collier-Macmillan, 1965); A. Hyman and J. Walsh *Philosophy in the Middle Ages: the Christian, Islamic and Jewish Traditions* (New York, Evanston and London; Harper & Row, 1967); C. Vollert, L. Kendzierski, P. Byrne *On the Eternity of the World* (Milwaukee; Marquette UP, 1964) – texts by Aquinas, Bonaventure and Siger of Brabant
ADAM WODEHAM	Commentary on *Sentences* 1,1,1, ed. in G. Gál, 'Adam of Wodeham's question on the "*complexe significabile*" as the immediate object of scientific knowledge', FS, 37, 1973, pp. 66–102
ALAN of LILLE	*Regulae Caelestis Iuris/Theologicae*, ed. N. Haring, AHDLMA, 48, 1981, pp.97–226; Summa 'Quoniam homines', ed. P. Glorieux, AHDLMA, 20, 1953, 113–364; *Anticlaudianus*, ed. P. Bossuat (Paris; Vrin, 1955) – there is a translation by J. Sheridan (Toronto; Pontifical Institute of Mediaeval Studies, 1973); *De Planctu Naturae*, ed. N. Haring, *Studi Medievali*, 3rd series – 19, 1978, pp.797–879 – there is a translation by J. Sheridan (Toronto; Pontifical Institute of Mediaeval Studies, 1980). Some other texts are published, with useful notes and introduction, in

M.–T. d'Alverny *Alain de Lille. Textes inédits*
(Paris; Vrin, 1965)

ALBERT the
GREAT

The edition of the complete works, ed. A.
Borgnet (Paris; Vives, 1890–1899) is being
replaced by a new critical edition, ed. B. Geyer
(Münster; Aschendorff, 1951–)

ALEXANDER of
HALES

Commentary on the *Sentences* ed. PP. Collegii S.
Bonaventurae, 4 vols (BFSMA:, 1951, 1952,
1954, 1957); the *Summa Fratris Alexandri* –
attributed to Alexander but not, in the main his
own work, is ed. by the PP. Collegii S.
Bonaventurae, 6 vols. (Quaracchi; Collegium S.
Bonaventurae, 1924–1979)

ANONYMOUS:
Treatises
ANONYMOUS:
Commentaries on *De
Anima*

Liber de Causis Primis et Secundis, ed. in R. de Vaux
Notes et textes. . . (below II.3.2)
De Anima et de Potenciis Eius, ed. R. Gauthier, 'Le
traité . . .' (below II.3.2)
Lectura in Librum de Anima (by a master of arts, c.
1245–1250), ed. R. Gauthier (SBon: 1985). Three
commentaries from the 1260s and 1270s are ed.
M. Giele, F. van Steenberghen, B. Bazan *Trois
commentaires anonymes sur le traité de l'âme d'Aristote*
(PM:1971)

BOETHIUS
BOETHIUS of
DACIA

Works, MPL 64
Collected works in CPD IV–VI, VIII MS = *Modi
significandi sive Quaestiones super Priscianum
Maiorem*, ed. J. Pinborg and H. Roos in vol. IV–I
(1969); *De Aeternitate Mundi* and *De Summo Bono*,
ed. N. Green-Pedersen in vol. VI–2 (1966)

BONAVENTURE

Collected works, 9 vols. (Quaracchi; Collegium
S. Bonaventurae, 1882–1902)
A useful edition of the *Itinerarium Mentis ad Deum*,
with commentary and French translation, is by
H. Duméry (Paris; Vrin, 1960). The work is
translated into English by G. Boas (Indianapolis,
New York, Kansas City; Bobbs-Merrill, 1953).
The *Breviloquium* is translated into English by E.
Nemmers (St Louis, Missouri, London; Herder,
1947). Texts on the eternity of the world are
translated in *On the eternity* . . . (under
ANTHOLOGIES above)

GILES, of
ROME
GODFREY, of
FONTAINES

Errores Philosophorum, ed. J. Koch, trsl. J. Riedl
(Milwaukee, Wisconsin; Marquette UP, 1944)
Quodlibets I–IV, ed. M. de Wulf and A. Pelzer
(PBel: 1904); V–VII, ed. M. de Wulf and J.
Hoffmans (PBel: 1914); VIII, ed. J. Hoffmans
(PBel: 1924; XIII and 3 *quaestiones ordinariae*, ed. O.

Lottin (PBel: 1937)

GUNDISSALINUS *De Anima* – Chapter 10 ed. in de Vaux *Notes et textes...* (below 11.3.2); *De Divisione Philosophiae*, ed. L. Baur (BGPM: 1903); *De Immortalitate Animae*, ed. G. Bülow (BGPM: 1897); *De Processione Mundi*, ed. G. Bülow (BGPM: 1925); *De Unitate*, ed. P. Correns (BGPM: 1891)

HENRY, of GHENT A critical edition of his works, ed. R. Macken and others (Leiden; Brill, 1979–) (M) is in progress. S = *Summae Quaestionum Ordinarium*, 1520 ed., reprinted, 2 vols. (FIP: 1953). Q = Paris, 1518 ed. (reprinted Louvain; bibliothèque S. J. de Louvain, 1961); Quodlibet I, x ed. R. Macken (M: 1979, 1981); Commentary on the *Liber de Causis* (probably by Henry, ed. J. Zwanpoel (PM: 1974)

HENRY, of HARCLAY *Quaestio de Significato Conceptus Universalis*, ed. G. Gál, FS, 31, 1971, pp.178–234

HUGH, of St VICTOR *De Sacramentis*, MPL 176, col. 173 ff.

JOHN BURIDAN *Sophismata*, ed. T. Scott (Stuttgart, Bad Cannstaat; Frommann-Holzboog, 1977); an English translation exists of this work by Scott (New York; Appleton-Century-Crofts, 1966); and there is an English translation with introduction and philosophical commentary of Chapter 8: G. Hughes *John Buridan on Self-reference* (Cambridge UP, 1982)
De Consequentiis, ed. H. Hubien (PM: 1976)

JOHN DUNS SCOTUS A critical edition of the complete works is being made under the editorship of C. Balić (Vatican City; Typ. Polygl. Vatic., 1950–). For the parts of his work not yet in this edition, the best printed text is in the revised version of L. Wadding's seventeenth-century edition: *Opera Omnia*, 26 vols (Paris; Vives, 1891–5 – reprinted Westmead; Gregg, 1969)
O = *ordinatio* of commentary on *Sentences*: I and II, d.1–3 – ed. Balic, II–VII; for the rest – ed. Vives, XII–XXI
M = *Quaestiones Subtilissimae* on *Metaphysics* – ed. Vives, VII
Q = Quodlibets – ed. Vives, XXV-XXVI; there is a translation of Q by F. Alluntis and A. Wolter (*God and Creatures*), 2 vols (Princeton; Princeton UP, 1975); there is also a translation of extracts from Scotus's writings. ed. A. Wolter

JOHN BLUND	(Edinburgh; Nelson, 1962) *Tractatus de Anima*, ed. D. Callus and R. Hunt (London; British Academy, 1970)
JOHN of READING	Commentary on *Sentences*, 1,3,3, ed. G. Gál, 'Quaestio Iohannis de Reading de necessitate specierum intelligibilium: defensio doctrinae Scoti', FS, 29, 1969, pp.66–156
JOHN OF RIPA	*Determinationes*, ed. A. Combes (Paris; Vrin, 1957); Commentary on *Sentences* I, 2 vols, ed. A. Combes and (for vol. 2) F. Ruello (Paris; Vrin, 1961, 1970); *Quaestio de Gradu Supremo*, ed. A. Combes and P. Vignaux (Paris; Vrin, 1964)
JOHN WYCLIF	*De Universalibus*, ed. I. Müller, P. Spade and A. Kenny, 2 vols. (Oxford UP, 1984)
LAMBERT, of AUXERRE	*Logica*, ed. F. Alessio (Florence; La Nuova Italia, 1971)
MARTIN, of DACIA	Collected words ed. H. Roos (CPD: 1961, vol. II) MS = *Modis Significandi*, ed. cit.
PETER AUREOLUS	Commentary on *Sentences* I, 2 vols., ed. E. Buytaert (FIP: 1952,1956)
PETER JOHN OLIVI	Commentary on *Sentences* II, 3 vols. (BFSMA: 1922, 1924, 1926)
PETER THE LOMBARD	*Sentences* 2 vols (SBon: 1971, 1981)
PETER, of POITIERS	*Sentences*, ed. P. Moore, M. Dulong and J. Garvin, 2 vols. (Notre Dame, Indiana; Notre Dame UP, 1943, 1950)
PETER, of SPAIN	*Tractatus* (often called *Summule Logicales*), ed. L. de Rijk (Assen; van Gorcum, 1972). There is an English translation by J. Mullally (Notre Dame, Indiana; Notre Dame UP, 1945)
RADULPHUS BRITO	A = commentary on *De Anima*: I,6 ed. as appendix to J. Pinborg, 'Radulphus Brito on universals', CIMAGL, 35, 1980, pp.56–142; Bk. III, ed. W. Fauser (BGPM:1974) PM = *Quaestiones super Priscianum Minorem*, ed. H. Enders and J. Pinborg (Stuttgart, Bad Cannstatt, 1980) Sophism on second intentions, ed. J. Pinborg, 'Radulphus Brito's sophism on second intentions', *Vivarium*, 13, 1975, pp.119–152; *Quaestiones super Porphyrium* 5–8 in Pinborg. 'Radulphus Brito on universals' (above)
ROBERT GROSSETESTE	Philosophical works, ed. L. Baur (BGPM: 1912); commentary on the *Physics*, ed. R. Dales (Boulder, Colorado; Colorado UP, 1963); commentary on the *Posterior Analytics*, ed. P.

Rossi (Florence; Olschki, 1981). The *De Luce* (ed.
in Baur, above) has been translated by C. Riedl
(Milwaukee, Wisconsin; Marquette UP, 1942)

ROBERT, of
MELUN

Works, ed. R. Martin and others (SSL) *Sentences*:
Vol. III, parts 1 and 2, ed. R. Martin and, for part
2, R. Gallet (SSL: 1947, 1952)

ROBERT
HOLCOT

Quodlibets: one is edited in E. Moody, 'A
quodlibetal question of Robert Holcot, O.P., on
problem of objects of knowledge and belief',
Speculum, 39, 1964, pp.53–74 (= Moody *Studies in
Medieval Philosophy*. . . [below II. 6.1]); another in
J. Muckle, 'Utrum theologia sit scientia: a
quodlibet question of Robert Holcot O.P.', MS
20, 1958, pp.127–153; and three in H. Gelber
*Exploring the Boundaries of Reason. Three Questions
on the Nature of God by Robert Holcot, OP* (PIMS:
1983)

ROGER BACON

Opus Maius, ed. J. Bridges, 2 vols (Oxford UP,
1897, 1900): there is a translation by R. Burke, 2
vols. (Philadelphia; Pennsylvania UP, 1928); the
Opus Minor, Opus Tertium and other works are
ed. J. Brewer (*Opera Quaedam Hactenus Inedita*)
(London; Longman, Green, Longman and
Roberts, 1859). Other works are ed. R. Steele
(*Opera Hactenus Inedita*), 16 fascicules (Oxford
UP, 1905–1940)

SIGER, of
BRABANT

M = commentary on *Metaphysics*, ed. W.
Dunphy (PM: 1981), A. Maurer (PM: 1983)
AI = *De Anima Intellectiva*, ed. B. Bazán, along
with commentary on *De anima* II and *De
Aeternitate Mundi* (PM: 1972). This is translated in
On the Eternity of the World. . . (under
ANTHOLOGIES above)
Commentary on *Liber de Causis*, ed. A. Marlasca
(PM: 1972); further writings are ed. B. Bazán in
*Siger de Brabant: écrits de logique, de morale et de
physique* (PM: 1974)

SIMON, of
TOURNAI

Disputationes, ed. J. Warichez (SSL: 1932)

THOMAS
AQUINAS

The Leonine edition (Leon), begun in 1882, will
eventually provide critical editions of all of
Aquinas's works. Some of the recent volumes,
such as Father Gauthier's edition of the
commentary on the *De Anima*, contain very full
and valuable introductions. Many of Aquinas's
works – in the Leonine text, where it has been

available, are conveniently available in editions
published by Marietti of Turin (Mar)
quA = *Quaestiones de Anima*: the best ed. is by J.
Robb (PIMS: 1968); Mar – in *Quaestiones
Disputatae*, ed. R. Spiazzi, 2 vols. (1964, 1965),
vol. II; there is a translation by J. Rowan (St
Louis, Missouri, London; Herder, 1949)
quV = *Quaestiones de Veritate*, ed. Leon – XXII,
Mar – *Quaestiones Disputatae* I; there is a
translation by R. Mulligan, 3 vols. (Chicago;
Regnery, 1952, 1953, 1954)
SG = *Summa contra Gentiles*, ed. Leon – XIII–XV;
Mar – ed. P. Marc, C. Pera and P.Caramello, 3
vols. – I (an introduction by P. Marc) 1967, II and
III (1961); there is a translation by A. Pegis and
others, 4 vols. (Notre Dame/London; Notre
Dame UP, 1975 – this ed.)
SDE = commentary on the *De Interpretatione*, ed.
Leon – I; Mar – ed. R. Spiazzi (1964 – 2nd ed.);
there is a translation by H. Oesterle (Milwaukee,
Wisconsin; Marquette UP, 1962)
SM = commentary on the *Metaphysics*, Mar – ed.
M. – R. Cathala, revised by R. Spiazzi (1964);
there is a translation by J. Rowan, 2 vols
(Chicago; Regenery, 1964)
ST = *Summa Theologia*, ed. – Leon IV–XII; Mar –
ed. P. Caramello, 4 vols. (1948). There is a cheap
edition of the Leonine text in the *Biblioteca de
Autores Cristianos* of Madrid, 5 vols. The best
translation is by T. Gilby and others, issued with
facing Latin text, 61 vols. (London/New York;
Eyre & Spottiswood/McGraw Hill, 1964–1980).
Translated selections comprise *Basic Writings of
Saint Thomas Aquinas*, ed. A. Pegis, 2 vols. (New
York; Random House, 1945)
T = commentary on Boethius *De Trinitate*
(incomplete). The best ed. is by B. Decker
(Leiden; Brill, 1955). The work is translated
completely by R. Brennan (St Louis, Missouri,
London; Herder, 1946) and partially (qu. 5 and 6)
in *The Divisions and Methods of the Sciences*, ed. A.
Maurer (Toronto; Pontifical Institute of
Mediaeval Studies, 1963)
U = *De Unitate Intellectus contra Averroistas*, ed.
Leon – XLIII, pp.243–314; Mar – in *Opuscula
Philosophica*, ed. R. Spiazzi (1954), pp. 59–90; it
accompanies Brennan's translation of the *De*

Trinitate commentary (above) and has also been translated by B. Zedler (Milwaukee, Wisconsin; Marquette UP, 1968)

De Aeternitate Mundi, ed., Leon – XLIII, pp.49–89; Mar – in *Opuscula Philosophica* (above), pp. 103–8; it is translated in *On the Eternity of the World. . .* (under ANTHOLOGIES above)

Commentary on *De Memoria et Reminiscentia*, Mar – ed. R. Spiazzi (along with commentary on *De Sensu et Sensato*) (1973 – 3rd ed.);

Commentary on the *De Anima*, ed. Leon – XLV; Mar – ed. A. Pirotta (1959 – 5th ed.); there is a translation by K. Foster and S. Humphries (London; Routledge & Kegan Paul, 1951)

Commentary on the *Liber de Causis*: the best ed. is by H. -D. Saffrey (Fribourg/Louvain; Société Philosophique/Nauwelaerts, 1954)

Commentary on *Sentences*, ed. P. Mandonnet and M. Moos, 4 vols (Paris; Léthielleux, 1929, 1933, 1947)

ULRICH of STRASBOURG   *Summa de Bono* I ed. J. Daguillon (BT: 1930)

VITALIS, of FURNO   *Quaestiones disputatae on knowledge*, ed. F. Delorme, AHDLMA 2, 1927, pp.151–337

WALTER BURLEIGH   *De Puritate Artis Logicae* – long and short versions, ed. P. Boehner (FIP: 1955); commentary on *De Interpretatione*, ed. S. Brown, FS, 33, 1973, pp.42–134; *quaestio* commentary on *De Interpretatione*, ed. S. Brown, FS, 34, 1974, pp.200–295

WALTER CHATTON   Commentary on *Sentences* (*reportatio*), I,3,2, ed. G. Gal. 'Gualteri de Chatton et Guillelmi de Ockham controversia de natura conceptus universalis', FS, 27, 1967, pp.191–212

WILLIAM, of AUVERGNE   Complete works (Orleans, Paris; Billaine, 1674), 2 vols. (there is a reprint of this edition: Frankfurt: Minerva, 1963)
A = *De Anima*, in 1674 ed., II, supplement
U = *De Universo* in 1674 ed., I; two works have been given modern editions – *De Bono et Malo*, ed. J. O'Donnell, MS, 8, 1946, pp.245–299; 16, 1954, pp.219–271; *De Trinitate*, ed. B. Switalski (PIMS: 1976)

WILLIAM, of AUXERRE   *Summa aurea*, ed. J. Ribaillier, 3 vols so far published (SBon, 1980–)

WILLIAM, of OCKHAM   There is a complete edition of the philosophical and theological works (St Bonaventure, New York; College of St Bonaventure, 1967) (SB).

The political works are ed. H. Offler, J. Sikes and others, 3 vols (Manchester UP, 1940–1963). For works not yet edited critically, the edition of Lyons, 1494–6 (reprinted Gregg, 1962) must be used.

O = commentary on *Sentences* i (*ordinatio*), in SB, *Opera Theologica* i–iv
H = commentary on *De Interpretatione* in SB, *Opera Philosophica* ii
Q = quodlibets, in SB. *Opera Theologica* ix
R = commentary on *Sentences* ii–iv (*reportatio*), Bks ii and iii in SB, *Opera Theologica* v, vi
SL = *Summa totius Logicae* in SB *Opera Philosophica* i; Part i has been translated (*Ockham's Theory of Terms*) by M. Loux (Notre Dame UP, 1974), and Part ii (*Ockham's Theory of Propositions*) by A. Freddoso and H. Schuurman, (Notre Dame UP, 1980)
A selection of extracts in translation is given by P. Boehner *Philosophical Writings: A Selection – William of Ockham* (Edinburgh, London; Nelson, 1957)

WILLIAM, of   *Introductiones in Logicam*, ed. M. Grabmann,
SHERWOOD   SBAW, 1937, no. 10; there is a translation with introduction and notes by N. Kretzmann (Minneapolis; Minnesota UP, 1966).
Syncategoremata, ed. J. O'Donnell, MS, 3, 1941, pp.46–93; there is a translation by N. Kretzmann (Minneapolis; Minnesota UP, 1968)

SECTION II: SECONDARY WORKS

(0.1) Some general books on (later) medieval thought

There are many general histories of medieval philosophy, the majority of which devote a great deal of space to the period from 1150–1350. Among the most useful are (in chronological order): E. Gilson *A History of Christian Philosophy in the Middle Ages* (London: Sheed and Ward, 1955 – translated ed.) – Gilson's views are sometimes peculiar, but no other general account has the range or consistent clarity of his; G. Leff *Medieval Thought from Saint Augustine to Ockham* (Harmondsworth; Penguin, 1958) – a brief but thorough account; P. Vignaux *Philosophy in the Middle Ages*, trans. E. Hall (London; Burns and Oates, 1959) – a sophisticated and intelligent discussion, which is carefully selective: especially valuable for stressing the difficulties of seeing medieval thinkers as 'philosophers'; J. Weinberg *A Short History of Medieval Philosophy* (Princeton, NJ; Princeton UP, 1964) – includes Arab and Jewish as well as Christian thought:

concentrates on the abstract problems which are presented with admirable clarity; CHLMP (*Cambridge History of Later Medieval Philosophy*) – written by a team of specialists, this provides a guide to the subject topic by topic. The chapters, many of them based on new research, are usually sophisticated and condensed. The bibliography is up-to-date and very full. There is also M. Haren *Medieval Thought. The Western Intellectual Tradition from Antiquity to the Thirteenth Century* (Houndmills, Basingstoke and London; Macmillan, 1985) – the best short account of the subject from an historian's point-of-view, with excellent bibliography; L.M. De Rijk *La Philosophie au moyen âge* (Leiden: Brill, 1985) – historiographical and methodological discussion, followed by studies of selected problems. For general books, see also below 4.4 and 5.3.

Chapter 1   Teaching and learning in the universities

(1.1)   The universities as institutions

General works
The fullest study remains H. Rashdall *The Universities of Europe in the Middle Ages*, revised by F. Powicke and A. Emden (Oxford UP, 1936) – Paris is treated in Volume I, Oxford in Volume III. G. Leff *Paris and Oxford Universities in the Thirteenth and Fourteenth Centuries: an Institutional and Intellectual History* (New York, London, Sydney; Wiley, 1968), Chapters I and II – usefully detailed; J. Verger *Les universités au moyen-âge* (Paris; Presses Universitaires de France, 1973); A. Cobban *The Medieval Universities: their Development and Organisation* (London; Methuen, 1975) – a sophisticated introduction.

Paris
Die Auseinandersetzungen an der Pariser Universität im XIII. Jahrhundert, ed. A. Zimmerman (MM: 1976) – a collection of essays on conflicts, intellectual and administrative, in the thirteenth-century university of Paris.

Oxford
The History of the University of Oxford, Volume One *The Early Oxford Schools*, ed. J. Catto (Oxford UP, 1984) – comprehensive and detailed.

Other universities A. Sorbelli *Storia della Università di Bologna*, I (Bologna; Zanichelli, 1940); A. Cobban. *The King's Hall within the University of Cambridge in the Later Middle Ages* (Cambridge UP, 1969 – suggests that Cambridge may have been of considerable importance by the fourteenth century; *The Universities in the Late Middle Ages* ed. J. Ijsewijn and J. Paquet (Louvain; Louvain UP, 1978) – a collection of essays.

Mendicants
A. Little *The Grey Friars in Oxford* (Oxford; Oxford Historical Society, 1892), and his 'The Franciscan School of Oxford in the Thirteenth Century, *Archivium Franciscanum Historicum*, 19, 1926, pp.803–874; W. Courtenay *Adam Wodeham: an Introduction to His Life and Writings* (Leiden; Brill, 1978), pp.45–53 – an excellent summary of information on Franciscan education in fourteenth-century England.

Offical university documents The documents relating to Paris as a university are collected in the *Chartularium universitatis parisiensis*, I, ed. H. Denifle (Paris; Delalain, 1889); those relating to Oxford in *Statuta antiqua universitatis oxoniensis*, ed. S. Gibson (Oxford UP, 1931). L. Thorndike *University Records and Life in the Middle Ages* (New York; Columbia UP, 1944 – reprinted 1971) – a collection of translations.

(1.2) Methods and organization of studies before the thirteenth century

M. Grabmann *Die Geschichte der scholastischen Methode* 2 vols. (Freiburg im Breisgau; Herder, 1909/11) is the fullest study of the whole area, but is outdated in many respects.
Methods of studying secular texts
E. Jeauneau *Lectio philosophorum* (Amsterdam; Hakkert, 1973) – essays on William of Conches, Thierry of Chartres and others and their study of the ancient philosophers; L. de Rijk *Logica modernorum* II–i (Assen; Van Gorcum, 1967 – on logical commentaries and textbooks.
Methods of theology
J. de Ghellinck *Le mouvement théologique du XIIe siècle* (Bruges, Brussels, Paris; De Tempel, L'Édition Universelle, de Brouwer, 1948 – 2nd ed.). For the development of the *quaestio*, see the introduction by R. Martin to *Oeuvres de Robert de Melun* III (above, Section I–ii) and M.-D. Chenu *Towards Understanding Saint Thomas*, trsl. (with addition and corrections) A.-M. Landry and D. Hughes (Chicago; Regnery, 1964), pp.80–93. For the origins of disputations, see introduction to J. Warichez *Les Disputationes de Simon de Tournai* (above, Section I–ii).
Peter the Lombard *Petri Lombardi Sententiae. . .* (above, Section I–ii) I–i *Prolegomena* replaces previous studies of his life, methods of work and sources. For the early influence of the *Sentences*, see de Ghellinck *Le mouvement théologique* and O. Lottin 'Le premier commentaire connu des Sentences de Pierre Lombard', *Recherches de théologie ancienne et médiévale*, 11, 1939, pp. 86–71 (reprinted in his *Psychologie et morale au XIIe et XIIIe siècles* VI [Gembloux; Duculot, 1960], pp.9–18).

(1.3) Methods and organization of studies in the thirteenth and fourteenth centuries
The general histories of the universities cited in (1.1) give some information about a student's career: see especially, Rashdall *The Universities. . .*, I, pp.439–496 (Paris); III, pp.152–160 (Oxford), and Leff . . . *Paris and Oxford*, pp.137–184. CHLMP, Chapter 1, 'Medieval philosophical literature', by A. Kenny and A. Pinborg, esp. pp.13–34, gives a brief, up-to-date summary.
Arts faculty
J. Weisheipl, 'Curriculum of the Faculty of Arts at Oxford in the Early Fourteenth Century', MS, 26, 1964, pp.143–185
Theology faculty
A. Little and F. Pelster *Oxford Theology and Theologians* (Oxford UP,

1934); P. Glorieux, 'L'enseignement au moyen âge. Techniques et méthodes en usage à la faculté de théologie de Paris, au XIII siècle', AHDLMA, 35, 1968, pp.65–186.

Disputations
P. Glorieux *La littérature quodlibetique*, 2 vols (Paris; Vrin, 1925, 1935). A modern account is given in CHLMP, pp.21–9.

Works of reference on university masters
P. Glorieux *La faculté des arts et ses maîtres au XIIIe siècle* (Paris; Vrin, 1971); P. Glorieux *Répertoire des maîtres en théologie de Paris au XIII siècle* 2 vols (Paris; Vrin, 1933); A. Emden *A Biographical Register of the University of Oxford to A.D. 1500* 3 vols (Oxford UP, 1957–9), *A Biographical Register of the University of Cambridge to 1500* (Cambridge UP, 1963)

(1.4) Forms of logical, philosophical and theological writing
Sentence commentaries
F. Stegmüller *Repertorium commentariorum in Sententias Petri Lombardi* (Würzburg; Schöningh, 1947) – a list of commentaries with introduction: there are two supplements to it – V. Doucet, 'Commentaires sur les Sentences: supplément au répertoire de M. Frédéric Stegmueller', *Archivium Franciscanum Historicum*, 47, 1954, pp.88–170, and J. Van Dyk, 'Thirty years since Stegmüller', FS, 39, 1979, pp.255–315; P. Glorieux, article 'Sentences, commentaires sur les' in DTC xiv, col. 1860–1884.
Quaestiones ordinariae/quodlibetales Glorieux *La littérature quodlibetique* (above. 1.3).
Sophisms M. Grabmann *Die Sophismaliteratur des 12. und 13. Jahrhunderts mit Textausgabe eines Sophisma des Boethius von Dacien* (BGPM: 1940).
Commentaries on Aristotle C.H. Lohr 'Medieval Latin Aristotle commentaries' in *Traditio*, 23–4, 26–30, 1967–8, 1970–1974. Fuller lists of commentaries in manuscripts in individual countries or centres include one by W. Senko for Parisian libraries (Warsaw; Akademia Teologii Katolickiej, 1982), 2 vols; by L. De Rijk and O. Weijers for the Netherlands (Amsterdam, Oxford, New York; North-Holland, 1981). M. Grabmann, 'Methoden und Hilfsmittel des Aristotelesstudiums im Mittelalter', SBAW, 1939, no. 5 = GAA ii, pp.1447–1638. For Aquinas's commentaries, see below, 4.3.
University manuscripts – copying and transmission
J. Destrez *La pecia dans les manuscrits universitaires du XIIIe et du XIVe siècle* (Paris, 1935); A. Dondaine *Secrétaires de Saint Thomas* (Rome; editori di San Tommaso, 1956); G. Fink-Errera, 'Une institution du monde médiéval: la "pecia" ', *Revue philosophique de Louvain*, 60, 1962, pp.184–243; J. Brounts, 'Nouvelles précisions sur la "pecia" ', *Scriptorium*, 24, 1970, pp.343–352.

Chapter 2 The techniques of logic

(2.1) General books on medieval logic
W. and M. Kneale *The Development of Logic* (Oxford UP, 1962), is an intelligent introduction to the history of formal logic from antiquity to

recent times; pp.224–297 deal with the main outlines of later medieval logic. P. Boehner *Medieval Logic* (Manchester UP, 1952) gives a clear and concise account (using modern symbolism) of formal logic, especially in the fourteenth century. J. Pinborg *Logik und Semantik im Mittelalter: ein Überblick* (Stuttgart/Bad Cannstatt; Frommann-Holzboog, 1972) – a fundamental introduction to philosophical logic in the whole period. D.P. Henry *Medieval Logic and Metaphysics: a Modern Introduction* (London; Hutchinson, 1972) – specialized studies, using the logical systems of Lesniewski to translate medieval arguments into symbolic form. Parts III, IV and V (pp.99–381) of CHLMP are devoted to logic and provide the most detailed and up-to-date survey of the field.

Collections
Modern Studies in Medieval Logic, Semantics and Philosophy of Science, ed. S. Knuuttila (Dordrecht; Reidel, 1979) (= *Synthese* 40, 1979).

Bibliographies
E. Ashworth *The Tradition of Medieval Logic and Speculative Grammar* (Toronto; Pontifical Institute of Mediaeval Studies, 1978); P. Spade *The Mediaeval Liar: a Catalogue of* Insolubilia *Literature* (Toronto; Pontifical Institute of Mediaeval Studies, 1975), 'Recent Research on Medieval Logic' in S. Knuuttila (ed.) *Modern Studies. . .* (above), pp.3–18.

(2.2)   The *Isagoge* and the *Categories*
Useful commentary on the *Categories* is given in the translation by J. Ackrill (Oxford UP, 1963). CHLMP Chapter 5 (pp.128–142), 'Predicables and categories', by D.P. Henry discusses the doctrines of these two works. M. Grabmann, 'Bearbeitungen und Auslegungen der aristotelischen Logik aus der Zeit von Peter Abaelard bis Petrus Hispanus. Mitteilungen aus Handschriften deutscher Bibliotheken', *Abhandlungen der Preussischen Akademie der Wissenschaften*, Phil.-Hist. Klasse, 1937, no. 5 (= GAA II, pp.1361–1418), contains useful material, especially on the *logica vetus* in the late twelfth and early thirteenth century.

(2.3)   The *De Interpretatione* and *Prior Analytics*
Ackrill translates and comments on the *De Interpretatione* in the same volume as the *Categories* (above, 2.2). J. Isaac *Le Peri hermeneias en occident de Boèce à Saint Thomas* (Paris; Vrin, 1953) discusses the assimilation and understanding of the *De Interpretatione*. There are a number of modern accounts of Aristotle's syllogistic: J. Lukasiewicz *Aristotle's Syllogistic from the Standpoint of Modern Formal Logic* (Oxford UP, 1957 – 2nd ed.) is the most famous.

(2.4)   Topical reasoning and the theory of consequences
E. Stump *Boethius's* De topicis differentiis. *Translated, with notes and essays on the text* (Ithaca/London; Cornell UP, 1978) discusses fully the theory of topics. She contributes a chapter (14: pp.273–299) to CHLMP on 'Topics: their development and absorption into consequences'. On this subject, see also J. Pinborg. 'Topik und Syllogistik im Mittelalter' in *Sapienter ordinare*.

Festgabe für Erich Kleineidam (Leipzig; St Benno, 1969), pp.157–178 (reprinted in MSem, no. 1). For the theory of consequences, see E.A. Moody *Truth and Consequences in Mediaeval Logic* (Amsterdam; North-Holland, 1953) and CHLMP Chapter 15, 'Consequences' by I. Boh.

(2.5) The *De Sophisticis Elenchis* and the theory of the properties of terms
L. de Rijk's *Logica modernorum* (Assen; Van Gorcum) is the fundamental study: vol. I (1962) examines the commentaries on the *De Sophisticis Elenchis* in the twelfth century; vol. II–i (above 1.2) discusses the origin of the theory of the properties of terms and vol. II–ii (1967) prints relevant texts. Vol. I may be complemented by S. Ebbesen *Commentators and Commentaries on Aristotle's Sophistici Elenchi: a Study of Post-Aristotelian and Medieval Writings on Fallacy*, 3 vols, (CLCAG: 1981) De Rijk summarizes some of his findings in CHLMP Chapter 7 (pp.161–173), 'The origins of the theory of the properties of terms'. On the differences between terminist theories, see J. Pinborg, 'The English contribution to logic before Ockham', *Synthese*, 40, 1979, pp.19–42 and CHLMP Chapter 8 (pp.174–187), 'The Oxford and Paris traditions in logic' by A. de Libera.

(2.6) The *Posterior Analytics*
The translation of the *Posterior Analytics* by J. Barnes (Oxford UP, 1975) contains a helpful introduction and commentary; see also his 'Aristotle's Theory of Demonstration' in *Articles on Aristotle 1 – Science* ed. J. Barnes, M. Schofield, R. Sorabji (London; Duckworth, 1975), pp.65–87. For early thirteenth-century use of the *Posterior Analytics*, see S. Marrone *William of Auvergne and Robert Grosseteste. New ideas of Truth in the Early Thirteenth Century* (Princeton UP, 1983), especially Part II (on Robert Grosseteste). For later thirteenth-century use, see Pinborg *Logik und Semantik. . .* (above 2.1, pp.77–87. CHLMP Chapter 24, 'Demonstrative science' (pp.496–517) by E. Serene discusses the wider influence of the concept of demonstration.

Chapter 3   Philosophy: the ancients, the Arabs and the Jews

(3.1)   The translations
Aristotle
The fullest guide is provided by the introductions to the volumes of AL. A complete list of manuscripts is given in the three AL *Codices volumes – Pars Prior* (Rome; Libreria dello Stato, 1939), *Pars Posterior* (Cambridge UP, 1955) and *Supplementa Altera* (1961). L. Minio-Paluello *Opuscula. The Latin Aristotle* (Amsterdam; Hakkert, 1972) collects together very important essays by this scholar on the subject. A very clear, up-to-date summary is provided by B. Dodd in CHLMP Chapter 2 (pp.45–79), 'Aristoteles latinus'. L. Minio-Paluello, 'Aristotele dal mondo Arabo a quello Latino' in *Settimane di studio del centro italiano di studi sull'alto medioevo: 'L'occidente e l'islam nell'alto medioevo'*, II (Spoleto; Centro Italiano di Studi sull'Alto

Medioevo, 1965), pp.603–637 (= *Opuscula* [above], pp.501–536) – on translations of Aristotle from the Arabic. On William of Moerbeke, see M. Grabmann *Guglielmo di Moerbeke O.P., il Traduttore delle Opere di Aristotele* (Rome; Pontificia Università Gregoriana, 1946).

Antique commentaries on Aristotle

M. Grabmann, 'Mittelalterliche lateinische Übersetzungen von Schriften der Aristoteles–Kommentatoren Johannes Philoponus, Alexander von Aphrodisia und Themistius', SBAW, 1929, no. 7 (= GAA ɪ, pp.497–564); E. Cranz, 'Alexander of Aphrodisia' in *Catalogus translationum et commentariorum*, ɪ, ed. P. Kristeller (Washington DC; Catholic University of America press, 1960), pp.77–135; much information is also to be found in the introductions to the editions in the CLCAG series.

The Toledan translators

R. Lemay, 'Dans l'espagne du XIIe siècle. Les traductions de l'arabe au latin', *Annales, économies, sociétiés, civilisations*, 18, 1963, pp.639–665; the best discussion of the identity of Avendeuth and his relations with Gundissalinus is in the preface to the edition by S. Van Riet of Avicenna's *De anima* vol. ɪ (above, Section ɪ-i).

Alfarabi

D. Salman, 'The medieval Latin translations of Alfarabi's works', *The New Scholasticism*, 13, 1939, pp.245–261.

Avicenna

M.-T. d'Alverny 'Notes sur les traductions médiévales d'Avicenne', AHDLMA, 19, 1952, pp.337–358.

Algazel

D. Salman, 'Algazel et les latins', AHDLMA, 10, 1935, pp.103–127; M. Grignaschi, 'Les traductions latins des ouvrages de logique arabe et l'abrégé d'Alfarabi', AHDLMA, 39, 1972, pp.41–89.

Averroes

H. Wolfson, 'Revised plan for the publication of a Corpus commentariorum Averrois in aristotelem', *Speculum*, 38, 1963, pp.88–104– a prospectus which lists the known translations. R. De Vaux's often cited 'La première entrée d'Averroes chez les latins', RSPT, 22, 1933, pp.193–245 must now be corrected by R. Gauthier, 'Notes sur les débuts (1225–40) du premier "averroisme" ', RSPT, 66, 1982, pp.321–374 – esp. pp.331–334 for the date of the translations.

Plato and Platonic works

R. Klibansky *The Continuity of the Platonic Tradition during the Middle Ages* (New York/London/Nendeln, Liechtenstein; Kraus, 1982 – new and augmented edition). This edition includes his 'Plato's Parmenides in the Middle Ages and the Renaissance', orginally published in *Mediaeval and Renaissance Studies*, ɪ, 1943, pp.1–55.

Other translations

M. Steinschneider, 'Die europäische Übersetzungen aus dem arabischen bis Mitte der 17. Jahrhunderts', *Sitzungsberichte der phil.-hist. Klasse der kaiserlichen Akademie der Wissenschaften*, 149, 1905, no.4; 151, 1906, no.1 – no more recent survey is equally comprehensive.

(3.2) Greek, Arabic and Jewish philosophy: availability and use
A clear, detailed account of the whole question is given by F. van Steenberghen *La philosophie au XIIIe siècle* (Louvain; Béatrice-Nauwelaerts, 1966). An earlier and shorter version of van Steenberghen's work is available in English: *Aristotle in the West* (trsl. L. Johnston) (Louvain; Nauwelaerts, 1970 – 2nd ed.). Van Steenberghen's represents the commonly accepted view which is questioned at a number of points in this chapter.

Use of the new texts up to 1215
R. de Vaux *Notes et textes sur l'avicennisme latin aux confins des XIIe–XIII siècles* (BT: 1934); *Autour du décret de 1210: (1) David de Dinant* by G. Théry; (3) *Amaury de Bène* by G. Capelle (BT: 1925, 1932); R. Hunt *The Schools and the Cloister: the Life and Writings of Alexander Nequam (1157–1217)*, ed. M. Gibson (Oxford UP, 1984).

The prohibitions M. Grabmann *I divieti ecclesiastici di Aristotele sotto Innocenzo III e Gregorio IX* (Rome; Saler, 1941).

The use of Aristotle, 1215–1260
M. Grabmann 'Eine für Examinazwecke abgefasste Questionensammlung der Pariser Artistenfakultät aus der ersten Hälfte des 13. Jahrhunderts', *Revue néoscolastique de philosophie*, 36, 1934, pp.211–226 (= MG II, pp.183–199); 'Die Aristoteleskommentatoren Adam von Bocfeld und Adam von Bouchermefort. Die Anfänge der Erklärung des "neuen Aristoteles" in England', SBAW, 1934 = MG II, pp.138–182; D. Callus, 'Introduction of Aristotelian learning to Oxford', *Proceedings of the British Academy*, 29, 1943, pp. 229–281. A wealth of information about the early study of the *De Anima* is to be found in the introduction to R. Gauthier's (Leonine) edition of Aquinas's commentary on the *De Anima* (above, Section I–ii), pp.235*–270*.

The influence of Avicenna
M.-T. d'Alverny *Avicenna Latinus* in AHDLMA 28–39, 1961–1972 – a catalogue of all Latin manuscripts containing translations of Avicenna; E.Gilson, 'Pourquoi Saint Thomas a critiqué Saint Augustin', AHDLMA, 1, 1926/7, pp.5–127 and 'Les sources gréco-arabes de l'augustinisme avicennisant', AHDLMA, 4, 1929, pp.5–149 – influential articles, putting forward a view of 'avicennising augustinism' no longer universally accepted. Gilson summarizes his views and takes account of criticisms in 'Avicenne en occident au moyen âge', AHDLMA, 36, 1969, pp.89–121.

The use of Averroes
R. Gauthier 'Notes' (above, 3.1) replaces all earlier studies; see also his 'Le traité *De Anima et Potenciis Eius* d'un maître ès arts (vers 1225): introduction et texte critique', RSPT, 66, 1982, pp.3–55. See also references in section 4.2 below, for 'Latin Averroists' in the 1260s and 1270s.

Use of Jewish philosophy
J. Dienstag *Studies in Maimonides and St Thomas Aquinas* (–; Ktav, 1975) – a collection of reprinted essays, wider in scope than its title suggests.

(3.3) Greek philosophy: its main characteristics
Aristotle
There is an enormous amount of modern work on Aristotle. Good general
introductions include G. Lloyd *Aristotle: the Growth and Structure of his
Thought* (Cambridge UP, 1968) and J. Barnes *Aristotle* (Oxford UP, 1982).
A valuable collection of philosophical studies will be found in *Articles on
Aristotle*, 4 vols, ed. J. Barnes, M. Schofield and R. Sorabji (London;
Duckworth, 1975–9). The translations of Aristotle in the *Clarendon
Aristotle* series, general editor J. Ackrill (Oxford UP) include full commen-
tary and discussion.
The Platonic tradition
A useful guide is provided by *The Cambridge History of Later Greek and
Early Medieval Thought* ed. A. Armstrong (Cambridge UP, 1970).

(3.4) Arabic philosophy
General works
A. Badawi *Histoire de la philosophie en Islam* 2 vols (Paris; Vrin, 1968) – the
second volume deals with the Aristotelian tradition – is full, scholarly,
excellent for bibliography but not analytical; M. Fakhry *A History of Islamic
Philosophy* (London/New York; Longman; Columbia UP, 1983 – 2nd ed) –
a briefer, but more discursive account of some major figures; O. Leaman
An Introduction to Medieval Islamic Philosophy (Cambridge UP, 1985) –
sophisticated philosophical discussion, concentrating on Algazel, Averroes
and Maimonides; R. Walzer 'Islamic philosophy' in his *Greek into Arabic:
Essays on Islamic Philosophy* (Oxford; Cassirer, 1962), pp.1–28.
Access to and use of Greek sources
F. Peters *Aristotle and the Arabs: the Aristotelian Tradition in Islam* (New
York; New York UP, 1968); A. Badawi *La transmission de la philosophie
grecque en monde arabe* (Paris; Vrin, 1968) – important on the *Theology of
Aristotle* and the *Liber de Causis*; G. Anawati, 'Le néoplatonisme dans la
pénsee musulmane: état actuel des recherches' in *Plotino e il Neoplatonismo
in Oriente e Occidente* (Rome; Accademia Nazionale dei Lincei, 1974),
pp.339–405.
Avicenna
A.-M. Goichon *The Philosophy of Avicenna and its Influence on Medieval
Europe*, trsl. M. Khan (Delhi/Patna/Varanasi; Banarsidas, 1969). The
clearest and most thorough western studies of his *Metaphysics* and *De
Anima* are those by G. Verbeke in the Introductions to the editions of these
works in Latin translation in AvL (above, Section 1–i).
Averroes
L. Gauthier *Ibn Rochd (Averroes)* (Paris; Presses Universitaires de France,
1948; S. Gomez Nogales 'Saint Thomas, Averroes et l'averroisme' in
Aquinas and the Problems of his Time Louvain, UP, 1976 – on the
differences between Averroes's real views and those attributed to him by
Aquinas.

(3.5) Jewish philosophy
General studies and catalogues
M. Steinschneider *Die hebräischen Übersetzungen des Mittelalters und die Juden als Dolmetscher* (Berlin: Bibliographische Bureau, 1893); G. Vajda *Introduction à la pensée juive du moyen âge* (Paris; Vrin, 1947): C. Sirat *A History of Jewish Philosophy in the Middle Ages* (Cambridge and Paris: Cambridge University Press and La Maison des Sciences de l'Homme, 1985).
Bibliography
G. Vajda *Jüdische Philosophie* (BE: 1950)
Avencebrol
J. Schlanger *La philosophie de Salomon ibn Gabirol; étude d'un néoplatonisme* (Leiden; Brill, 1968).
Maimonides
Essays on Maimonides: an Octocennial Volume, ed. S. Baron (New York; Columbia UP, 1941) – especially interesting is 'The literary character of the *Guide for the Perplexed*' by L. Strauss, pp.37–91; L. Strauss, 'How to begin study of the Guide of the perplexed' in the translation of the *Guide* ed. S. Pines (above 1–i), pp.xi–lvi.

Chapter 4   The aims of arts masters and theologians

(4.1)   Philosophia and its divisions
J. Weisheipl, 'The nature, scope and classification of the sciences' in Lindberg (ed.) *Science in the Middle Ages* (above 0.1), pp.461–482 and 'Classification of the sciences in medieval thought', MS, 27, 1965, pp.54–90.

(4.2)   Faith and reason
Siger of Brabant
F. van Steenberghen *Maître Siger de Brabant* (PM: 1977) largely replaces his *Siger de Brabant d'après ses oeuvres inédites*, 2 vols, (Louvain; L'Institut Supérieur de Philosophie, 1931/42). R. Gauthier has revised Steenberghen's widely accepted views in 'Notes sur Siger de Brabant', RSPT, 67, 1983, pp.201–232; 68, 1984, pp.3–49).
Boethius of Dacia
J. Pinborg 'Zur Philosophie des Boethius de Dacia. Ein Überblick', *Studia mediewistyczne*, 15, 1974, pp.165–185 (= MedSem, no. 11).
Aquinas and the controversies about Aristotle and the arts faculty.
E. Wéber *La controverse de 1270 à l'université de Paris et son retentissement sur la pensée de S. Thomas d'Aquin* (BT: 1970), *Dialogue et dissensions entre Saint Bonaventure et Saint Thomas d'Aquin à Paris* (BT: 1974).
The unity of the possible intellect
For Averroes's position, see the works cited in 3.3 above; for the various discussions in the west and their sources, see below, 5.1–7.4. See also the introductions to *Trois commentaires anonymes*. . . (above, Section 1–ii, under **anonymous**, commentaries on Aristotle's *De Anima*).
The eternity of the world

214 Later Medieval Philosophy

An excellent background to the problem is provided by R. Sorabji *Time, Creation and the Continuum: Theories in antiquity and the Early Middle Ages* (London; Duckworth, 1983), esp. Part III, pp.191–283; A. Zimmermann, ' "Mundus est aeternus". – Zur Auslegung dieser These bei Bonaventura und Thomas von Aquin' in *Auseinandersetzungen*. . . (above 1.1), pp.317–330; J. Wippel, 'Did Thomas Aquinas defend the possibility of an eternally created world?', *Journal of the History of Philosophy*, 19, 1981, pp.21–37.

The condemnations of 1277
R. Hissette *Enquête sur les 219 articles condamnés à Paris le 7 mars 1277* (PM: 1977) – a systematic discussion of the sources of each condemned article; J. Wippel, 'The condemnations of 1270 and 1277 at Paris', *Journal of Medieval and Renaissance Studies*, 7, 1977, pp.169–201; CHLMP Chapter 26, 'The effect of the condemnation of 1277' by E. Grant emphasizes the importance of God's absolute power for those who formulated the Paris condemnation; D. Callus *The Condemnations of St Thomas at Oxford* (Oxford; Blackfriars, 1946).

(4.3) Theology, metaphysics and Aristotelian science
Metaphysics
Die Metaphysik im Mittelalter: ihr Ursprung und ihre Bedeutung, ed. P. Wilpert (MM: 1963) – a collection of essays; A. Zimmermann *Ontologie oder Metaphysik? Die Diskussionen über den Gegenstand der Metaphysik im 13. und 14. Jahrhundert* (Leiden; Brill, 1965); J. Pinborg 'Diskussionen um die Wissenschaftstheorie an der Artistenfakultät' in *Auseinandersetzungen*. . . (above 1.1), pp.240–268 (= Med Sem no. III).
Aquinas and the schools of ancient thought
R. Henle *St Thomas and Platonism: a Study of the* Plato *and* Platonici *texts in the writings of St Thomas* (The Hague; Nijhoff, 1956) – fundamental on this aspect of Aquinas's work; M. Grabmann, 'Die Aristoteleskommentare des heiligen Thomas von Aquin', MG I, pp.266–314 (revised version). The introduction to R. Gauthier's (Leonine) edition of the commentary on the *De Anima* (above, Section I–ii) discusses Aquinas's purposes as an Aristotelian commentator – see esp. pp.288–294. For the commentary on the *Liber de causis* see the introduction to Saffrey's edition (above, Section I–ii).
Theology as a science
M.-D. Chenu *La théologie comme science au XIIIe siècle* (Paris; Vrin, 1957 – 3rd ed.); R. Guelluy *Philosophie et théologie chez Guillaume d'Ockham* (Louvain/Paris; Nauwelaerts/Vrin, 1947).

Conclusion to Part One

(4.4) Approaches to medieval philosophy
The fullest discussion of the different 'schools' of historians of medieval philosophy is provided by F. van Steenberghen *Introduction a l'étude de la philosophie médiévale. Recueil de travaux offert à l'auteur*. . . (PM: 1974) – a collection of some of van Steenberghen's own pieces – pp.35–77. No attempt will be made to reproduce his extensive bibliography here.

CHLMP Chapter 46, 'Neoscholasticism' (pp.838–852) by P. Fitzpatrick illustrates some of the background against which scholarly interest in medieval philosophy grew up.
Rationalists
B. Hauréau *Histoire de la philosophie scolastique*, 2 vols – vol. II in 2 parts (Paris; [Durand et] Pedone-Lauriel, 1872, 1880 – 2nd ed.).
Separationists
Van Steenberghen gives a detailed defence of his separationist position in *Introduction*. . . (above), pp.78–113 and also in *La philosophie au XIIIe siècle* (above 3.2).
Christian philosophy
E. Gilson *Introduction à la philosophie chrétienne, Le philosophe et la théologie* – both (Paris; Vrin, 1960); see also Gilson's *A History of Christian Philosophy*. . . (above, 0.1), *The Christian Philosophy of St Bonaventure* (below, 7.4) and *The Christian Philosophy of St Thomas Aquinas* (below 7.1) and see below, 7.4, for works on St Bonaventure which discuss the problem of 'Christian philosophy', especially Quinn *The Historical Constitution*. . .
The modern analytical approach
Besides the Introduction to CHLMP by N. Kretzmann, a concise statement of some of the aims and presuppositions of this approach is made by A. Kenny in *Wyclif* (Oxford/New York; Oxford UP, 1985), pp.5–8. Kenny's own work on Aquinas provides an outstanding example of the approach (below 7.1, 7.2).
Other approaches
P. Vignaux everywhere stresses the theological interests of medieval thinkers: see his *Philosophy in the Middle Ages*. . . (above 0.1) and also the essays collected in his *De Saint Anselme à Luther* (Paris; Vrin, 1976).

Chapter 5   Intellectual knowledge: the problem and its sources

(5.1)   The problem in antiquity
Non-propositional thought
A. Lloyd, 'Non-discursive thought – an enigma of Greek philosophy', *Proceedings of the Aristotelian Society*, 70, 1969–70, pp. 261–274, puts forward the commonly accepted view which is challenged by R. Sorabji *Time, Creation and the Continuum*. . . (above 4.2), pp.137–156, where he denies that 'non-propositional thinking is found in Plato, Aristotle, or Plotinus, at any of the points where it has most commonly been detected' (p.137).
The Platonic approach
E. Gilson *The Christian Philosophy of St Augustine*, trs. C. Lynch (London; Gollancz, 1961), esp. pp. 66–126; R. Roques *L'univers dionysien: structure hiérarchique du monde selon le Pseudo-Denys* (Paris: Editions du Cerf, 1983 – a reprint of the original ed. of 1954), esp. pp.200–244.
Aristotle
For general bibliography, see above 3.3. The translation of *De Anima* II and III by D. Hamlyn in the Clarendon Aristotle series (Oxford UP, 1968)

contains a full analytical commentary and references to modern discussions of Aristotle's meaning.
Antique exegetes of Aristotle
P. Moraux *Alexandre d'Aphrodise. Exegète de la noétique d'Aristote* (Liège/ Paris; Faculté de Philosophie et Lettres/Droz, 1942) corrects previous accounts.

(5.2)   The problem in Arab philosophy
Gilson, 'Les sources gréco-arabes. . . ', (above 3.2) traces the Arab tradition which reached the west through Latin translations; R. Walzer, 'Aristotle's active intellect NOYC πOIHTIKOC in Greek and early Islamic philosophy', in *Plotino e il Neoplatonismo*. . . (above, 3.4), pp.423–436.
Avicenna
See above, 3.3 – the most thorough treatment of his *De Anima* is in the introduction the AvL edition.
Averroes
Haren ref. and G. Thery *Autour du décret de 1210. II. Alexandre d'Aphrodise. Aperçu sur l'influence de sa noétique* (BT: 1926) – despite the title, this work is especially useful on Averroes's theory of the soul; S. Gomez Nogales, 'Saint Thomas, Averroes. . .' (above 3.4).

(5.3)   Some works on intellectual knowledge in thirteenth and fourteenth-century thought which are not limited to a particular period or thinker
M. Grabmann, 'Mittelalterlichen Deutung und Umbildung der aristotelischen Lehre vom voûs ποιητίκοζ nach einer Zusammenstellung im Cod. B. III 22 der voûs Tiolntlkos Universitätsbibliothek Basel', SBAW, 1936, no. 6 (= GAA I, pp.1021–1122); C. Bérubé *La connaissance de l'individuel au moyen âge* (Montreal/Paris; Montreal UP/Presses Universitaires de France, 1964) – an important study; G. Nuchelmans *Theories of the Proposition. Ancient and Medieval Conceptions of the Bearers of Truth and Falsity* (Dordrecht; North-Holland, 1973); *Sprache und Erkenntnis im Mittelalter*, ed. W. Kluxen and others, 2 vols (MM: 1981).

Chapter 6   William of Auvergne

(6.1)   Studies of William of Auvergne
General studies
A. Masnovo *Da Guglielmo d'Auvergne a s. Tommaso d'Aquino*, 3 vols, (Milan; Vita e Pensiero, 1945, 1946 – 2nd ed.)
Intellectual knowledge
M. Baumgartner *Die Erkenntnislehre des Wilhelm von Auvergne* (BGPM: 1893) – thorough but outdated; E. Gilson, 'Pourquoi Saint Thomas. . .' (above 3.2), pp.46–80 – puts forward the view of William as an 'Avicennising Augustinian'; E. Moody, 'William of Auvergne and his treatise *De Anima*' in his *Studies in Medieval Philosophy, Science and Logic* (Berkeley, Los Angeles, London; California UP, 1975), esp. pp.59–83; S. Marrone

William of Auvergne. . . (above 2.6), pp.3–134. Marrone's study proposes a new interpretation of William's philosophy of mind, in which the influence of Aristotle's *Posterior Analytics* is emphasized; although the account of William given in this *Introduction* differs substantially from Marrone's, it owes much to his clear and detailed analysis.

(6.2) Other early thirteenth century thinkers
W. Principe *The Theology of the Hypostatic Union in the Early Thirteenth Century*, ɪ – William of Auxerre, ɪɪ – Alexander of Hales, ɪɪɪ – Hugh of Saint-Cher, ɪv – Philip the Chancellor (PIMS: 1963, 1967, 1970, 1975) – a wider discussion than the title might suggest.
William of Auxerre
C. Ottaviano *Guglielmo d'Auxerre, la vita, le opere, il pensiero* (Rome; L'Universale, 1931).
Grosseteste
J. McEvoy *The Philosophy of Robert Grosseteste* (Oxford UP, 1982) – a comprehensive general study; *Robert Grosseteste: Scholar and Bishop*, ed. D. Callus (Oxford UP, 1955) – a collection of essays; A. Crombie *Robert Grosseteste and the Origins of Experimental Science* (Oxford UP, 1953).

Chapter 7 Thomas Aquinas

(7.1) General works on Aquinas
Biography
J. Weisheipl *Friar Thomas d'Aquino: His Life, Thought and Works* (Oxford; Blackwell, 1974); A. Kenny *Aquinas* (Oxford UP, 1980), pp. 1–31 – a good, brief sketch.
Canon
M. Grabmann *Die Werke des hl. Thomas von Aquin: eine literarhistorische Untersuchung und Einführung* (Munster; Aschendorff, 1949); 'A brief catalogue of authentic works' in Weisheipl *Friar Thomas.* . . (above), pp.355–405
Bibliography
P. Mandonnet and J. Destrez *Bibliographie thomiste* (BT: 1921); P. Wyser *Thomas von Aquin, Der Thomismus* (BE: 1950, 1951). Further bibliography will be found in the *Bulletin thomiste* (1924–1965), continued as *Rassegna di Letteratura Tomistica* (1966–).
Manuscripts
Codices manuscripti operum Thomae de Aquina, ɪ (Libraries: A–F), ed. H. Dondaine and H. Schooner, ɪɪ (Libraries: G–M) ed. H. Schooner (Rome; Commissio Leonina, Editori di San Tommaso, 1967, 1973; Dondaine *Secrétaires* (above, 1.4)
General expositions of his work
A.-D. Sertillanges *La philosophie de S. Thomas d'Aquin*, 2 vols (Paris; Aubier, 1940 – new ed.); G. Manser *Das Wesen des Thomismus* (Frieburg, Switzerland; Paulus, 1949 – 3rd ed.); E. Gilson *The Christian Philosophy of*

St Thomas Aquinas (New York; Random House, 1956) – explains in detail Gilson's particular view of Aquinas the Christian philosopher; M.-D. Chenu *Towards Understanding Saint Thomas* (above 1.2) – examines the various forms in which Aquinas worked; Kenny *Aquinas* (above – sharply-focused philosophical studies of the concept of being and the philosophy of mind in Aquinas follow a biographical sketch); 'Aquinas' by P. Geach in G. Anscombe and P. Geach *Three Philosophers* (Oxford; Blackwell, 1961)

Collections
Aristote et Saint Thomas d'Aquin – journées d'études internationales (Louvain, Paris; Publications Universitaires de Louvain, Béatrice–Nauwelaerts, 1957); *Aquinas: a Collection of Critical Essays*, ed. A. Kenny (Notre Dame UP, 1976) – essays on many aspects of Aquinas's work, mostly from the modern philosophical point of view; *St Thomas Aquinas* 1274–1974. *Commemorative Studies*, 2 vols, ed. A. Maurer (Toronto; Pontifical Institute of Medieval Studies, 1974); *Aquinas and the Problems of his Time* (above 3.4); *Thomas von Aquin* in the series *Wege der Forschung*, 2 vols (Darmstadt; Wissenschaftliche Buchgesellschaft, 1978, 1981) – articles reprinted (in German translation where necessary: vol. I contains studies of chronology, biography and sources, vol. II contains philosophical studies).

(7.2)   Intellectual knowledge and the soul in Aquinas
The soul
A. Pegis *Saint Thomas and the Problem of the Soul in the Thirteenth Century* (Toronto; St Michael's College, 1934); J. Mundhenk *Die Seele im System des Thomas Von Aquin: ein Beitrag zur Klärung und Beurteilung der Grundebegriffe der thomistischen Psychologie* (Hamburg; Meiner, 1980 ed. of a book first published 1934).

Knowledge and the intellect.
J. Peghaire *'Intellectus' et 'ratio' selon S. Thomas d'Aquin* (Paris/Ottawa; Vrin/Institut d'Etudes Médiévales, 1936) – fundamental: many of Peghaire's views have been adopted in this *Introduction*; B. Lonergan *Verbum. Word and Idea in Aquinas*, ed. D. Burrell (Notre Dame UP, 1967) – a very thorough and subtle study, especially of the different stages in an act of intellectual cognition; A. Kenny, 'Intellect and imagination in Aquinas' in A. Kenny (ed.) *Aquinas: a Collection. . .* (above 7.1), pp.273–296 – an attempt to analyze as exactly as possible what Aquinas means when he describes an act of intellectual cognition; A. Kenny *Aquinas* (above 7.1), pp.61–81 reworks some of the same material; A. Kenny, 'Intentionality: Aquinas and Wittgenstein' in A. Kenny *The Legacy of Wittgenstein* (Oxford; Blackwell, 1984), pp.61–76 – continues the investigation.

(7.3)   Some studies of other aspects of Aquinas's thought
Aesthetics
U. Eco *Il Problema Estetico in Tommaso d'Aquino* (Milan; Bompiani, 1970 2ed.).
Analogy G. Klubertanz *St Thomas Aquinas on Analogy* (Chicago; Loyola

UP, 1960); R. McInerny *The Logic of Analogy. An Interpretation of St Thomas* (The Hague; Nijhoff, 1971); D. Burrell *Aquinas: God and Action* (London; Routledge & Kegan Paul, 1979).

Being
E. Booth *Aristotelian Aporetic Ontology in Islamic and Christian Thought* (Cambridge UP, 1983), esp. pp. 205–267.

Ethics
W. Kluxen *Philosophische Ethik bei Thomas von Aquin* (Mainz; Grünewald, 1964); R. McInerny *Ethica thomistica, The Moral Philosophy of Thomas Aquinas* (Washington, D.C.; Catholic University of America Press, 1982).

Metaphysics
L.-B Geiger, 'Saint Thomas et la Metaphysique d'Aristote' in *Aristote et Saint Thomas* . . . (above 7.1); J. Doig *Aquinas on Metaphysics: Historico-doctrinal Study of the Commentary on the Metaphysics* (The Hague; Nijhoff, 1972); J. Wippel *Metaphysical Themes in Thomas Aquinas* (Washington D.C.; Catholic University of America Press, 1984).

Natural theology
A. Kenny *The Five Ways* (London; Routledge & Kegan Paul, 1969)

(7.4)   Mid-thirteenth century thinkers
St Bonaventure
E. Gilson *The Philosophy of St Bonaventure*, trsl. I. Trethowan and F. Sheed (London; Sheed & Ward, 1938) – a controversial view; J. Bougerol *Introduction to the Works of Bonaventure* (Paterson, New Jersey, St Anthony's Guild, 1964 – translated ed.); J. Quinn *The Historical Constitution of St Bonaventure's Philosophy* (PIMS: 1973).

Albert the Great and his Followers
I. Crämer-Rügenberg *Albertus Magnus* (Munich; Beck, 1980) – a useful introduction. On Albert and intellectual knowledge, see A. Schneider *Die Psychologie Alberts des Grossen* (BGPM: 1903) and P. Michaud-Quentin *La psychologie de l'activité chez Albert le Grand* (BT: 1966). Collections of essays on Albert include: *Studia Albertina*, ed. H. Ostlender (BGPM: 1952), *Albert der Grosse: seine Zeit, sein Werk, seine Wirkung*, ed. A. Zimmermann (MM: 1981), *Albertus Magnus and the Sciences. Commemorative Essays*, ed. J. Weisheipl (Toronto; Pontifical Institute of Mediaeval Studies, 1980). On Albert's influence, see esp. M. Grabmann, 'Studien über Ulrich von Strassburg. Bilder wissenschaftichen Lebens und Strebens aus der Schüle Alberts des Grossen', MG I, pp.147–221, revised version, and 'Der Einfluss Alberts des Grossen auf das mittelalterlichen Geistesleben. Das deutsche Element in der mittelalterliche Scholastik und Mystik', MG II, pp.324–412, revised version.

Roger Bacon
T. Crowley *Roger Bacon. The Problem of the Soul in his Philosophical Commentaries* (Louvain/Dublin; L'Institut Supérieur de Philosophie/Duffy, 1950); S. Easton *Roger Bacon and his Search for a Universal Science* (Oxford; Blackwell, 1952).

Chapter 8   Modes and intentions: some arts masters on intellecutal knowledge

(8.1)   Arts masters: their lives and work

Information on arts masters in general will be found in P. Glorieux *La faculté des arts. . .* (above 1.3).

Boethius of Dacia

See above, 4.2.

Radulphus Brito

The fullest study is in the preface to the edition of his *quaestiones* on Priscian (above 1–ii).

(8.2)   Modes

J. Pinborg *Die Entwicklung der Sprachtheorie im Mittelalter* (BGPM: 1967) is the fundamental study of grammatical theory and the *modi significandi*. Pinborg summarizes some of his views in parts of his *Logik und Semantik. . .* (above 2.1), and he provides a concise introduction to the topic in CHLMP Chapter 13, 'Speculative grammar' (pp.254–269). Other introductions to modistic grammar include I. Rosier *La grammaire spéculative des modistes* (Lille, 1983); M. Covington *Syntactic theory in the High Middle Ages* (Cambridge UP, 1984).

(8.3)   Intentions

CHLMP Chapter 23, 'Intentions and impositions' (pp.479–495) by C. Knudsen is a useful, though not always clear, survey.

Avicenna and Aquinas

K. Gyekye 'The terms "prima intentio" and "secunda intentio" in Arabic logic', *Speculum*, 46, 1971, pp.32–38, esp., pp.35–37; H. Simonin 'La notion d'intentio dans l'oeuvre de S. Thomas D'Aquin', RSPT, 19, 1930, pp.445–463.

Arts masters

J. Pinborg, 'Die Logik der Modistae', *Studia Mediewistyczne*, 16, 1975, pp.39–97 (= MedSem no. V), 'Zum Begriff der *Intentio Secunda*: Radulphus Brito, Hervaeus Natalis und Petrus Aureoli in Diskussion', CIMAGL, 13, 1974, pp.49–59 (= MedSem no. VI), 'Radulphus Brito's Sophism. . .' (above Section 1–ii).

Chapter 9   Henry of Ghent

(9.1)   Studies of Henry of Ghent

Chronology

J. Gomez Caffarena, 'Cronologia de la "suma" de Enrique de Gante', *Gregorianum*, 38, 1957, pp.116–133.

Manuscripts

R. Macken *Bibliotheca manuscripta Henrici de Gandavo* – vols I and II of the new, critical edition (above Section 1–ii).

General studies

J. Paulus *Henri de Gand. Essai sur les tendances de sa métaphysique* (Paris; Vrin, 1938).
Intellectual knowledge
The fullest study is E. Bettoni *Il Processo Astrattivo nella Concezione di Enrico di Gand* (Milan; Vita e Pensiero, 1954). T. Nys *De Werking van het Menselijk Verstand volgens Hendrik van Gent* (Louvain; Nauwelaerts, 1949) – summarized and criticized by J. Paulus, 'A propos de la théorie de la connaissance d'Henri de Gand', *Revue philosophique de Louvain*, 47, 1949, pp.493–6 – is unusual in recognizing that Henry's view of intellectual knowledge changed; but Nys sees the evolution as being from a more Aristotelian to a more Augustinian theory.

(9.2) Later thirteenth-century thinkers
D. Sharp *Franciscan Philosophy at Oxford in the Thirteenth Century* (Oxford/London; Oxford UP/Milford), 1930 – concentrates especially on this period.
Followers of St Thomas and their adversaries
F. Roensch *Early Thomistic School* (Dubuque, Iowa; Priory, 1964); R. Zavalloni *Richard de Mediavilla et la controverse sur la pluralité des formes* (PM: 1951).
Vitalis of Furno
J. Lynch, 'The knowledge of singular things according to Vital de Four', FS, 29, 1969, pp.271–301.
Giles of Rome
P. Bruni *Le opere di Egidio Romano* (Florence; Olschki, 1936).
Godfrey of Fontaines
M. de Wulf, 'Un théologien-philosophe du XIIIe siècle: étude sur la vie, les oeuvres et l'influence de Godefroid de Fontaines', Académie Royale des Belges, Classe des Lettres, n.s. i–ii (Brussels, 1905).
Peter John Olivi
E. Bettoni *Le Dottrine Filosofiche di Pier di Giovanni Olivi* (Milan; Università del S. Cuore, 1959).

Chapter 10   Duns Scotus: intuition and memory

(10.1)   General works of Duns Scotus
Biography and canon
C. Balić 'The life and works of John Duns Scotus' in *John Duns Scotus, 1265–1965*, ed. J. Ryan and B. Bonansea (Washington; Catholic University of America), 1965, pp. 1–27.
Bibliography
O. Schaefer *Johannes Duns Scotus* (BE: 1953), 'Resenha abreviada sa bibliografia escotista mais recente (1954–1966)', *Revista Portuguesa de Filosofia*, 23, 1967, pp.338–363.
Manuscripts
De ordinatione Ioannis Duns Scoti disquisitio historico-critica = *Opera omnia* ed. Balić (above, Section i–ii), 1.

222 _Later Medieval Philosophy_

General studies of his work
C. Harris _Duns Scotus_ 2 vols. (Oxford UP, 1927) – rather outdated; E.
Gilson _Jean Duns Scot: introduction à ses positions fondamentales_ (Paris; Vrin,
1952) – the best general study; E. Bettoni _Duns Scotus: the Basic Principles of
his Philosophy_, trsl. B. Bonansea (Washington; Catholic University of
America Press, 1961) – straightforward exposition, not analytical; L.
Honnefelder _Ens inquantum ens. Der Begriff des Seienden als Solchen als
Gegenstand der Metaphysik nach der Lehre des Johannes Duns Scotus_ (BGPM:
1979).
Collections
John Duns Scotus. . . ed. Ryan and Bonansea (above) – contains the most
analytical examinations of Scotus to have been written; _The Monist_, 49, no.
4 – October 1965 – is a collection on the 'Philosophy of John Duns Scotus,
in commemoration of the 700th anniversary of his birth'; _De doctrina
Ioannis Duns Scoti_, 7 vols. (Rome; Commision Scotistica, 1968) –
proceedings of a conference.

(10.2) Memory and intuitive cognition
A detailed discussion of Aristotle's _De Memoria et Reminiscentia_ is found in
R. Sorabji's translation: _Aristotle on Memory_ (London; Duckworth, 1972).
The two most useful discussions of intuitive cognition in Scotus are
Gilson's in _Jean Duns Scot. . ._ (above 10.1), and that by Bérubé in _La
connaissance de l'individuel. . ._ (above 5.3), pp.134–224, esp. pp.188–220
(discussed and criticized in the chapter). Honnefelder – _Ens inquantum ens_
(above 10.1) pp.218–267, esp. pp.238–241 – follows the main lines of
Bérubé's interpretation of this aspect of Scotus's work. S. Day _Intuitive
Cognition. A Key to the Significance of the Later Scholastics_ (St Bonaventure,
New York: Franciscan Institute, 1947) presents a useful collection of texts
but is not reliable as an interpreter.

Chapter 11   William of Ockham

(11.1) General works on Ockham
Biography
L. Baudry _Guillaum d'Occam: sa vie, ses oeuvres, ses idées sociales et politiques_
(Paris; Vrin, 1949).
Bibliography
J. Reilley 'Ockham bibliography, 1950–1967', FS 28, 1968, pp.197–214.
Chronology and revision of his works
Boehner's contributions on this subject, which form the first 10 items in
BCAO, should be corrected by the introductions to the new edition of
Ockham's complete works (above Section 1–ii).
General expositions and guides to his thought
E. Hochstetter _Studien zur Metaphysik und Erkenntnislehre Wilhelms von
Ockham_ (Berlin, Leipzig; De Gruyter, 1927), L. Baudry _Lexique philosophi-
que de Guillaume d'Occam: étude des notions fondamentales_ (Paris: Léthielleux,

1975); G. Leff *William of Ockham: the Metamorphosis of Scholastic Discourse* (Manchester/Totowa, NJ; Manchester UP/Rowman and Littlefield, 1975); K. Bannach *Die Lehre von der doppelten Macht Gottes bei Wilhelm von Ockham. Problemgeschichtliche Voraussetzungen und Bedeutung* (Wiesbaden; Steiner, 1975).

Collections
BCAO – Boehner's articles have been of great importance in the re-evaluation of Ockham.

(11.2) Studies of particular areas of Ockham's works
Logic and language
E. Moody, *The Logic of William of Ockham* (London; Sheed and Ward, 1935) – still useful, although Moody exaggerates the closeness of Ockham to Aquinas; P. Boehner, 'Ockham's theory of signification', 'Ockham's theory of supposition and the notion of truth', FS 6, 1946, pp.143–170, 261–292 (= BCAO, pp.201–232, 232–267); P. Vignaux *Nominalisme au XIVe siècle* (Montreal/Paris; Institut D'Études Médiévales/Vrin, 1948); Pinborg *Logik und Semantik* (above 2.1) pp. 127–139. CHLMP Chapter 20, 'Universals in the early fourteenth century' (pp.411–439), by M. Adams, sets Ockham's discussions into the context of the arguments of his contemporaries; A. Kenny *Wyclif* (above 4.4), esp. pp.5–8, provides a useful comparison between medieval and modern realism and anti-realism, which is used in this chapter.

Intuitive cognition
P. Boehner, 'The notitia intuitiva of non-existents according to William of Ockham', *Traditio* 1, 1943, pp.223–275 (= without ed. of a text BCAO, pp.268–300). Boler's chapter in CHLMP (pp. 461–78) is particularly perceptive about Ockham's abstractive cognition: see esp. pp.466–473.

Theology
Guelluy *Philosophie et théologie . . .* above (4,.3).

Political ideas
A. McGrade *The Political Thought of William of Ockham* (Cambridge UP, 1974).

(11.3) Some other fourteenth-century thinkers
General studies
La philosophie au XIVe siècle (Frankfurt; Minerva, 1969) – a collected reprint of articles published in the 1920s; P. Vignaux *Justification et prédestination au XIVe siècle: Duns Scot, Pierre d'Auriole, Giullaume d'Occam, Grégoire de Rimini* (Paris; Leroux, 1934), art. 'Nominalisme' in DTC XII, col. 717–784; S. Romeo *Guillermo de Ockham y la filosofia del siglo XIV* (Madrid; Consejo Superior de Investigaciones Cientificas, 1966); R. Paqué *Der pariser Nomi-nalistenstatut. Zur Entstehung der Realitätsbegriff der neuzeitlichen Naturwissens-chaft (Occam, Buridan und Petrus Hispanus, Nikolaus von Autrecourt und Gregor von Rimini)* (Berlin; de Gruyter, 1970); on logic in this period, see Pinborg *Logik und Semantik. . .* (above, 2.1), pp.139–177; J. Weisheipl, 'Ockham and some Mertonians', MS, 30, 1968, pp.163–213, 'Repertorium mer-

tonense', MS, 31, 1969, pp. 174–224, 'Ockham and the Mertonians' in *The History* . . . *of Oxford* (above, 1.1), pp. 607–658 – this chapter, especially, provides an excellent introduction to the area.
Hervaus Natalis
E. Allen, 'Hervaeus Natalis: an early Thomist on the notion of being', MS, 22, 1960, p. 1–14; F. Kelley, 'Some observations on the "fictum" theory in Ockham and its relation to Hervaeus Natalis', FS, 38, 1978, pp. 260–282.
Buridan
A. Ghisalberti *The Logic of John Buridan*, ed. J. Pinborg (Copenhagen; Museum Tusculanum, 1976) – a collection of papers.
Walter Burley
C. Martin, 'Walter Burley' in *Oxford Studies Presented to Daniel Callus* (Oxford UP, 1964)
Peter Aureolus
R. Dreiling *Der Konzeptualismus in der Universalienfrage des Franziskaner Erzbischofs Petrus Aureoli* (BGPM: 1913).
Robert Holcot
F. Hoffmann *Die theologische Methode des Oxford Dominikanelehrers Robert Holcot* (BGPM: 1972).
Adam Wodeham
Courteney *Adam Wodeham*. . . (above 1.1).
Wyclif
Kenny *Wyclif* (above 4.4)
Gregory of Rimini
G. Leff *Gregory of Rimini. Tradition and Innovation in Fourteenth Century Thought* (Manchester UP, 1961).
Thomas Bradwardine
G. Leff *Bradwardine and the Pelagians* (Cambridge UP, 1957)
John of Ripa
A. Combes, 'Présentation de Jean de Ripa', AHDLMA 23, 1956, pp. 145–242.

Addendum (cf. 9.1)
After this book was complete, S. Marrone *Truth and Scientific Knowledge in the Thought of Henry of Ghent* (Cambridge, Mass.; Mediaeval Academy of America, 1985) became available. Marrone's lucid and thorough analysis differs from that here, but shares its scepticism towards traditional presentations of Henry.

Index

Abelard, Peter, 3, 7, 10, 41
abstraction, 75, 102, 106, 110, 114-15,
  119, 125-6, 128-9, 134-5; abstractive
  cognition, *see* cognition, abstractive
accident, *defined* 37
act: and potency, 65, 75, 96-105, 107-8,
  110-11, 119, 149-50, 156, 165-6; and
  disposition, 125
actuality (*entelecheia*), 96-7, 100-1, 103
Adam of Balsham (Parvipontanus), 7,
  and see Fallacie Parvipontane
Adam Wodeham, 188
Aegidius Romanus, *see* Giles of Rome
al-Farabi, 53-4, 59-60
Algazel (al-Ghazzālī), 53, 62
al-Kindī, 53, 59
Alan of Lille, 10, 54, 57
Albert the Great, 3, 15, 24, 27, 68-9, 77,
  88
Alexander IV, Pope, 16
Alexander of Aphrodisias, 52, 102, 109,
Alexander of Hales, 15, 17-18, 26, 33-4,
  116
Alexander Nequam (Neckam), 55
Alfred of Sareshel, 55
ampliation (of supposition), 44-5
analogy, 48, 94,
angels: their knowledge, 94, 115, 117-
  21, 127, 130-1, 135, 149, 152, 157,
  159, 190; as messengers, 112
Anselm of Canterbury, 29, 42
Anselm of Laon, 11
appellation, *see* reference, types of
Aquinas, *see* Thomas Aquinas
Arabic: knowledge of, 50-2; translation
  from, 51-7, 74

Aristotle, 32, 58, 66, 181; ancient
  commentaries on, 50, 52, 58, 66, 69,
  102-3; Aquinas's view of, 77-9; and
  the Arabs, 59-62; on eternity of
  world, 71-2; on intellectual
  knowledge, 95-102, 110, 113, 116-17,
  119-20, 129, 131, 133, 139, 149-50,
  156, 169, 171, 178-80, 189-90; on
  memory, 160-3; on metaphysics, 58,
  60-1; 'radical aristotelianism', 74;
  translations of, 50-7; wish to appear
  faithful to, 150-1, 181; *Categories*, 35-
  8; *De Anima*, 17, 29, 51-2, 55, 58,
  68-70, 93, 95-103, 109, 120, 132, 189-
  90; *De Caelo*, 51-2, 58; *De Generatione
  et Corruptione*, 51, 55, 57-8; *De
  Interpretatione*, 35, 38, 93, 99, 137; *De
  Memoria et Reminiscentia*, 98, 160-4;
  De Sophisticis Elenchis, 41-2, 52;
  Ethics, 16, 51-2, 54, 56, 58, 202; logic
  (books of), 12-13, 16, 51; *Metaphysics*,
  17, 21, 51-2, 54-7, 59-61, 75, 77-8,
  120; *Meteorologica*, 51, 55, 58; natural
  philosophy (books of/*libri naturales*),
  17, 21, 54-7; *Parva Naturalia*, 51;
  Physics, 17, 51-2, 56-8; *Politics*, 51;
  Posterior Analytics, 36, 47-9, 51-2, 56-
  7, 101, 152; *Prior Analytics*, 36, 38-9;
  Topics, 12-3, 36, 41, 72
arts, faculties of: their studies and
  organization, 14-21, 66
arts, masters of: and the faith, 67-74;
  and *philosophia*, 66-7; value and
  limitations of their work, 2, 87, 132,
  143, 190
Augustine, 3, 29, 32, 84, 101, 181; on

Empedocles, 63
entelecheia, see actuality
eternity of world, 68, 71-2, 133
evidence: evident knowledge, *see*
  knowledge, evident; God's existence
  not self-evident, 61; self-evident (*per
  se nota*) propositions, 40-1, 48, 66,
  72-3, 75-6, 80-1, 88, 101, 104, 108,
  111, 120-1, 127, 132, 147, 183, 187
examinations, 14

faculties, *see* arts, faculties of; theology,
  faculties of
Fallacie Parvipontane, 42
form, 64, 96-8, 103-5, 108, 110, 112-13,
  115-19, 120, 122-4, 129, 134, 149
formal distinctions, *see* distinctions,
  formal
Franciscans, 15-16, 24

genus: defined, 36-7
Gerard of Cremona, 51, 53
Gilbert of Poitiers, 3, 10, 42
Giles of Rome (Aegidius Romanus), 27
Gilson, E., 85, 87
God: as active intellect, 102-3, 116;
  existence of, 28-9, 61, 65, 134; as final
  cause, 61; formal distinctions in, 175;
  his knowledge, 12, 94, 113, 115, 117-
  18, 130-1, 135, 149, 152, 176-7; as
  object of beatific vision, 149-50, 156,
  158-9, his perfection, 33-4; his power,
  12, 74, 81, 148-9, 184-5, 187; ways of
  being known, 111, 135, 150; *see also*
  Christ, Trinity
Godfrey of Fontaines, 3, 32, 155
grammar, 10, 16-17, 21, 43, 132, 182;
  authorities in, 9; textbooks of, 26;
  speculative, 93, 136-9
Greek: knowledge of, 50-1; translations
  from, 50-7
Gregory IX, Pope, 56
Grosseteste, *see* Robert Grosseteste
Gundissalinus, 52, 54

Hamlyn, D.W., 100
Hebrew, 53
Heidelberg, University of, 7
Henry of Ghent, 2, 32, 87, 95; on
  intellectual knowledge, 144-53, 155,
  178, 189-90; Quodlibets, 144, 149-52;
  Summa Quaestionum Ordinarium, 144-

8, 151
Henry of Harclay, 178
Hermannus Alemannus (the German),
  52
Hervaeus Natalis, 3, 178
Hugh of St Victor, 3, 11, 29

ibn Rushd, *see* Averroes
ibn Sīnā, *see* Avicenna
ideas: Platonic, 77-8, 94-6, 117; in God's
  mind, 77, 146, 176-7
illumination, 95, 103, 112, 116-17, 144-
  9
imagination, 97-8, 103, 108, 119, 160
impositions: first and second, 136-7,
  181-2
individuals (here used synonymously
  with *singulars*), 96, 104, 106-7, 134,
  142, 157, 171-80; intellectual
  cognition of, 113-5, 128-30, 151-2,
  156-60, 164, 168-9, 178-86
Innocent IV, Pope, 16
intellect: active, 56, 62, 99-101, 106,
  108-110, 112, 116-17, 126, 142, 151;
  the Ideas are contemplated by it, 94-5;
  its knowledge, 2, 28-9, 38, 58, 78,
  93-191; meaning grasp of first
  principles (intuition), 101, 120;
  material (*nous hulikos*), 102, 106, 108;
  potential, 99-101, 106, 116-17, 123,
  126, 142, 151, 178; speculative/made,
  108; *and see* individuals, intellectual
  cognition of
Intelligences, 61, 64, 109; agent
  Intelligence (*intelligentia agens*), 104-6,
  110, 117, 161
interpretation: allegorical, 18, 64; of
  authoritative texts, 9-10, 30, 110; by
  Avicenna of Aristotle, 60-1; biblical,
  18; Siger of Brabant's attitude to,
  69-70
intention (*intentio*): first and second,
  139-43, 181-2; meaning 'purpose', 90,
  140; meaning 'concept', 105-6, 108,
  126, 132-3
intuition: grasp of first principles, *see*
  intellect, meaning grasp of first
  principles; a type of knowing which is
  like vision, *see* cognition, intuitive
Islam, *see* Muslims
Isaac Israeli, 53-4
Isidore of Seville, 54